Dance Psychology for Artistic and Performance Excellence

Jim Taylor, PhD
Elena Estanol, PhD, MFA

Human Kinetics

Library of Congress Cataloging-in-Publication Data

Taylor, Jim, 1958-
 Dance psychology for artistic and performance excellence / Jim Taylor, Elena Estanol.
    pages cm
 Includes bibliographical references and index.
1. Dance--Psychological aspects. 2. Dance--Social aspects. 3. Performing arts--Social aspects. I. Estanol, Elena
II. Title.
 GV1588.5.T38 2014
 792.8019--dc23
                                2014021487

ISBN: 978-1-4504-3021-0 (print)

Permission notices for photos reprinted in this book from other sources can be found on page xi.
The web addresses cited in this text were current as of March 2015, unless otherwise noted.

Acquisitions Editor: Gayle Kassing, PhD
Developmental Editor: Bethany J. Bentley
Managing Editor: Carly S. O'Connor
Copyeditor: Tom Tiller
Indexer: Laurel Plotzke
Permissions Manager: Dalene Reeder
Senior Graphic Designer: Keri Evans
Cover Designer: Keith Blomberg
Photograph (cover): © Larry Williams/Lithium/age fotostock
Photo Asset Manager: Laura Fitch
Visual Production Assistant: Joyce Brumfield
Photo Production Manager: Jason Allen
Art Manager: Kelly Hendren
Associate Art Manager: Alan L. Wilborn
Illustrations: © Human Kinetics, unless otherwise noted
Printer: Versa Press

Printed in the United States of America   10 9 8 7 6 5 4 3 2 1

The paper in this book is certified under a sustainable forestry program.

Human Kinetics
Website: www.HumanKinetics.com

United States: Human Kinetics
P.O. Box 5076
Champaign, IL 61825-5076
800-747-4457
e-mail: humank@hkusa.com

Canada: Human Kinetics
475 Devonshire Road Unit 100
Windsor, ON N8Y 2L5
800-465-7301 (in Canada only)
e-mail: info@hkcanada.com

Europe: Human Kinetics
107 Bradford Road
Stanningley
Leeds LS28 6AT, United Kingdom
+44 (0) 113 255 5665
e-mail: hk@hkeurope.com

Australia: Human Kinetics
57A Price Avenue
Lower Mitcham, South Australia 5062
08 8372 0999
e-mail: info@hkaustralia.com

New Zealand: Human Kinetics
P.O. Box 80
Mitcham Shopping Centre, South Australia 5062
0800 222 062
e-mail: info@hknewzealand.com

E5723

First and foremost, I express my deepest gratitude to my coauthor, Elena, for her passion for dance; her deep knowledge of this remarkable art form; and her unwavering commitment, perseverance, and good cheer in completing *Dance Psychology for Artistic and Performance Excellence* in the face of significant personal challenges (i.e., a severely broken ankle and three surgeries). Elena, it has been a joy to share the experience of writing this book with you.

I also express my love and thanks to my late mother (and coauthor of my first dance book), Ceci Taylor, who instilled in me a great love for dance and who first ignited my interest in exploring how the mind can help deepen the dance experience.

Finally, I express my love to my wife, Sarah, and our daughters, Catie and Gracie, with whom I joyously share the dance of life.

JT

My most sincere gratitude goes to my coauthor, Jim, for giving me the opportunity to collaborate with him on this book and bringing to fruition my dream of writing my first book for dancers; applying performance psychology principles to dance—my most enduring love. I appreciate his patience, encouragement, and understanding as I struggled to write about dance when I myself could not dance due to a severe injury. It has been an honor.

I am thankful to the countless dancers I have danced with, taught, choreographed for, and worked with as a performance psychologist. You have taught me about dance, love, and following one's passion.

I honor Barbara Hamblin, my first academic dance mentor, who always encouraged me to write and to continue on my academic journey in addition to dancing.

I am also thankful for the encouragement and modeling given to me by my family—Bruno, Alicia, and Iliana—that we may be artists and scientists all rolled into one. Most important, I express my deep love and never-ending appreciation to my husband, Shayn, for his support, encouragement, and donation of his precious time to allow this book to blossom.

EE

CONTENTS

Part I   *Building a Foundation*   **1**

1   Dancing Your Best   **3**
Consistently achieve prime dance performance.

2   Knowing Yourself   **19**
Gain an understanding of yourself to enable efficient and focused dance training and performance.

Part II   *Prime Dance Pyramid*   **31**

3   Motivation   **33**
Understand what motivates you to dance.

4   Confidence   **47**
Believe you can succeed in your dance training, performances, and life.

5   Intensity   **71**
Determine the level at which you dance your best.

6   Focus   **93**
Improve your focus and avoid distractions to dance your best.

7   Emotions   **111**
Manage the ups and downs of a rigorous schedule of training and performance.

PREFACE

If you're like most of the dancers with whom we have worked, you have chosen to become a dancer because something inside of you compels you to feel the music, to express yourself in your movement—to dance! This passion is the reason you embarked on your technical, artistic, and creative journey. You understand the dedication, diligence, patience, perseverance, and tenacity required to be a dancer. You know what it's like to wake up, day in and day out, feeling the fatigue and pain that often accompany your commitment to dance. You've experienced firsthand the challenges of balancing your devotion to dance with your education, social life, and other interests.

You forget about all of that, however, once you arrive at the studio, rehearsal hall, or performance venue—and especially once the music starts. As you become absorbed in the rhythm of the music and the movement of your body, you feel your spirits soar. This special experience is what brings you to dance every day and inspires you to work through challenges as you refine your technique and express your artistry in the choreography. It is a transcendent experience culminating in an indescribable feeling of awe, exhilaration, joy, and peace. And this is the moment that you live for every day in your dance.

We have written *Dance Psychology for Artistic and Performance Excellence* to benefit dancers at all levels. Whether you are a beginner, a seasoned dancer, or a top professional, the information and tools we provide here can help you achieve your training objectives and performance dreams. Specifically, the book achieves the following goals: (1) to provide clear and understandable information about the mental aspects of dance, (2) to offer simple and practical techniques that you can use easily to raise your dance to a new level, (3) to enable you to perform your best when it really counts, and (4) to help you gain the greatest possible satisfaction and joy from your involvement in this special art form.

When you participate in dance, you perform on two levels. The first and most obvious level is the dance performance itself—whether in a class, rehearsal, audition, show, or competition. The second and more significant performance occurs in your mind. If you succeed in your internal performance, you will succeed in any performance on the stage.

Contrary to what many dancers believe, the physical aspects of dance do not usually determine who is most successful. Technique does not determine who gets a standing ovation. At any level of dance—whether youth, university, or professional—once you get to a certain level, your mind is your most powerful tool or your most harmful weapon. Is Misty Copeland a better dancer than Wendy Whelan? Is Sascha Radetsky stronger than Desmond Richardson? In both cases, the answer is most likely no, and this may be true for you and the dancers with whom you perform or compete for the best roles. On any given day, what separates the best dancers from the good ones is their mental preparation to perform their best, regardless of the circumstances that dance or life may throw at them. The dancers who are the most motivated to train, who have the greatest confidence in themselves, who perform their best under pressure, who stay focused on their performance, who keep their emotions under control, and who direct their emotions to elevate their performance and technique to true artistry—these are the most successful and revered dancers.

People come to watch the same show performed by different casts of dancers because they want to see the characterization of a role by each individual dancer. They come to see not the technical aspects of the choreography but the embodiment of a role as it is imbued with the emotion and artistry of each performer. The dancers who are most successful and most sought after are those who connect to their choreography and to the story line and who use their body and emotions to portray a character.

In recent years, more and more dancers have realized that traditional methods of dance education do not necessarily prepare them for the demands of a career in dance. Similarly, perhaps you have recognized that reaching your potential, both technically and artistically, requires much more than just the time-honored approaches that have been taught for generations. Like many dancers, you may have realized that technique alone does not propel you to artistic and performance excellence, to acceptance by a dance school or company, or to a coveted role. Rather, you may have come to recognize that your mind affects how well you dance and how you feel about your dance.

With this richer perspective, many dancers have asked deeper questions about dance:

- Why can't I dance in performances as well as I do in classes and rehearsals?
- How can I overcome my doubts and anxiety about my ability before auditions, performances, and examinations?
- Why does my confidence seem to rise and fall depending on the roles I get or how I perform each time?
- How can I keep my motivation high in spite of disappointments, criticism, and difficult choreography and technical changes?
- How can I stay focused on what matters during classes, rehearsals, and performances in spite of the many distractions around me?
- What can I do to avoid burnout?
- Why do I struggle with my eating and health?
- How can I balance my devotion to dance with my commitments to relationships and school or career?

Addressing these questions, and others, is the reason that we wrote this book. It provides you with an understanding of the psychological issues that are most influential in dance. It offers you scientifically proven and practical information, as well as tools that enable you to maximize the quality of your dancing and enhance your experience of dance. Just as important, the book helps you explore your relationship with dance—and its relationship with your life as a whole. The ultimate goal of the book is to help you develop a healthy and life-affirming relationship with dance as you attain performance excellence, fulfillment, and personal and professional growth.

Historically, dance has relied on tradition-bound methods of preparing dancers. Recently, however, advances in exercise science and psychology have come together with a motivation in the field of dance to increase dancers' sophistication and professionalism. This confluence has created a need for dancers to obtain clear and practical information about psychological issues and preparation. This void is filled by *Dance Psychology for Artistic and Performance Excellence*, which integrates the latest scholarly information in diverse topic areas, presents it in a clear and understandable format, and provides simple and practical techniques that you can use regularly in both your dance life and your personal life.

This book includes four major sections that progress from the person as a dancer to the dancer as a person. Part I, Building a Foundation, introduces you to the concept of prime dance that serves both as the overall basis of the book and as the goal to be achieved through the remainder of the book. This part explores the attitudes and beliefs that underlie dance psychology. It also gives you tools to increase your self-knowledge as both a dancer and a person.

Part II, Prime Dance Pyramid, lays out the framework and practical information that you need in order to fully develop your psychological capabilities as a performer and take your technique and performances to a new level. Topics discussed in this section include motivation, confidence, intensity, focus, and emotions. These chapters describe strategies that you can use in order to develop to your fullest capacity in these areas and thereby maximize your technical and artistic expression. The overall goal of part II is to help you become the most motivated, confident, relaxed, focused, and emotionally balanced dancer that you can be.

Part III, Prime Dance Tools, describes three essential psychological tools for getting the most from your dance: goal setting, mental imagery, and routines. This section also shows you how to incorporate the information and strategies discussed in parts I and II into a structured mental training program that optimizes their value to your dancing. The overall goal of part III is to help you use all of the information we offer in the most effective and efficient way possible as you pursue your dance dreams.

Finally, part IV, Special Concerns for Dancers, explores the "dark side" of dance—that is, the side of dance that can hurt your mental and physical health through burnout, pain and injury, and disordered eating. This section helps you ensure that dance plays a positive role for you and supports you in leading a life that is mentally and physically healthy. It concludes with a chapter discussing how you can embrace the "light side" of dance and all of the joy and fulfillment that it offers.

In sum, *Dance Psychology for Artistic and Performance Excellence* helps you develop an appreciation for and an understanding of the role that your mind—in the form of attitudes, thoughts, and emotions—plays in your dance life. We hope that considering these issues helps you accomplish two essential goals in your dance. First, you can maximize your performance, both technical and artistic, in your roles as student, dancer, and person. Second, you can ensure that your dance experience is fun and fulfilling and provides a means for personal and professional growth and enrichment.

How to Use This Book

Our motivation for writing *Dance Psychology for Artistic and Performance Excellence* is to provide you with a down-to-earth, holistic guide that allows you to maximize your performance, enjoyment, and growth in dance. The ultimate goal is for you to thrive in this most demanding of art forms. Given the wealth of information presented in this text, we encourage you to take your time in absorbing each section. Indeed, you may need to read some chapters more than once. Just as it takes time to develop your physical and technical abilities, it also takes time to develop your mental capabilities. Be patient and commit yourself to your mental training just as you are committed to your physical and technical training.

The book is organized on the basis of what we believe to be the most important psychological contributors to dance performance. This structure enables you to select the areas most relevant to your level of training and performance. It allows you to find out exactly what you need to know at your level of dance participation and development. The book presents in detail the information and skills you need to develop in the mental areas that are most important to you. It also explains the exercises you need to practice in order to train your mind to achieve your goals for dance training and performance.

We suggest the following process for using this book to the greatest possible benefit. First, read the book all the way through. As you read, note specific topics that are important to you. After reading the entire book, identify the issues that are most relevant to you and reread the relevant sections to better familiarize yourself with them. Then select two or three areas on which you want to focus. Experiment with different techniques to develop in these areas, then select the ones you like best and implement them in your training program.

Now, let's begin the exciting journey that culminates in your gaining mastery over your mind as you strive for excellence and artistry in your dance.

ACKNOWLEDGMENTS

We express our sincerest gratitude to Taryn Brandt, a former dancer and graduate student of Jim's, who tirelessly and punctually contributed her time and energy in compiling the research and quotations for this book. We would also like to extend our deepest appreciation to Canyon Concert Ballet, as well as the following individual dancers for allowing us to use their images as part of this book: McKenzie Northburg, Marie Ritschard, Nicole Ferreri, Jacob Machmer, Claire Snyder, Conner Horak, and Laurel Brubcher. We also express enormous gratitude to our Human Kinetics editors, Gayle Kassing and Bethany Bentley, for their suggestions, encouragement, and patience with our busy schedules and with the progression of this book.

PHOTO CREDITS

How to Access the Web Resource

Throughout *Dance Psychology for Artistic and Performance Excellence,* you will notice references to a web resource. This online content is available to you free of charge when you purchase a new print or electronic version of the book. The web resource offers 32 worksheets that you can print, save, and either complete electronically or edit to suit your needs. The worksheets are grouped by chapter to help you locate them easily. To access the online content, simply register with the Human Kinetics website. Here's how:

1. Visit www.HumanKinetics.com/DancePsychologyForArtisticAnd PerformanceExcellence.

2. Click the first edition link next to the corresponding first edition book cover.

3. Click the Sign In link on the left or at the top of the page. If you do not have an account with Human Kinetics, you will be prompted to create one.

4. Once you have registered, if the online product does not appear in the Ancillary Items box at the left, click the Enter Pass Code option in that box. Enter the following pass code exactly as it is printed here, including any capitalization and hyphens: TAYLOR-3W9HM-WR.

5. Click the Submit button to unlock your online product.

6. After you have entered your pass code for the first time, you will never have to enter it again in order to access this online product. Once you have unlocked your product, a link to the product will appear permanently in the menu on the left. All you need to do to access your online content on subsequent visits is sign in to **www.HumanKinetics.com/DancePsychologyForArtisticAnd PerformanceExcellence** and follow the link!

If you need assistance along the way, click the Need Help? button on the book's website.

PART I

BUILDING A FOUNDATION

Artistic excellence and performance excellence in dance do not result from chance or from trial and error. Instead, both of these types of excellence require you to know what you're striving for in your dance experience and to develop a deep understanding of who you are as a dancer and as a person.

To help you meet these needs, part I of *Dance Psychology for Artistic and Performance Excellence* lays the groundwork for the rest of the book in several ways. Chapter 1 introduces you to prime dance, a concept that can serve as the goal you work toward in your dance. It also explores fundamental attitudes that enable you to perform at your highest level and enjoy the best possible dance experience. These approaches include taking a healthy perspective toward dance, accepting the ups and down of this art form, understanding why you dance, and defining success and failure in dance-affirming ways. This chapter also describes what it takes to become a prime dancer, the importance of mental preparation, and how you can ascend the prime dance pyramid, which consists of the essential mental contributors to artistic and performance excellence.

Chapter 2 introduces you to the important role that self-knowledge plays in developing yourself mentally and dancing your best. It encourages you to embrace your greatest strengths as a dancer while also acknowledging areas that may hold you back. It also introduces you to prime dance profiling, which allows you to assess your strengths and weaknesses in both the mental and physical aspects of your dance. The results of this assessment help you focus your attention and efforts on the areas in which you most need to improve, and they set the stage for your reading of the remainder of the book.

CHAPTER 1

Dancing Your Best

"I do not try to dance better than anyone else. I only try to dance better than myself."

Mikhail Baryshnikov

*D*ancing your best requires that you lay a solid foundation of physicality and technique as you develop your skills and learn your choreography. Your foundation must also enable you to develop mentally. To that end, we introduce you in this chapter to several key concepts that act as the foundation for the remainder of *Dance Psychology for Artistic and Performance Excellence*.

One of the most popular phrases heard in achievement-oriented environments is "peak performance." It was first used by athletes, coaches, and sport psychologists and was then incorporated into the vocabulary of business, the performing arts, and other high-performance settings. Peak performance is typically defined as the highest level of performance that a person can achieve, and it is often viewed as the goal toward which all performers should strive. Despite its widespread usage, however, this received wisdom is not without its problems, as Jim realized soon after coming out of graduate school. Here is his description:

"At first, peak performance was what I wanted to help performers achieve. But as I became more experienced as a consultant and writer, I began to appreciate the power of words and how vital it is to use words that communicate specifically. In turn, I began to see several difficulties with the phrase 'peak performance.' For one thing, dancers can maintain a peak for only a very short time. Would you be satisfied if you danced well in one performance, then did poorly in subsequent ones? Also, once that peak is reached, there is only one way to go—down. Finally, you may peak too early or too late for an important performance.

"For several years, I searched for a phrase that would accurately describe what I wanted performers to achieve. One day, while walking through the meat section of a supermarket, I saw a piece of beef labeled as 'prime cut.' This was an aha moment—I knew I was onto something. I looked up *prime* in the dictionary and found that it means 'of the highest quality or value.' Thus was born the term 'prime performance.'"

Prime performance, or in our case prime dance, involves dancing at a consistently high level under the most challenging conditions. The power of this definition hinges on two essential words: *consistently* and *challenging*. In terms of consistency, we want you to be able to dance at a high level day in and day out, week in and week out, and month in and month out. Prime dance is not about being "on" 100 percent of the time—that is impossible. Rather, it means performing at a high level while experiencing only minimal ups and downs instead of the large swings in training and performance that are so common among dancers.

The second key word is *challenging*. It's easy to dance well under ideal conditions when you're healthy and rested, when you have an easy role, and when you're performing in a familiar venue in front of a small and friendly audience. What makes great dancers so successful, however, is their ability to perform their best in the worst possible conditions, in the most challenging roles, and under the greatest pressure in front of a large and potentially critical audience in a well-known venue. If you attain this prime level of performance, you will not only succeed but also gain immense enjoyment and satisfaction from your efforts. That is a goal worth achieving!

What does prime dance consist of? Although this book focuses on the mental components of dance, the mind is only one piece of the puzzle. For this reason, we have taken a holistic perspective that emphasizes the whole person and thus allows you to dance your best. In addition to being mentally prepared, you must also operate at a high level of physical health, which includes being well conditioned, well rested, well nourished through a balanced diet, and free from injury and illness. At the same time, your technical skills must be precise and well learned. If you are prepared in these three ways—mentally, physically, and technically—then you have the ability to achieve prime dance.

Have you ever experienced prime dance? Do you know what it feels like to perform at that level? Prime dance fosters the experience of flow, a state identified by the psychologist Mihaly Csikszentmihalyi and marked by the following characteristics:

- It is effortless—comfortable, easy, natural, and automatic.

- There is little thought. The body does what it knows how to do with no mental interference.

- You experience sharpened senses. You see, hear, and feel everything more acutely.

- Time is distorted. We've heard professionals say that when they're "on," their performance seems to fly by.

- You are totally absorbed in the experience and focused entirely on the process of artistry. You are free from distractions and unnecessary thoughts that might interfere with your performance.

- You have boundless energy. Your stamina seems never ending, and fatigue is simply not an issue.

- You experience what we call prime integration, in which everything works together. Specifically, the physical, technical, and mental aspects of your art are integrated into one focused effort of dancing with virtuosity and joy.

Before you begin the process of developing prime dance, you may find it helpful to create a foundation of attitudes about three areas of dancing. The first area involves your perspective on dance performance and competition—what you think of them, how you feel about them, and how you approach them. The second area involves your view of yourself as a dancer—how you perform in rehearsal versus in performance or competition. And the third area involves your attitude toward success and failure—how you define success and failure and whether you know the essential roles that they play in your process of becoming the best dancer you can be. We encourage you to explore your attitudes in these three areas in order to develop a personal philosophy that serves as your wellspring for understanding and shaping your own experience of prime dance.

Maintaining a Healthy Perspective on Dance

You have a passion for dance, and it is important to you. You put a great deal of time and effort into your dance training and performance. When you dance well, of course, you feel thrilled and fulfilled. When you dance poorly, you feel disappointed. These feelings—both positive and negative—are natural because they are normal expressions of your love for dancing. It is possible, however, to lose perspective, in which case your feelings about dance can hurt your training and performance.

This problem sometimes takes the form of falling into what we call the "too zone." Of course, you care about your dance participation, but do you care *too* much? Dance is important to you, but is it too important? You try to perform your best, but do you try too hard? You can lose healthy perspective when your self-identity becomes overly connected to your dance—when the way you feel about yourself is overly determined by how you dance rather than by a holistic picture of yourself that incorporates all aspects of who you are.

In the too zone, dance is no longer a positive aspect of your life—it *is* your life! As a result, dance is no longer about having fun and achieving your goals. Instead, you invest your very ego—how you feel about yourself as a person—in your training and performance. Therefore, if training and performance don't go well, you feel bad about yourself and beat yourself up. If you feel this way, step back and regain perspective. Reevaluate what dance means to you, the role it plays in your life, and how it affects your happiness. You may find that it plays too big a role. If dance defines how you feel about yourself, this disproportion may affect your performance and the satisfaction you derive from this art form.

You have also crossed over into the too zone if the way you feel about yourself depends on whether or not you're cast in a coveted role. If this is the case for you, pull back and regain perspective. Find the middle ground where you care and feel motivated—where you value dance as one part of your identity—without overinvesting and caring so much that dance becomes the dominant part of your identity. That kind of commitment detracts from your dance.

So, to perform your best and have fun, approach dance with a healthy perspective. Remember why you dance. It's fun and a great way to socialize. You enjoy the movement and the music. You find it fulfilling to master your body, as well as a particular piece of choreography. And you enjoy performance, competition, and achievement.

Even if you're a professional dancer, take care to maintain your perspective about your career. Most of us become dancers (whether paid or not) because we *love* to dance, to feel the music, to experience the synchrony in our body, and to enjoy the satisfaction of mastering a challenging piece. If you've lost your love, your fun, or your passion, and dance has become just a job, then you've crossed into the too zone and it's time to take a step back and remember what got you where you are in the first place. The prime dance perspective approaches dance as a healthy and balanced part of your life that enhances you physically, mentally, socially, and spiritually. If you have fun, give your best effort, and enjoy the process of dance, then you will perform better and attain more of your goals.

"I dance because I'm happy. Dance is so powerful. Not only does it have the ability to bring people together, but it also has the power to heal. I dance because I'm free."

Antoine Hunter, award-winning dancer and choreographer

Accepting the Ups and Downs

Another aspect of the prime dance perspective is recognizing and accepting the ups and downs of the art form. Even the greatest dancers in history—those such as Mikhail Baryshnikov, Martha Graham, Savion Glover, Ann Reinking, Gelsey Kirkland, José Manuel Carreño—experience ebb and flow, whether within a single performance, across roles, or in the course of a season. Therefore, focus not on whether you have ups and downs but on the height of the peaks and the depth of the valleys—and how you respond to them. This book is devoted to helping you smooth out the bumps in your dance performance.

In a down period, it's also easy to get down on *yourself*. You may feel disappointed and helpless to reverse the downward trend. You may want to give up. Addressing these feelings is an essential skill for dancers. Successful dancers know how to maintain a positive attitude and helpful emotions, which enable them to stop the decline and return to a high level of performance as quickly as possible.

The first step in reversing your descent is to keep the ups and downs in perspective by acknowledging that they're a natural and expected part of the art form. This attitude reduces the pressure in down moments by easing (though not completely alleviating) your frustration and disappointment. Thus, it enables you to stay positive and motivated. Most important, never give up. Stay focused on your dance performance goals. Look for the cause of your decline and find a solution. Maintaining this healthy perspective helps you keep the down periods short and return quickly to the highs.

Remembering Why You Dance

It's easy to lose sight of why you dance when you're caught up in the cycle of rehearsal, performance, and competition. There are the many other dancers with wonderful bodies and great talent. There are the costumes, sets, choreographers, directors, teachers, judges, and audiences. And of course there is the spotlight, with ovations and bravos and accolades. These external aspects of dance can cause you to lose sight of the deeper, more meaningful reasons for which you participate.

When external aspects of the art form come to dominate your focus, remind yourself of what dance means to you. Dance is like child's play. You're engaging in an activity that children love to do. Every time you go to class or rehearsal, you have the opportunity to reconnect with the simplicity and purity of childhood. Remember the joy that dance brought you when you were young—the love that you felt when you twirled, jumped, and moved your body to the music. Realize that you were not motivated then by the notion of receiving praise from a choreographer, getting a coveted role, or basking in the warm glow of a standing ovation.

Rather, you were drawn by the simple pleasure of being absorbed in the music and moving your body to it—perhaps being part of a mosh pit with your friends, or simply experiencing the pleasure of spinning until you were dizzy and jumping until you were out of breath. What a wonderful gift! You can still experience these feelings—and more. Beyond the childlike joy of movement, dance can inspire you and help you grow as a person, enhancing all aspects of your life. Ultimately, the best reason to dance is that it provides you with potentially unparalleled meaning, fulfillment, and joy.

Infuse your movement with passion.

Measuring Success and Failure

Your attitude toward dance, and your feelings about it, are also affected by your attitude toward success and failure. Indeed, your definition of success and failure determines your ability to consistently perform at your best and enjoy the art form. Too often, success and failure are defined narrowly in dance culture: If you're accepted into a dance company or get a coveted solo role, you succeed; if not, you fail.

Yet one of the wonderful aspects of dance is the fact that everyone can succeed. For some dancers, success means having fun, performing in the corps, being with friends, or just staying healthy after a series of injuries. For others, success means performing a role that they never imagined possible. For still others, it means performing consistently or allowing their artistry to shine through. And for the rare few, success involves earning a college scholarship, a place in a prestigious company, or a prized role.

With this perspective in mind, we define success as giving your best effort, performing to the best of your technical ability, expressing yourself through your artistry, and enjoying the performing experience. That alone is success; everything else is icing on the cake. Moreover, because this definition of success lies entirely within your control, you have the power to pursue and achieve success at will.

Unfortunately, however, dance culture does not always approach success and failure in such a healthy way. In fact, it has created many myths and misconceptions that prevent dancers from taking a healthy perspective on success and failure. For example, many dancers believe that the only way to succeed is to have always been successful—that people who are a success rarely or never fail. The reality is that the greatest dancers both succeed and fail. When they do poorly, they are disappointed, but they benefit from the failure by learning the lessons offered by the experience. In this way, they use failure to set the stage for future success.

Therefore, we recommend that as part of your healthy definition of success and failure, you attend to their value in achieving prime dance. Success—whether defined as we have suggested here or in the more traditional sense—builds your confidence and reinforces your belief that you can perform well and meet the challenges of dance. At the same time, success can breed complacency. If you succeed all the time, you have little motivation to improve, and you may not even recognize areas in need of improvement. As a result, you miss the opportunity to develop them and improve as a dancer. Sooner or later, however, as you move up the performance ladder, you come up against others who are just as good as or better than you are. When this happens, if you haven't put in the time and effort to improve, you won't be as good as you could be.

Failure, on the other hand, can be immensely beneficial to your development as a dancer, whether it occurs in class, audition, rehearsal, or performance. Failure provides you with information about your progress. It shows you what you're doing well and, more important, what you need to work on. A setback shows you what doesn't work, which helps you identify what works best. For example, failure may highlight an aspect of technique that you need to change in order to use proper biomechanics and move more efficiently. Poor performance also teaches you how to respond positively to adversity, which is an inevitable part of both dance and life.

Finally, setbacks teach you humility and an appreciation for what it takes to be successful. Because dance frequently confronts you with diverse challenges and teaches you painful lessons, you develop a healthy respect both for the art form itself and for your ability to learn its lessons. Therefore, rather than letting poor performance discourage you, focus on how it helps you become a better dancer.

If you learn the valuable lessons offered by both success and failure, you gain wisdom and a perspective on dance that allows you to achieve prime dance. Like life, dance is more about the process than about the outcome. Every time you step into a class, rehearsal, or performance, you have a unique opportunity to learn about yourself so that, regardless of the short-term outcome, you can grow.

Becoming a Prime Dancer

Looking back at great dancers over the years—Baryshnikov, Graham, Margot Fonteyn, José Limón, Merce Cunningham, Fred Astaire, Ginger Rogers, Gregory Hines, Michael Jackson, Mia Michaels, Paloma Herrera—you see the unique ability, style, and personality of each one. You also see several essential characteristics they have held in common. All of these dancers and choreographers developed top physical conditioning, technical proficiency, and strong artistic presence.

These same qualities, however, are also possessed by many dancers who don't achieve greatness. Indeed, these qualities alone only make you a good dancer. Becoming a prime dancer requires something more. There's a considerable difference between dancing well in training (in class and rehearsal) and dancing well in the most important performance of your life. The ability to handle this difference is what separates prime dancers from the rest.

It is true that you must first master the physical, technical, and artistic aspects of dance. Indeed, becoming a prime dancer requires that you maximize every aspect of your physical and artistic ability, and the process starts at the physical level. Optimal fitness results from committing yourself to a high-quality training program geared toward helping you achieve your dance goals. Although dance is not often seen by lay people as a difficult art form, those in the know realize that each dance discipline makes particular technical and artistic demands that a dancer must master in order to perform at a high level. In order to meet these demands, you must develop an ingrained and automatic technique that withstands fatigue.

With physical fitness as the foundation, you also achieve an exquisite level of technical competence. Though you may be considered a naturally talented dancer, what enables your often breathtaking expressions of dance is the many hours spent in the classroom honing your technique, as well as your mental training.

You must also develop a strong artistic presence through which you integrate choreographic steps and themes into both your body and your mind and make them your own. You must then find ways to express the choreography, music, and narrative in ways that are unique and authentic to you. All of these efforts, however, take you only part of the way down the road to becoming a prime dancer.

The final piece of the puzzle is the mental aspect. If you fully develop yourself mentally, then you position yourself to achieve prime dance. What separates prime dancers from others is how they respond to adversity and pressure. In important performances, under difficult conditions, when facing their toughest critics, they raise their performance to a new level of artistry and excellence. Everything that turns negative for most dancers shifts positively for prime dancers, and this ability to rise to the occasion propels them to their very best dancing.

At the heart of all prime dancers is an unwavering determination to be their best. They are driven to improve constantly. They feel great passion for hard work. They spend long hours each day training and rehearsing to improve their dancing. They embrace the repetition of training and are willing to suffer in order to succeed.

Prime dancers also have a deep and enduring belief in themselves. They have the confidence to push their limits, endure discomfort in training, see performance as a challenge rather than a threat, enjoy the process, and never give up. This belief enables them to be *inspired* by failure and disappointment, and it allows them to keep faith in their ability even when faced with adversity. As a result, they approach difficult conditions and tough competition as exciting opportunities to showcase their skills.

In addition, prime dancers can raise their performance level in order to succeed. They thrive on the pressure of important events, such as the first night of a new role or the final performance of a season. They've developed the ability to stay calm and focused when a crucial performance is on the line. Most fundamentally, prime dancers perform their best in the most important performances of their lives.

Being a prime dancer does not require you to be a professional or prepro-fessional. Every dancer can become a prime dancer. The attributes described here have nothing to do with natural ability or with being the best. Rather, they are about being *your* best. Each of these qualities can be developed by any dancer motivated to achieve her or his personal best. With this beauty of possibility in mind, this book is devoted to helping you be thoroughly pre-pared—physically, technically, artistically, and mentally—to perform your best.

> *"Why I dance changes constantly. On my best days, dancing— pushing myself to my physical and emotional limits—lets me express my deepest truths."*
>
> Paloma McGregor,
> dancer at Urban Bush Women and cofounder of Angela's Pulse

Preparing Mentally

Experienced dancers will tell you that once you have rehearsed and practiced enough, a dance performance is less a physical challenge than a mental one. Later in the performance, when your body starts to break down, you may struggle to remain positive and motivated. The best way to tap into a last reserve of energy and get to the final curtain is to use your mind to encour-age, cajole, and persuade your body to keep going in the face of fatigue. You can say, for example, "Keep at it. This is what I've worked so hard for. I will not give up." Or you might say, "I have rehearsed this many times and was able to keep up. I can certainly do it now." When you use your mind to make such a statement, your body listens, and you can dance your best until the curtain falls.

Here are some good times to recognize that your mind is in charge: when you are comparing yourself with other dancers, doubting your ability, or worrying about how you look in your costume or who will be in the audience judging you. At such times, you can remind yourself of the following truths: "All I can do is be the best version of myself. I know I have worked very hard in class and rehearsal, and worrying won't help me achieve my goals." Take several deep, slow breaths and remind yourself of that inner child—twirling, jumping, and enjoying the movement of your body to the music. Remind yourself, "This is the moment I've worked so hard for. I can enjoy the opportunity to move, express myself, and share my gift with the world." Then go out and focus on the moment, on what you're doing, on what you're expressing, and on what's coming next. That's it.

Mental preparation translates to synchronicity with your partner.

Some dancers hold misconceptions about the mental side of dance. They believe that mental abilities are inborn—that either you have them or you don't. But mental abilities are skills, and, as with technical skills, you can develop them. Therefore, you can approach mental skills in the same way that you approach the physical and technical parts of dance. In other words, if you consistently work on your mental skills, you will improve them, and your overall performance will benefit.

Ascending the Prime Dance Pyramid

The goal of this book is to help you experience the feeling and performance of dancing your very best. This goal is accomplished by ascending the prime dance pyramid (see figure 1.1), which consists of five essential mental factors: motivation, confidence, intensity, focus, and emotional mastery. These five mental factors are ordered such that later ones build on previous ones in a sequence that leads to prime dance.

At the base of the prime dance pyramid lies motivation, which is essential for maintaining the desire, determination, and perseverance to train. Prime motivation ensures that you put in the necessary time and effort to be totally prepared to dance your best.

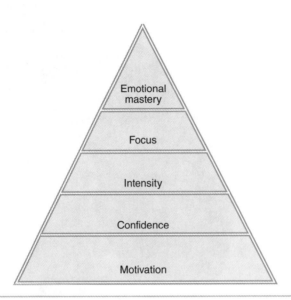

Figure 1.1   Prime dance pyramid.

From motivation to train and prepare comes confidence in your physical, technical, and artistic capabilities and in your ability to achieve your goals. Prime confidence gives you the desire to perform and a core belief that you can dance your best.

From confidence comes the ability to manage your intensity and respond positively to the pressures of performance. Prime intensity enables you to maintain your ideal level of intensity during each performance.

From intensity comes the ability to focus properly during classes, rehearsals, and performances. Prime focus lets you stay focused and avoid distractions.

Finally, from motivation, confidence, intensity, and focus comes the ability to master your emotions. Prime emotional mastery ensures that your emotions act as a useful tool while you are training and performing.

Once you ascend the prime dance pyramid, you possess the tools to achieve prime dance. Moreover, the attitude you hold influences not only how you dance but also how you approach every aspect of your life. To put it the other way around, your ability to achieve prime dance is determined in part by your philosophy and perspective on life—how you view the inevitable ups and downs of life and how you define success and failure outside of dance. Whether or not you believe that your mind can control much of what life throws at you, the same attitudes that you hold about dance can help you find meaning, satisfaction, and joy in your relationships, in school and work, and in just plain life.

Center Stage: Zoey

Maintaining a Healthy Perspective

At age 17, Zoey was somewhat new to modern dance but already showed considerable promise. A former ballet and lyrical dancer, she quickly picked up modern dance and emerged as a top dancer at her school, where she was also a cheerleader. Zoey was "trying out" modern dance, and she enjoyed learning, moving differently, and experimenting with syncopation and uneven music. Her training wasn't organized or intensive—she was just having fun and developing quickly.

After several very successful performances and a third-place finish at a national competition, Zoey accepted a contract to dance professionally with a modern dance company. She also hired a private instructor and established a highly structured training program. Her dance life became her daily life, which revolved around training, nutrition, and rest. As a result, Zoey lost touch with her friends outside of dance friends and gave up several hobbies.

Then, contrary to her expectations, Zoey had a terrible dance season. She found classes and rehearsals a chore—monotonous and boring. Before performances, she was so nervous that she thought she was going to be ill. Her performances were a struggle; the ease and freedom with which she had moved were gone, and her dance suffered. She seemed to be going backward. Following a string of poor performances, Zoey was disconsolate, frustrated, and angry. This pattern continued all year until Zoey was just glad to have the season over with.

When the company did not continue Zoey's contract, she returned to school and decided to dance just for fun again. She cut back on her training, did only what she felt like doing, reconnected with her friends, and got back into her hobbies. Almost immediately, her dancing improved and she enjoyed herself again. At her first performance, she wasn't a bit nervous; in fact, she had fun and, much to her surprise, reconnected with her technique, movement, and artistry and received a standing ovation.

Then Zoey experienced an epiphany: What had changed was not her dancing but her attitude toward it. Before joining the company, she had danced for fun, joy, and expression. With the company, however, she had created strict expectations that exerted pressure on her to perform. Then, when she hadn't danced well, she had become negative and critical of herself. Now, she had returned to that initial attitude of enjoyment and freedom, and it showed in her pure delight in dancing!

ENCORE

- Prime dance involves dancing at a consistently high level under the most challenging conditions.

- Prime dance is an experience involving effortlessness; a clear mind; sharpened senses; ease and artistry of movement; total absorption; boundless energy; and an integration of body, mind, and spirit.

- Experiencing prime dance requires having a healthy philosophy of dance.

- The too zone is a state in which a dancer is excessively invested in dance.

- By nature, dance involves ups and downs.

- Dance is about love of yourself, others, and the art form.

- Prime dance values both success and failure as essential to your development as a dancer.

- Prime dancers have the following characteristics: They master the physical, technical, and artistic aspects of dance; they have an unwavering determination to be their best; they believe deeply in their capabilities; and they can dance their best when it matters most.

- Prime dance involves believing that your mind is in charge of your dance.

- Prime dance involves developing skills that help you dance your best.

- The prime dance pyramid consists of the five most important mental contributors to dance: motivation, confidence, intensity, focus, and emotional mastery.

- The knowledge and skills you gain from prime dance help you excel and find meaning, fulfillment, and joy in every part of your life.

References

Bennett, J.G., & Pravitz, J.E. (1982). *The miracle of sports psychology*. Englewood Cliffs, NJ: Prentice-Hall.

Bennett, J.G., & Pravitz, J.E. (1987). *Profile of a winner: Advanced mental training for athletes*. Ithaca, NY: Sport Science International.

Butler, R.J., & Hardy, L. (1992). The performance profile: Theory and application. *The Sport Psychologist, 6*(3), 253–264.

Csikszentmihalyi, M. (1990). *Flow: The psychology of optimal experience*. New York: Harper & Row.

Dishman, R.K. (1983). Identity crisis in North American sport psychology: Academics in professional issues. *Journal of Sport Psychology, 5*, 123–134.

Doyle, L., & Landers, D. (1980). *Psychological skills in elite and subelite shooters*. Unpublished manuscript.

Gauron, E.F. (1984). *Mental training for peak performance*. Lansing, NY: Sport Science Associates.

Gould, D., Dieffenbach, K., & Moffet, A. (2002). Psychological characteristics and their development in Olympic champions. *Journal of Applied Sport Psychology, 14*(3), 172-204.

Graham, M. (1974). A modern dancer's primer for action. In S.J. Cohen (Ed.), *Dance as a theatre art: Source readings in dance history from 1581 to the present* (pp. 135-142). New York: Dodd, Mead.

Greenspan, M.J., & Feltz, D.L. (1989). Psychological interventions with athletes in competitive situations: A review. *The Sport Psychologist, 3*, 219-236.

Hanrahan, S.J. (1996). Dancers' perceptions of psychological skills. *Revista de Psicologia del Deporte, 5*(2), 19-27.

Hanrahan, S.J. (2005). On stage: Mental skills training for dancers. In M.B. Andersen (Ed.), *Sport psychology in practice* (pp. 109-127). Champaign, IL: Human Kinetics.

Harris, D.V., & Harris, B.L. (1984). *The athlete's guide to sports psychology: Mental skills for physical people*. New York: Leisure Press.

Hays, K. (2002). The enhancement of performance excellence among performing artists. *Journal of Applied Sport Psychology, 14*, 299-312.

H'Doubler, M.N. (1968). *Dance: A creative art experience*. Madison: University of Wisconsin Press.

Hunter, A. (2013, September). Why I dance: Antoine Hunter. *Dance Magazine*, 21-25.

Kamata, A., Tenenbaum, G., & Hanin, Y. (2002). Individual zone of optimal functioning (IZOF): A probabilistic conceptualization. *Journal of Sport & Exercise Psychology, 24*, 189-208.

Klockare, E., Gustafsson, H., & Nordin-Bates, S.M. (2011). An interpretive phenomenological analysis of how professional dance teachers implement psychological skills training in practice. *Research in Dance Education, 12*(30), 277-293.

Locke, E.A. (1966). The relationship of intentions to level of performance. *Journal of Applied Psychology, 50*, 60-66.

Mahoney, M., & Avener, M. (1977). Psychology of the elite athlete: An explorative study. *Cognitive Therapy and Research, 1*, 135-141.

Martens, R., & Burton, D. (1984). *Psychological skills training*. Unpublished manuscript.

McGregor, P. (2009, June). Why I dance: Paloma McGregor. *Dance Magazine*, 17-21.

Meyers, A., Cooke, C., Cullen, J., & Liles, L. (1979). Psychological aspects of athletic competitors: A replication across sports. *Cognitive Therapy and Research, 3*, 361-366.

Orlick, T. (1990). *In pursuit of excellence* (2nd ed.). Champaign, IL: Human Kinetics.

Orlick, T., & Partington, J. (1986). *Psyched*. Ottawa: Coaching Association of Canada.

Ravizza, K. (2010). Increasing awareness of sport performance. In J.M. Williams (Ed.), *Applied sport psychology: Personal growth to peak performance* (pp. 149-161). Palo Alto, CA: Mayfield.

Rushall, B.S. (1979). *Psyching in sport*. London: Pelham.

Seligman, M.E.P. (2002). *Authentic happiness: Using the new positive psychology to realize your potential for lasting fulfillment*. New York: Free Press.

Sorell, W. (1971). *The dancer's image: Points and counterpoints*. New York: Columbia University.

Taylor, J. (1988). Psychological aspects of teaching and coaching tennis. In J.L. Groppel (Ed.), *The USPTA sport science and sports medicine guide* (pp.133–147). Wesley Chapel, FL: USPTA.

Taylor, J. (2001). *Prime sport: Triumph of the athlete mind*. New York: iUniverse.

Taylor, J., & Schneider, T. (2005). *The triathlete's guide to mental training*. Boulder, CO: Velopress.

Weinberg, R.S. (1984). Mental preparation strategies. In J.M. Silva III & R.S. Weinberg (Eds.), *Psychological foundations of sport* (pp. 145–156). Champaign, IL: Human Kinetics.

Williams, J.M. (2010). Integrating and implementing a psychological skills training program. In J.M. Williams (Ed.), *Applied sport psychology: Personal growth to peak performance* (pp. 301–324). Palo Alto, CA: Mayfield.

CHAPTER

Knowing Yourself

"Your dancing is really 95 percent [made up of] what your mind is. It's just this little bit of skin, bone, muscle, and connective tissue that makes it happen. But the whole source is what you think, how you imagine, and how you know yourself."

Natalie Desch, Doug Varone and Dancers

ecoming the best dancer you can be is a complex process, which of course requires time. In addition, you probably have enormous time commitments for school or work, as well as family, social life, and other activities. In the midst of these commitments, one way to help yourself focus and work efficiently in your dance training and performance efforts is to develop an understanding of yourself. By developing greater self-understanding, you can recognize both your strengths and the areas in need of improvement.

Although most dancers enjoy focusing on and displaying their strengths, they often have difficulty seeing or acknowledging areas that aren't yet fully developed. In fact, some dancers think that they're as good as their greatest strengths. The truth, however, is that dancers are only as good as their most significant weakness. For example, a certain former collegiate dancer joined a small regional company, where he was often seen practicing his turns even though he was already a fantastic turner. His reason? "Because it's fun!" However, the advantage provided by his turning ability was neutralized by his lack of the power necessary to lift his partners. He would have benefited, therefore, from devoting some of his practice time to working on his lifts.

Recognizing the areas in which you can improve provides two benefits: It fosters your development, and it enhances your strengths. If, as in the preceding example, power is not one of your strengths but turning or artistry is an asset, you can optimize your performance by increasing your power. It may help to think of your dancing in terms of a mathematical equation:

strengths + weaknesses = overall dance performance

For example, if a dancer is an excellent turner (rating of 10 on a scale of 10) but a weak jumper (rating of 2) with mediocre extension (rating of 6), then her overall performance is low ($10 + 2 + 6 = 18$). However, if she improves her jumps (to a rating of 5) and her leg extensions (to a rating of 8), then her overall performance rises considerably ($10 + 5 + 8 = 23$). In this way, the more you improve your less developed areas, the greater the gains you can make in your overall dance performance.

You may find it challenging to grasp the mental aspects of dance because they are intangible and therefore not as easily measured as the physical and technical dimensions of dance. To learn about your physical strengths and areas of challenge, you can go through a physical testing program that provides you with objective data about your physical condition. For example, you might assess your strength and flexibility. Similarly, your technical capabilities can be assessed objectively with the aid of video analysis or observation by an instructor. In contrast, there are no direct ways to measure your mental abilities related to dance.

You can, however, measure your "mental muscles" indirectly through the use of pencil-and-paper inventories. This process, called prime dance profiling, enables you to test your mind in a way that makes psychological contributors more concrete. Prime dance profiling increases your self-understanding so that you can take active steps to maintain your strengths and develop in areas that have held you back.

Approach the prime dance profiling process with an open mind. Consider the information in a positive and constructive way. Finding areas in need of improvement doesn't mean that you're incapable of dancing well. Perhaps you simply haven't had to use the less developed skills at your current level, or perhaps you've been able to cover for them with your strengths.

In any case, it's best to know both your strengths and your areas of challenge. Knowing your strengths gives you confidence in your ability to meet the challenges of dance. Knowing which aspects of your dancing need work gives you a starting point for minimizing your limitations and turning them into strengths.

Psychological Profile

The prime dance psychological profile consists of 12 mental, emotional, and performance factors that influence your dancing. To complete the Psychological Profile worksheet (available in the web resource), read the following descriptions of each factor and rate yourself on a scale of 1 to 10 by shading in the appropriate portion of the worksheet diagram.

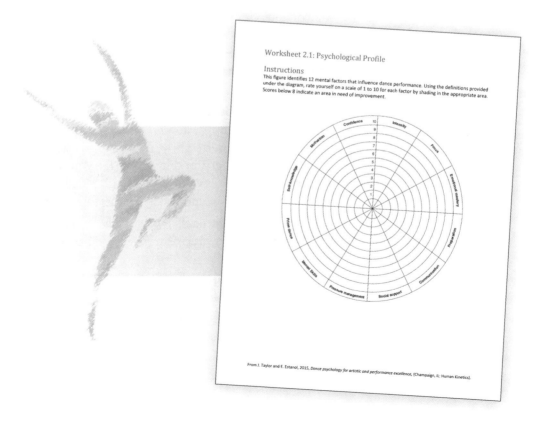

Worksheet 2.1: Psychological Profile

Instructions
This figure identifies 12 mental factors that influence dance performance. Using the definitions provided under the diagram, rate yourself on a scale of 1 to 10 for each factor by shading in the appropriate area. Scores below 8 indicate an area in need of improvement.

From J. Taylor and E. Estanol, 2015, *Dance psychology for artistic and performance excellence*, (Champaign, IL: Human Kinetics).

1. **Self-knowledge** in this context refers to knowing your mental strengths and areas of challenge. Do you understand what helps and hurts you mentally in dance? (1 = don't know myself, 10 = know myself well)

2. **Motivation** refers to how determined you are to train and perform in order to achieve your dance goals. Motivation affects all aspects of your preparation, including your desire to invest time and energy in your physical conditioning, your technical and artistic development, and your mental preparation. Do you work hard consistently on all aspects of dance, or do you ease up or even give up when you get tired, bored, or frustrated? (1 = not at all motivated, 10 = very motivated)

3. **Confidence** depends on how strongly you believe in your ability to achieve your goals. It is reflected in how positive or negative your self-talk is during training, performance, and competition. Confidence includes the ability to maintain positive beliefs during performance and competition, especially when you face challenging conditions. When you face a difficult situation, or when you're not dancing well, do you stay confident and positive, or do you lose confidence and become negative? (1 = very negative, 10 = very positive)

4. **Intensity** determines whether your physical state helps or hurts you during a performance. Do you stay calm and relaxed, or do you become too anxious before or during a performance? (1 = very anxious, 10 = very relaxed)

5. **Focus** refers to how well you keep your mind on performing your best and avoiding distractions before and during a performance. Do you stay focused on what you need to address in order to perform well, or do you become distracted by things that hurt your performance? (1 = very distracted, 10 = very focused)

6. **Emotional mastery** involves how well you control your emotions before and during a performance. When you approach an important performance, face difficult conditions, or dance poorly, do you stay excited and inspired, or do you get frustrated, angry, or depressed? Do you experience emotions that help or hurt you in performances? (1 = negative emotions, hurt performance; 10 = positive emotions, help performance)

7. **Preparation** refers to how physically, technically, artistically, and mentally ready you usually feel before a dance performance. (1 = not at all prepared; 10 = very prepared)

8. **Communication** is how well you are able to communicate with instructors and other dancers. (1 = poorly; 10 = well)

9. **Social support** is the degree of social support you are receiving from instructors, other dancers, family, and friends. (1 = none; 10 = considerable)

10. **Pressure management** refers to how well you are able to manage the pressure of leading roles, demanding choreography, or difficult performing conditions and dance your best during performances. (1 = not at all well; 10 = very well)

11. **Mental skills** refers to the degree to which you incorporate mental skills into your dance training and performances. (1 = not at all; 10 = a great deal)

12. **Prime dance** refers to how consistently you are able to achieve and maintain your highest level of dance performance. (1 = never; 10 = often)

Physical Profile

The Physical Profile worksheet, available in the web resource, identifies 12 physical factors that are critical to dance performance. When you identify and track the physical elements that affect your dance, you can set clearer goals that help you maximize your training and achieve prime dance. Follow the same directions given for the Psychological Profile worksheet to rate yourself on the following factors.

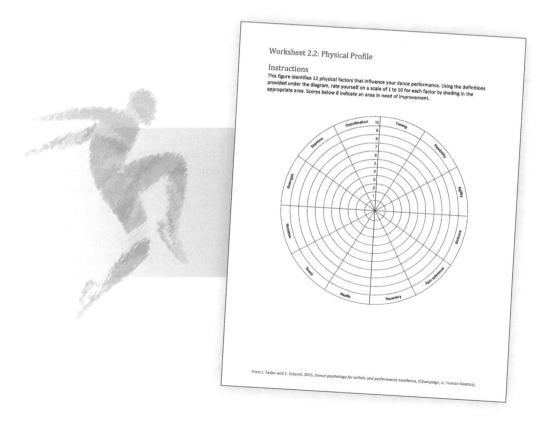

1. **Strength**: The amount of force you can generate for a specific muscle group (e.g., deep pliés). (1 = low; 10 = high)

2. **Stamina**: Ability to sustain dance for a long period of time (e.g., a lengthy solo). (1 = poor; 10 = excellent)

3. **Coordination**: Your ability to execute complex movements and combinations. (1 = poor, 10 = excellent)

4. **Timing**: Ability to coordinate dance movements and time choreography with other dancers. (1 = poor; 10 = excellent)

5. **Flexibility**: Ability of muscle to lengthen (e.g., leg lift). (1 = poor; 10 = excellent)

6. **Agility**: Ability to change direction with quickness and power (e.g., quick turns). (1 = poor; 10 = excellent)

7. **Balance**: Ability to maintain center of gravity and equilibrium during an activity (e.g., on pointe). (1 = poor; 10 = excellent)

8. **Pain tolerance**: Ability to endure pain and discomfort from training and injury (e.g., during and after class, rehearsal, and performance). (1 = poor; 10 = excellent)

9. **Recovery**: Ability to recover from intense training period (e.g., maintain high intensity in training, no burn-out). (1 = poor; 10 = excellent)

10. **Health**: Degree of injury, illness, or fatigue you now have (e.g., knee injury, flu, burn-out). (1 = poor; 10 = excellent)

11. **Sleep**: How well you are sleeping (e.g., length and quality). (1 = poor; 10 = excellent)

12. **Nutrition**: How well you eat and get sufficient nutrition (e.g., high carbohydrates, low fat, eating nutritious foods that help you maintain a healthy weight). (1 = poor; 10 = excellent)

In addition, the web resource for this book includes a blank Technical and Artistic Profile worksheet that you can use to note specific technical and artistic elements of your dance style as either strengths or areas of challenge. Examples might include pirouettes, syncopation, prances, and petit allegro.

The key in completing these profiles is to be completely honest with yourself—both about your strengths and about what you need to work on. If you find that you're unable to be completely accurate in your technical profile, ask an instructor to complete one about you as well and then compare notes.

Analyzing Your Profiles

Once you complete the prime dance profiles, you have a clear picture of what you believe to be your mental, physical, and technical strengths. You also know the areas in which your dancing is underdeveloped—generally, all areas with

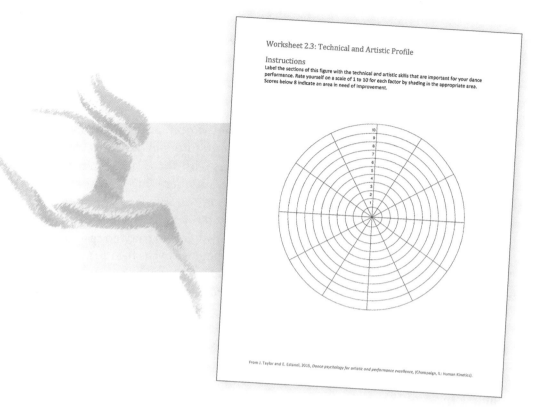

Worksheet 2.3: Technical and Artistic Profile

Instructions
Label the sections of this figure with the technical and artistic skills that are important for your dance performance. Rate yourself on a scale of 1 to 10 for each factor by shading in the appropriate area. Scores below 8 indicate an area in need of improvement.

From J. Taylor and E. Estanol, 2015, *Dance psychology for artistic and performance excellence*, (Champaign, IL: Human Kinetics).

a score below 8. Place a check mark next to each factor that you scored as 7 or below and consider working on these factors in your mental training program (see chapter 11).

For now, select three of your check-marked items to focus on immediately. It's most efficient to focus on a few areas, strengthen them, and then move on to others. First, ask which areas are most important for your development. For example, if your biggest obstacles to achieving your goals are your strength in holding a position and your flexibility, give these factors high priority.

Second, some less-developed parts of your dancing may be symptoms of other limitations. In such cases,

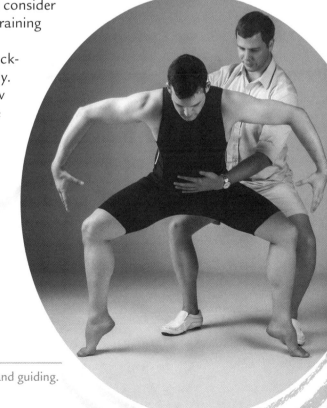

Instructors enhance learning by correcting and guiding.

dealing with one factor may also relieve another one without your having to work on the second one directly. For example, if you lack confidence, you may not handle adversity very well. If so, building your confidence will also improve your ability to overcome adversity.

Third, balance your immediate training and performance needs with your long-term development. Perhaps you identify motivation and confidence as the most important areas to address for your long-term future in dance. At the same time, perhaps you're also held back by struggles with focus and intensity and have an immediate need to prepare for an important upcoming performance. In this case, you might choose to work on your focus and intensity right now and address motivation and confidence over the long term.

Use the prime dance Priority Form worksheet, available in the web resource, to identify the three mental factors that you want to focus on in the near future. Then, after you finish reading the book, return to the chapters that address your selected areas in order to review techniques and exercises for strengthening them. To help you carry out this work, use the goal-setting program described in chapter 8.

You can also use prime dance profiling to measure progress in your training. Once a month, complete the profiles again and compare the results with those from your past profiles to see your improvement in the targeted areas. If you have a dance coach, teacher, choreographer, or training partner, ask that person to complete the profile based on her or his perceptions of you and of any positive changes in the relevant areas. When your ratings move above 7, select other factors to work on and follow the same procedure.

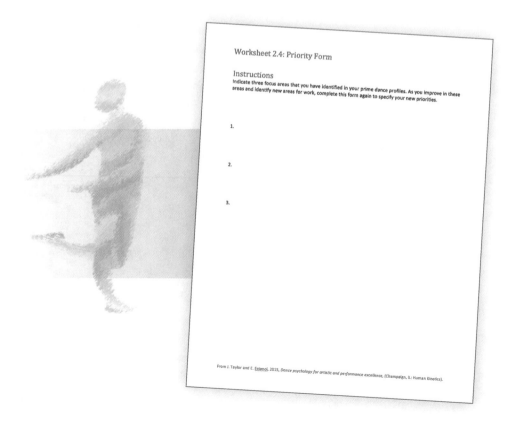

Worksheet 2.4: Priority Form

Instructions

Indicate three focus areas that you have identified in your prime dance profiles. As you improve in these areas and identify new areas for work, complete this form again to specify your new priorities.

1.

2.

3.

From J. Taylor and E. Estanol, 2015, *Dance psychology for artistic and performance excellence*, (Champaign, IL: Human Kinetics).

Center Stage: Sean

Cultivating Self-Knowledge

Sean, a 24-year-old, had been dancing professionally for a ballet company for three years. He enjoyed dancing but was frustrated by the fact that he never danced in performances as well as he did in classes and rehearsals. Sean gave his best effort in training, maintained excellent physical conditioning, and pursued realistic goals, but his performances were often disappointing. As a result, he had not progressed out of the corps as he had hoped.

Sean was confident that his training was sound and that he had no glaring technical weaknesses. A voracious consumer of dance-related literature, he began looking for articles in dance magazines to see if something was missing in his efforts. After reading an article about the psychology of dance, he realized that his problems might be mental. A self-proclaimed nonintrospective person, he began to explore the mental side of his dance and was surprised at how little he had even thought—much less done—anything about it. He completed the prime dance profiles and began to see patterns that held him back.

For one thing, as Sean looked back over past seasons, he realized that he didn't have much confidence in pushing himself, physically or artistically, during performances. True, he would *think* about pushing himself in performances like he did in rehearsals. However, he would fail to follow through on those thoughts because he was afraid that if he went to his limits, his efforts still might not be good enough, and then he would be disappointed. In other words, holding back gave him an excuse.

As he thought more about past seasons, Sean also realized that he didn't focus very well during performances. Specifically, he paid too much attention to who was watching and what they might be thinking and not enough to his own expression of the choreography. In addition, during most of his performances—especially when he had a bigger role—he was distracted from dancing his best by worries about his technique and how he appeared with his partner.

Sean applied this newfound self-awareness to his training and performances. In particular, he worked on being positive and trusting his technique and artistry while staying focused on his artistry and partners. To his pleasant surprise, his performances and company reviews improved noticeably over the season; as a result, he was given more challenging roles and even leading roles, and he had more fun than ever before.

ENCORE

- The first step in achieving prime dance is to develop self-knowledge.

- When you understand your strengths and your areas to work on, you can further develop your strengths and remove obstacles to your development.

- You can gain understanding of yourself as a dancer effectively and efficiently through prime dance profiling.

- Prime dance profiling makes the ethereal nature of the mind more tangible.

- In order to get the most out of prime dance profiling, keep an open and constructive mind; the goal is to help you dance your best.

- The prime dance psychological profile assesses 12 factors that we have found most influential on dance performance: self-knowledge, motivation, confidence, intensity, focus, emotional mastery, preparation, communication, social support, pressure management, mental skills, and prime dance.

- From your completed prime dance profiles, select three areas to develop first in your mental training program.

References

Bandura, A. (1986). *Social foundations of thought and action*. Englewood Cliffs, NJ: Prentice Hall.

Bandura, A., & Adams, N.E. (1977). Analysis of self-efficacy theory of behavioral change. *Cognitive Therapy and Research, 1*, 287–308.

Bandura, A., & Cervone, D. (1983). Self-evaluative and self-efficacy mechanisms governing the motivational effects of goal systems. *Journal of Personality and Social Psychology, 45*, 1017–1028.

Bandura, A., & Cervone, D. (1984). *Differential engagement of self-reactive influences in cognitive motivation*. Unpublished manuscript, Stanford University, Department of Psychology.

Bennett, J.G., & Pravitz, J.E. (1987). *Profile of a winner: Advanced mental training for athletes*. Ithaca, NY: Sport Science International.

Boud, D., Keogh, R., & Walker, D. (1985). *Reflection: Turning experience into learning*. New York: Routledge.

Buckroyd, J. (2000). *The student dancer: Emotional aspects of the teaching and learning of dance*. London, England: Dance Books.

Burke, S. (2011, January). Teach learn connection: Technique my way—Natalie Desch. *Dance Magazine*. www.dancemagazine.com/issues/January-2011/Teach-Learn-Connection-Technique-My-Way.

Butler, R.J., & Hardy, L. (1992). The performance profile: Theory and application. *The Sport Psychologist, 6*(3), 253–264.

Clark, L. (1960). Effect of mental practice on the development of a certain motor skill. *Research Quarterly, 31*, 560–569.

Cohn, P.J., Rotella, R.J., & Lloyd, J.W. (1990). Effects of a cognitive behavioral intervention on the preshot routine and performance in golf. *The Sport Psychologist, 4*, 33–47.

Cunningham, M. (1951). The function of a technique for dance. In W. Sorell (Ed.), *The dance has many faces* (pp. 250–251). New York: World.

Deci, E., & Ryan, R. (Eds.). (2002). *Handbook of self-determination research*. Rochester, NY: University of Rochester Press.

Dowd, I. (1981). *Taking root to fly: Seven articles on functional anatomy*. New York: Author.

Ellfeldt, L. (1976). *Dance: From magic to art*. Dubuque, IA: Brown.

Gauron, E.F. (1984). *Mental training for peak performance*. Lansing, NY: Sport Science Associates.

Gere, D. (1992, August). Mikko Nissinen: Strength regained, confidence restored. *Dance*, 32–37.

Gould, D., Dieffenbach, K., & Moffet, A. (2002): Psychological characteristics and their development in Olympic champions. *Journal of Applied Sport Psychology, 14*(3), 172–204.

Greenhill, J. (1992). A critical step toward a ballet career. *Dance Teacher Now, 14*, 53–58.

Hanrahan, S.J. (1996). Dancers' perceptions of psychological skills. *Revista de Psicologia del Deporte, 5*(2), 19–27.

Hanrahan, S.J. (2005). On stage: Mental skills training for dancers. In M.B. Andersen (Ed.), *Sport psychology in practice* (109–127). Champaign, IL: Human Kinetics.

Hays, K. (2002). The enhancement of performance excellence among performing artists. *Journal of Applied Sport Psychology, 14*, 299–312.

Jacobos, L. (2011, July). Russian soul: ABT principal Veronika Part brings elegance and intensity to her roles. *Dance Magazine*, 27–28.

Kanfer, F.H., & Karoly, P. (1972). Self-control: A behavioristic excursion into the lion's den. *Behavior Therapy, 3*, 398–416.

Kopelman, R.E. (1982–83). Improving productivity through objective feedback: A review of the evidence. *National Productivity Review, 24*, 43–55.

Loren, T. (1978). *The dancer's companion: The indispensable guide to getting the most out of dance classes*. New York: Dial Press.

Ravizza, K. (2010). Increasing awareness of sport performance. In J.M. Williams (Ed.), *Applied sport psychology: Personal growth to peak performance* (pp. 149–161). Palo Alto, CA: Mayfield.

Reivick, K., & Shatte, A. (2002). *The resilience factor: 7 essential skills for overcoming life's inevitable obstacles*. New York: Broadway Books.

Smith, R.E., Zane, N.S., Smoll, F.L., & Coppel, D.B. (1983). Behavioral assessment in youth sports: Coaching behaviors and children's attitudes. *Medicine and Science in Sports and Exercise, 15*, 208–214.

Taylor, J., & Schneider, T. (2005). *The triathlete's guide to mental training*. Boulder, CO: Velopress.

PRIME DANCE PYRAMID

This part of the book guides you through your next step toward experiencing prime dance. Specifically, it introduces you to the five mental dimensions that we believe are most essential to performance and artistic excellence in dance: motivation, confidence, intensity, focus, and emotional mastery.

Chapter 3 explores the vital role that motivation plays in every aspect of your dance experience. It also asks you to identify your deepest reasons for dancing. Given that motivation can ebb and flow in even the most determined dancers, we describe in this chapter the most common obstacles that can hurt your motivation. The chapter also provides you with many strategies for staying motivated through the inevitable challenges and setbacks of dance life.

Chapter 4 addresses confidence by highlighting the importance of your belief in your dance abilities. The chapter describes the positive effects of an upward spiral of confidence versus the negative effects of a vicious cycle of doubt. With this distinction in mind, we help you implement a key progression that leads to prime confidence, which is a deep and resilient belief in your ability to achieve your goals. The chapter also introduces you to practical techniques and exercises that you can use to build your confidence.

Chapter 5 delves into the powerful influence that physical intensity exerts on your dancing—in classes, rehearsals, and performances. This chapter teaches you the signs of both over-intensity and under-intensity so that you can recognize them when you are dancing. It also helps you identify your ideal intensity for dancing and introduces you to useful tools for reducing over-intensity and elevating under-intensity.

Chapter 6 explores the ways in which your ability to focus and avoid distractions is crucial to dancing your best. The chapter begins by helping you understand the basics of this often-misunderstood mental dimension of dance performance. More specifically, the chapter describes helpful cues to attend to when you're dancing, examines different styles of focus, and helps you identify which style best fits your dancing. It also emphasizes the importance of focus flexibility in various settings—class, rehearsal, and performance. The chapter concludes by offering you a variety of strategies for developing and maintaining your focus control.

Chapter 7 investigates the ways in which emotions affect your technique, artistry, and performance. It considers the most common causes of negative emotions and shows you how to interpret and differentiate your emotional experiences in dance. It also explores the most frequent emotional obstacles to prime dance, which include fear, frustration, despair, and postperformance depression. Finally, it describes essential ways to master your emotional dance life so that you can use your emotions as tools that facilitate—rather than weapons that harm—your performance and artistic excellence.

CHAPTER

3

Motivation

"*I intend to work for this dance of the future. I do not know whether I have the necessary qualities; I may have neither genius nor talent nor temperament. But I know that I have a Will; and will and energy sometimes prove greater than either genius or talent or temperament.*"

Isadora Duncan

Motivation lies at the base of the prime dance pyramid. It is the foundation on which you build everything you do in dance. Your motivation determines how you prioritize dance in your life, how much time you put into your training, how much mental preparation you perform, and how much you push yourself in training and performance. If you lack the desire and determination to train and perform, then all other mental factors—confidence, intensity, focus, and emotions—are meaningless, as are the physical, technical, and artistic elements of dance. Motivation is the key to maximizing your ability.

In scientific terms, motivation is a theoretical construct that refers to one's reason for doing something. In more practical terms, we might think of it as the inclination and ability to initiate and persist at a task. In particular, to achieve your dance goals, you must be motivated to begin the process of developing as a dancer and then to put in the necessary time and effort to achieve your goals.

Strong motivation is imperative in dance because you must be willing to maintain your efforts in the face of fatigue, boredom, pain, and other distractions. In the midst of these hindrances, your motivation determines your effort in training, rehearsal, and performance. More broadly, it determines the role that dance plays in your life and therefore the choices that you make about dance. In fact, it affects every aspect of your dance: physical conditioning, technical training, artistry, mental preparation, and aspects of life in general that affect dance (including sleep, diet, school or work, and relationships).

Motivation is one of three major contributors to dance performance. The other two are ability and difficulty, and we can express the relationship between these three factors in the following formula:

$$\textbf{ability} - \textbf{difficulty} + \textbf{motivation} = \textbf{performance}$$

Of these three major contributors to dance performance, motivation is the only one over which you can exercise complete control. Your physical ability, of course, can change over time due to training, but you are still limited by your genetic makeup (e.g., turnout, ligament looseness, body type, body fat content, cardiovascular efficiency, hip socket depth). Difficulty also lies beyond your control, whether it comes in the form of a challenging role or piece or in the form of competition among dancers.

In contrast, you dictate your own motivation, which directly influences your development and the level of performance that you ultimately achieve. If you're highly motivated to train, you put in the necessary time and effort to improve your conditioning and your technical, artistic, and mental skills. Motivation also determines how you react to fatigue, pain, and other forms of adversity.

Why Do You Dance?

To maximize your motivation, you need to understand why you dance. Motivators can be either internal or external, and internal motivators themselves can be either unhealthy or healthy. Unhealthy internal motivators for dance include fear of failure, desire to maintain a certain body appearance, and unmet need to feel worthwhile. Healthy internal motivators cover a wide range: passion for the art form, enjoyment of good fitness, the satisfaction of mastering new skills, the emotional high of performing, the rewards of meeting the challenges of partnering, the meaning and fulfillment that the art form can provide, and the sheer joy of movement and music.

External motivators can also lead to high motivation in dancers, but they can carry high costs as well. As social beings, dancers naturally value external rewards—for example, respect, appreciation, and financial benefits—which may motivate them to work hard. At the same time, research has demonstrated that behavior driven by outside forces can undermine internal motivation. As a result, an externally motivated dancer's efforts may become motivated primarily by a sort of "carrot," such as praise from parents, rather than by a deep devotion to dance.

As you explore what motivates you to dance, we encourage you to connect with your internal motivators and distance yourself from external motivators. Ask yourself why you dance and what you gain from participating in this art form. Knowing your motivations helps you create a dance life that best satisfies your true needs, maximizes your enjoyment, and ensures that you achieve your dance goals.

For example, if you love to go to class and rehearsal but find less enjoyment in performing, you might prefer an intense training program that focuses on only a few performances per year. If you dance for the simple love of the art form's physicality, you might choose not to perform at all. If, on the other hand, you particularly enjoy people, then a good option for you might be to find a school, team, or company with whom you enjoy dancing.

If your motivation in dance is to perform your best and strive for high goals, then you should ask yourself the following two questions: How motivated am I? Am I as motivated as I need to be in order to achieve my goals? You will not meet lofty goals unless you are motivated to devote the time and energy necessary to fulfill them. In other words, your motivation must be consistent with your goals. Are you willing to do what is necessary to reach your goals? If not, then you have two choices: either increase your motivation to attain your goals or set your sights on revised goals that you can achieve with your current level of motivation.

Motivation is also essential in your training. It is the force that impels you to get out of bed in the morning to train and pushes you to go to class or rehearsal after a long day of school or work. Therefore, it determines the nature of your training—that is, the frequency, volume, and intensity. Through it all, motivation keeps you going when you're tired, bored, stressed, struggling, dancing poorly, or simply not having fun.

To identify your internal and external motivators, complete the Why I Dance worksheet in the web resource.

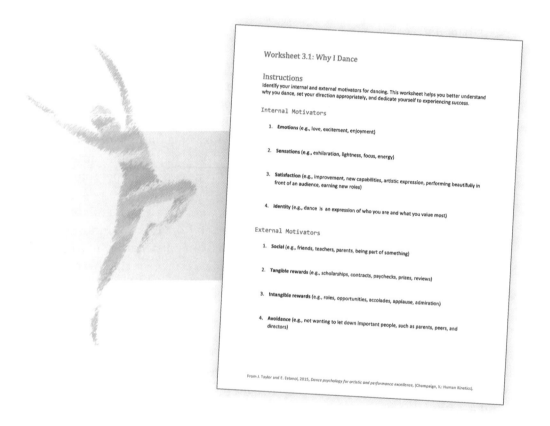

Worksheet 3.1: Why I Dance

Instructions
Identify your internal and external motivators for dancing. This worksheet helps you better understand why you dance, set your direction appropriately, and dedicate yourself to experiencing success.

Internal Motivators

1. **Emotions** (e.g., love, excitement, enjoyment)

2. **Sensations** (e.g., exhilaration, lightness, focus, energy)

3. **Satisfaction** (e.g., improvement, new capabilities, artistic expression, performing beautifully in front of an audience, earning new roles)

4. **Identity** (e.g., dance is an expression of who you are and what you value most)

External Motivators

1. **Social** (e.g., friends, teachers, parents, being part of something)

2. **Tangible rewards** (e.g., scholarships, contracts, paychecks, prizes, reviews)

3. **Intangible rewards** (e.g., roles, opportunities, accolades, applause, admiration)

4. **Avoidance** (e.g., not wanting to let down important people, such as parents, peers, and directors)

From J. Taylor and E. Estanol, 2015, *Dance psychology for artistic and performance excellence*, (Champaign, IL: Human Kinetics).

Three Ds of Motivation

Prime motivation involves putting in as much time, effort, and energy as you can in order to achieve your dance goals. It means training with sufficient frequency, volume, and intensity to get the most benefit from your involvement in dance. Prime motivation is based on the three Ds:

destination → decision → dedication → motivation

Before you can achieve prime motivation, you must first consider your destination—that is, where you would like to go with your dancing. Do you hope to become a professional dancer? Are you aiming for a scholarship at a well-known school? Do you have an upcoming audition, performance, or competition in which you would like to do well? Setting your destination guides every other action that you do. Granted, there are times when we aren't exactly sure where we want to go, but even then we have hopes or ideas, and considering them is an important step in your decision making.

The next element—decision—involves examining the paths available for your dancing and deciding which one to take. You have three choices: stop participating completely, continue at your current level, or adjust your efforts either up or down depending on what you want to accomplish. None of these decisions is better or worse than the others; they're simply your options. Your decision dictates the time and effort that you put into dancing and therefore how good a dancer you ultimately become. Therefore, this decision in some way also determines where you would like to end up—your destination. Once you have decided why you dance and where you want to take your dancing, you must set a course of action. As with travel, you can't arrive at your intended destination in dance without good directions for getting there. In dance, you must figure out the steps you need to take in order to reach your intended destination.

The final D refers to dedication. Once you've made your decision, actively dedicate yourself to it. Commit yourself wholeheartedly to pursuing your chosen course and achieving your goals. If you decide to become the best dancer you can be, then this last step is absolutely critical to realizing that goal. You must give top priority to your decision to be your best and dedicate yourself to dance. Only by completely dedicating yourself to your decision can you ensure that you achieve prime motivation.

Complete the Three Ds of Motivation worksheet in the web resource to help you examine your own expectations and clarify your three Ds.

Obstacles to Motivation

Despite your best efforts to stay motivated and committed to dance, many obstacles can arise and prevent you from fully expressing your desire and achieving your goals. Chances are that you have a busy life in which dance plays only one part. As a result, your motivation may sometimes ebb or even disappear in the midst of life stresses from school, career, family, friends, or other commitments. Additional causes of low motivation include overtraining, illness, injury, monotony, and loss of balance in life.

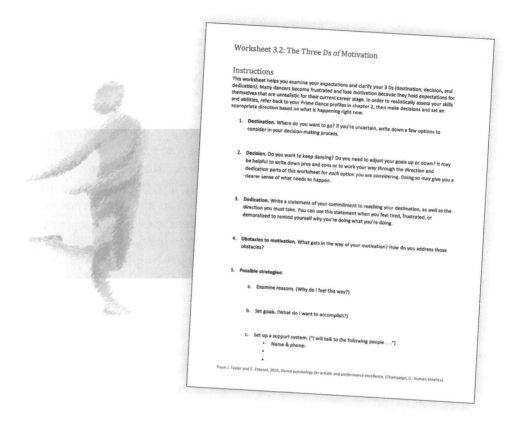

Worksheet 3.2: The Three Ds of Motivation

Instructions

This worksheet helps you examine your expectations and clarify your 3 Ds (destination, decision, and dedication). Many dancers become frustrated and lose motivation because they hold expectations for themselves that are unrealistic for their current career stage. In order to realistically assess your skills and abilities, refer back to your Prime Dance profiles in chapter 2, then make decisions and set an appropriate direction based on what is happening right now.

1. **Destination.** Where do you want to go? If you're uncertain, write down a few options to consider in your decision-making process.

2. **Decision.** Do you want to keep dancing? Do you need to adjust your goals up or down? It may be helpful to write down pros and cons or to work your way through the direction and dedication parts of this worksheet for each option you are considering. Doing so may give you a clearer sense of what needs to happen.

3. **Dedication.** Write a statement of your commitment to reaching your destination, as well as the direction you must take. You can use this statement when you feel tired, frustrated, or demoralized to remind yourself why you're doing what you're doing.

4. **Obstacles to motivation.** What gets in the way of your motivation? How do you address those obstacles?

5. **Possible strategies:**

   a. Examine reasons. (Why do I feel this way?)

   b. Set goals. (What do I want to accomplish?)

   c. Set up a support system. ("I will talk to the following people . . .")
      * Name & phone:
      *
      *

From J. Taylor and E. Estanol, 2015, *Dance psychology for artistic and performance excellence.* (Champaign, IL: Human Kinetics).

Low motivation is often indicated by certain signs. One clear sign is a lack of desire to train as much as you need to in order to achieve your goals. Another sign is giving less than 100 percent of your effort in class or rehearsal. When you train, do you work as hard as is necessary? Do you complete all aspects of your daily training program? Common specific signs of low motivation include skipping or shortening classes or rehearsals and finding excuses not to attend your dance training. If you're not motivated, it's easy to leave out or reduce parts of your training, particularly when it is difficult or not enjoyable.

Low motivation may also be indicated by a lack of enjoyment in your dancing. It's not likely that you're being forced to dance. Ideally, you do it because you have fun with it and gain a great deal from it. If training and performance consistently feel like chores, make some changes to put the fun back in your dance life and reconnect with your motivation for participating. For example, try a new style of dance, change teachers, or take different classes.

If you exhibit any of these signs of low motivation, it will be difficult for you to achieve your goals. If you're not as motivated as you want to be, do two things. First, ask yourself why you're not giving your best effort in training. Second, take active steps to increase your motivation for dance.

Your dedication to dance will shine through your performance.

"I dance because nothing else has the ability to bring about tears, joy, frustration, love, passion, and anger, both as a dancer and as a spectator. I dance for those moments onstage when exhaustion is overtaken by exhilaration in a matter of seconds simply by glancing at a colleague and drawing on their strength. I dance because I know it's a special gift that was given to me, and sharing it is what I want and need to do."

Laura Gilbreath, Pacific Northwest Ballet

Developing Motivation

You now have a better understanding of motivation and how it affects your dance efforts. If you find that you're not as motivated as you'd like to be, take heart—there are solutions. Specifically, you can improve your motivation by implementing one or more of the following strategies: setting goals, establishing a support system, acknowledging your accomplishments, cross-training, focusing on your greatest competitor, using motivational cues, and asking daily questions.

Setting Goals

Few experiences are more rewarding or motivating than setting a goal, working toward that goal, and reaching it. The resulting sense of achievement validates your efforts, increases your confidence, and motivates you to pursue additional goals. Therefore, it is valuable to establish clear goals for your dancing and to identify how you will achieve those goals. Chapter 8 shows you in detail how to create a goal-setting program.

Though it's important to put focused effort into your dancing, not all of the time that you devote to this effort will be enjoyable. We refer to this reality as the grind. It means putting great energy and many hours into your training, often beyond the point of fun and excitement. During the grind, when class or rehearsal is difficult and your motivation lags, focus not on the fatigue and boredom but on your long-term goals and the benefits to be gained from your committed effort—improved technical skills and artistry, better performance, more prestigious roles, and achievement of your goals.

Richly imagine what you want to accomplish. Remind yourself that the only way to reach your goals is to go through the grind. Imagine the feelings of fulfillment and joy that you'll experience when you reach your goals. This technique distracts you from the immediate unpleasantness, focuses you on what you want to achieve, and generates positive thoughts and emotions that help you get through the grind.

Establishing a Support System

Your dance training—indeed, all aspects of your life—are influenced by the people with whom you surround yourself. These people affect what you think, how you feel, and how you act. They also influence your motivation to dance; if you're around people who value and support your dance participation, you find it easier to stay motivated.

To constantly bolster your motivation, establish a support system made up of people who appreciate and encourage your dance efforts. This network can include immediate family members, friends, schoolmates, and coworkers. It can also include others who are committed to the art of dance—for example, an inspiring dance school or program, a supportive dance instructor or choreographer, and dance partners who are themselves highly motivated.

In addition, you can establish a more focused support system that directly reinforces your motivation. For example, it's difficult to be consistently motivated if you train alone; on some days, you just don't feel like going into the studio and moving your body. Therefore, no matter how much you try to push yourself, you can work harder if you have someone else pushing you as well. When you make a commitment to a training partner or class, you're more motivated to get out of bed in the morning for yoga or cross-training or to get yourself to the studio after school or work even when you're tired.

The best training partner is someone working at or near your level of ability and pursuing similar goals. You may have similar technical skills and may be training for the same show or performance. You may even be competing for a role or alternating roles in a particular piece. Whatever the details may be, you can work together and motivate each other to accomplish your goals. Indeed, when you work in this way, your training becomes a shared commitment and responsibility that you must uphold both for yourself and for your training partner. When someone relies on you, and you in turn depend on that person, the two of you create a collective motivation that is greater than the motivation of either individual alone.

Acknowledging Your Accomplishments

Another way to bolster your motivation is to purposefully acknowledge your training efforts and achievements and appreciate how they contribute to your dance progress. After every class and rehearsal, pause to take stock of what you just did. Review the specifics of what you accomplished. For example, if you finally mastered a difficult skill, note what you did well and celebrate it. Remind yourself of the effort you put forth in the face of discomfort in order to improve your technique and artistry. Then take a moment to look forward and think about how that effort helps you achieve your dance goals. Finally, give yourself a pat on the back and allow yourself to feel the satisfaction of a job well done.

Cross-Training

One potential problem with dance training arises when it becomes so routine that it feels monotonous and undermines your motivation. The singular nature of dance training can also lead to overtraining, burnout, and injury. Fortunately, both of these pitfalls can be avoided by cross-training with other physical activities, such as yoga, Pilates, and strength training. Those who are committed to becoming their best often find that cross-training provides them with both physiological and psychological benefits. Specifically, it allows them to remain motivated, fit, and strong and thus helps them enjoy a longer dance career.

Another way to vary your training is to take classes involving styles of dance other than the one you regularly perform. In fact, directors and choreographers increasingly seek out dancers who are well rounded and adaptable to different kinds of movement. Taking up other dance styles allows you to discover new ways of thinking about dance and connecting to music, all of which also enhances your ability to perform in the particular dance style to which you are committed. Training in various dance styles also gives you an advantage over other dancers who are less versed in multiple styles when you audition for jobs.

Still another way to stay motivated is to vary your dance training frequently; doing so keeps your training both interesting and challenging. You can alter your training by changing teachers or classes or by joining new dance clubs. Such variety keeps you engaged and motivated as you pursue your dance goals.

All of these ways to engage in new and creative training routines help motivate you because they keep you interested in and excited about your training. Varied workouts also help you maintain focus and intensity by requiring you to pay attention to new routines and to muster and sustain the energy needed to perform them properly. Such changes prevent you from falling into a rut and merely going through the motions. As a result, you enjoy consistent, high-quality training that challenges you to grow as a dancer.

Focusing on Your Greatest Competitor

Some dancers are motivated by the goal of outperforming a fellow dancer—for example, by winning a prized role or defeating the other dancer in a competition. For these dancers, focusing on their greatest competitor provides the impetus to work hard. If you feel that this approach might work for you, identify your biggest competitor and put her or his name or photo where you can see it every day. Ask yourself, "Am I working as hard as this person?" By using this motivation to sustain your best effort, you give yourself a chance to overcome your greatest competitor and achieve your goals.

Enjoyment is a great motivator.

Using Motivational Cues

Another way to stay motivated is to generate positive emotions associated with your efforts and goals. Feelings of pride and inspiration can bolster your motivation during classes, rehearsals, and performances. You can evoke such emotions in yourself by using motivational cues, such as inspirational phrases, images, and photographs. For example, if you come across a quote from (or picture of) a famous dancer that moves you, place it where you can see it regularly—perhaps in your bedroom, on your refrigerator door, or in your locker. Look at it periodically and allow yourself to experience the emotions it generates. This reminder, and the associated emotions, can inspire you to continue your efforts.

You may also find motivational cues in your own dance history. If you have a video of yourself performing beautifully, replay it often and focus on re-creating the feelings associated with that performance. Such images of your own success inspire you to continue giving your best effort in difficult classes, rehearsals, and performances.

Asking Daily Questions

It's easy to get caught up in the whirlwind of dance and forget *why* you put so much effort and energy into this art form. As a result, you might, for example, participate in a class or rehearsal by simply going through the motions and therefore never connect your efforts with your goals.

To ensure that you keep your eyes on the prize and maximize your efforts, ask yourself three questions each day. When you get up in the morning, ask, "What can I do today to become the best dancer I can be?" Then, before you start a class or rehearsal, take a deep breath and ask, "What things do I need to work on today to become a better dancer?" Finally, before you go to sleep, ask, "Did I do everything possible today to become the best dancer I can be?" If you can answer yes, give yourself a pat on the back for your great efforts. If the answer is no, ask what you can do better tomorrow. These three questions remind you daily of your goal and challenge you to stay motivated to become your best.

The techniques described in this chapter can help you increase your motivation in the short run, but long-term motivation comes from within. If you possess the passion to participate in dance, you are motivated to achieve your goals. In the final analysis, your motivation to train and dance depends on the fact that you love the *experience* of dancing more than the results. You perform because you just enjoy being out there and expressing your love of movement and music. If you truly love dance, the motivation to pursue your goals is almost always there when you take a class, rehearse a role, and step onstage for a performance. On those occasions when dancing is difficult (when you experience the grind, for example), your motivation will carry you through.

We have discussed motivation from the perspective of maximizing your dance performance and achieving your dance goals, but you can apply the same ideas to other areas of life—your health, your well-being, and your pursuit of goals outside of dance. These strategies for finding your motivation are equally beneficial in developing relationships, improving your diet, going smoke free, finishing school, and transitioning to another career after dance.

Center Stage: Julia

Finding the Motivation to Express Yourself

As a child, Julia developed a great passion for dance because her mother had been a ballerina and Julia basically grew up in the dance world. As a result, Julia took dance classes from an early age. Even so, as she grew up, she directed most of her energy to her education. She continued this pattern as an adult, continuing to take dance classes but devoting most of her time to her career, her marriage, and her children.

When Julia was 33, her mother died of cancer. This loss prompted Julia to reexamine her life, and she decided to make some changes, one of which was to prioritize her passion for dance. She wanted to honor her mother by reconnecting with her love of dance, and she set a goal of performing in a local modern dance production. During the next year, Julia committed to taking several classes a week and earned an invitation to join the local dance studio's performing company. At times, she felt overwhelmed by her many responsibilities and the resulting demands on her time. However, whenever she felt like she couldn't show up, she thought of her mother and of her own love for dance, and these thoughts inspired her to continue.

To help herself focus, Julia found a photograph of her mother dancing and placed it on her bedside table to remind herself of how proud her mother would be to see her dancing. She also communicated to her husband and children the importance of her dancing. As a result, they all rallied around her and encouraged her to continue with her classes and rehearsals. Her children helped out by doing more chores, and her husband rearranged his schedule so that he could be home while she was at class or rehearsal.

Julia stuck with her classes and rehearsals, and on opening night her entire family was there to support her and watch her achieve her goal. She enjoyed every moment of being onstage and felt that her mother was there in spirit watching her perform. After the performance, her family told her they could see how happy she was while dancing and promised to continue supporting her efforts to dance as long as she wanted to.

ENCORE

- Motivation provides the foundation for everything you do in dance.

- To understand your motivation, you must first determine why you dance.

- Obstacles to motivation include a busy and stressful life, overtraining, illness, injury, monotony, and loss of life balance.

- Signs of low motivation include lack of desire to take classes and rehearse, failure to give full effort in your dance training, and lack of enjoyment in dancing.

- Prime motivation requires the three Ds: destination, decision, and dedication.

- You can increase your motivation by setting goals, focusing on your long-term goals, establishing a support system, acknowledging your progress and accomplishments, cross-training, focusing on your greatest competitor, using motivational cues, and asking daily questions.

References

Bandura, A., & Cervone, D. (1983). Self-evaluative and self-efficacy mechanisms governing the motivational effects of goal systems. *Journal of Personality and Social Psychology, 45*, 1017–1028.

Bandura, A., & Cervone, D. (1984). *Differential engagement of self-reactive influences in cognitive motivation.* Unpublished manuscript, Stanford University, Department of Psychology.

Bandura, A., & Simon, K.M. (1977). The role of proximal intentions in self-regulation of refractory behavior. *Cognitive Therapy and Research, 1*, 177–193.

Carron, A.V. (1984). *Motivation: Implications for coaching and teaching.* London, Ontario: Sports Dynamics.

Csikszentmihalyi, M. (1975). *Beyond boredom and anxiety.* San Francisco: Jossey-Bass.

Csikszentmihalyi, M. (1990). *Flow: The psychology of optimal experience.* New York: Harper & Row.

Deci, E., & Ryan, R. (Eds.). (2002). *Handbook of self-determination research.* Rochester, NY: University of Rochester Press.

Doyle, L., & Landers, D. (1980). *Psychological skills in elite and subelite shooters.* Unpublished manuscript.

Duda, J.L., & Hall, H. (2001). Achievement goal theory in sport: Recent extensions and future directions. In R.N. Singer, H.A. Hausenblas, & C.M. Janelle (Eds.), *Handbook of sport psychology* (pp. 206–224). New York: Wiley.

Erez, M., & Zidon, I. (1984). Effects of goal acceptance on the relationship of goal difficulty to performance. *Journal of Applied Psychology, 69*, 69–78.

Feltz, D.L., & Albrecht, R.R. (1985). The influence of self-efficacy on approach/avoidance of a high-avoidance task. In J.H. Humphrey & L. Vander Velden (Eds.), *Current research in the psychology/sociology of sport* (Vol. 1) (pp. 97–116). Princeton, NJ: Princeton Book.

Feltz, D.L., & Riessinger, C.A. (1990). Effects of in vivo emotive imagery and performance feedback on self-efficacy and muscular endurance. *Journal of Sport and Exercise Psychology*, *12*, 132–143.

Gould, D. (2010). Goal setting for peak performance. In J.M. Williams (Ed.), *Applied sport psychology: Personal growth to peak performance* (pp. 133–148). Palo Alto, CA: Mayfield.

Halliwell, W. (1978). Intrinsic motivation in sport. In W.F. Straub (Ed.), *Sport psychology: An analysis of athlete behavior* (pp. 74–92). Ithaca, NY: Mouvement.

Landers, D.M. (1978). Motivation and performance: The role of arousal and attentional factors. In W.F. Straub (Ed.), *Sport psychology: An analysis of athlete behavior* (pp. 91–103). Ithaca, NY: Mouvement.

Landers, D.M., & Boutcher, S.H. (2010). Arousal-performance relationships. In J.M. Williams (Ed.), *Applied sport psychology: Personal growth to peak performance* (pp. 163–184). Palo Alto, CA: Mayfield.

Locke, E.A. (1968). Toward a theory of task motivation and incentives. *Organizational Behavior and Human Performance*, *3*, 157–189.

Locke, E.A., & Bryan, J.F. (1969). The directing function of goals in task performance. *Organizational Behavior and Human Performance*, *4*, 35–42.

Locke, E.A, Cartledge, N., & Knerr, C.S. (1970). Studies of the relationship between satisfaction, goal setting, and performance. *Organizational Behavior and Human Performance*, *5*, 135–158.

Locke, E.A., & Latham, G.P. (1985). The applications of goal setting to sports. *Journal of Sport Psychology*, *7*, 205–222.

Locke, E.A., Mento, A.J., & Katcher, B.L. (1978). The interaction of ability and motivation in performance: An exploration of the meaning of moderators. *Personnel Psychology*, *31*, 269–280.

Locke, E.A., Shaw, K.N., Saari, L.M., & Latham, G.P. (1981). Goal setting and task performance: 1969–1980. *Psychological Bulletin*, *90*, 125–152.

Passer, M.W. (1981). Children in sport: Participation motives and psychological stress. *Quest*, *33*, 231–244.

Taylor, J., & Schneider, T. (2005). *The triathlete's guide to mental training*. Boulder, CO: Velopress.

Taylor, J., & Taylor, C. (1987, June). Mental attitude: Motivation. *Dance Teacher Now*, 10–11.

Weinberg, R.S. (1984). The relationship between extrinsic rewards and intrinsic motivation in sport. In J.M. Silva & R.S. Weinberg (Eds.), *Psychological foundations of sport* (pp. 177–187). Champaign, IL: Human Kinetics.

Weinberg, R.S., & Ragan, J. (1979). Effects of competition, success/failure, and sex on intrinsic motivation. *Research Quarterly*, *50*, 503–510.

CHAPTER 4

Confidence

"The dancer with conviction has power; many a dance of poor quality has been "put across" just by the superb belief of the performer in the work. . . . If you believe in yourself, everybody else probably will, too."

Doris Humphrey

C onfidence may be the most important mental contributor to success in dance. We define confidence as a strong belief that you can perform your best and achieve your goals. Confidence affects every aspect of your training, your performances, and your life in general. Of course, confidence alone is not enough; you must also have the necessary ability. However, if you don't *believe* that you have the ability, then you won't perform at the level of which you're physically capable. For example, even if you have the fitness to perform in a full-length ballet and do the 32 fouettés required at the end of a variation, you won't succeed unless you also possess the confidence that you can achieve it.

The best dancers may possess better technique, strength, flexibility, and artistry than less successful dancers, but their achievements also depend on a profound belief in their ability to perform their best in the most important role on the biggest stage. These dancers believe that they can push their limits and achieve their goals. In contrast, less self-assured dancers may lack the confidence to take on more demanding roles, the willingness to engage in difficult competitions, or the courage to push themselves to perform difficult jumps and turns.

Maintaining confidence poses a particular challenge to dancers because dance involves so many types of fitness, skill, style, and artistry. Therefore, in order to be truly confident as a dancer, you must develop not only an overall confidence but also a strong belief in your ability to succeed in specific facets of the art, such as adagio, turning, and jumping. You might, for example, possess great confidence in your musicality or ability to learn new choreography yet harbor serious doubts about your artistry or jumping ability. Similarly, you might be positive about lyrical and modern dance but unsure of your ability to tap, swing-dance, or do ballet. Or you might be sure of your ability to dance barefoot but doubt your ability to dance well in shoes. Your goal, then, is not merely to develop your capabilities—physical, technical, and artistic—but also to build your confidence in all of these areas.

Upward Spiral Versus Vicious Cycle

To understand how confidence affects you as a dancer, begin by recalling a time when you lacked confidence in your dancing ability. Perhaps, for example, you were caught in a vicious cycle of low confidence and poor performance. In this kind of cycle, negative thinking leads to poor performance, which in turn leads to more negative thinking and even poorer performance. Now think of a time when you were supremely confident. In this period, you likely experienced an upward spiral, in which great confidence led to improved performance, which in turn bred even more confidence and even better performance (see figure 4.1). Beyond this direct effect on your performance, confidence also

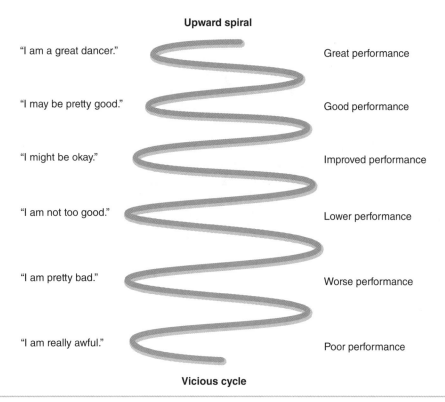

Figure 4.1   Upward and downward spiral.

affects every other mental factor in your dancing. To see how, let's take a closer look at the upward spiral and the vicious cycle.

Upward Spiral

Envision once more a time when you have been confident in your dancing abilities. In such a period, you have complete faith that you can achieve your goals. Your self-talk is positive: "I'm a good dancer. I can have a great performance." This positive talk motivates you to give your best effort and allows you to feel prepared, relaxed, and energized during your performance. You experience positive emotions, such as pride, inspiration, and excitement. You focus on positive aspects of your performance, and you are not distracted.

These mental factors—your positive thoughts, feelings of calm, sharp focus, and positive emotions—allow you to enjoy your training and performances, dance at your highest level, and minimize your risk of injury. As a result, you have more fun in both training and performance, and you deliver strong performances. Thus the significance of an upward spiral is that every positive factor supports and bolsters the others, so that you think, feel, and dance well in all settings.

Vicious Cycle

The vicious cycle may start with a period of poor training or a bad performance. You may get discouraged and begin to question your ability. You may think and talk negatively: "I'm in terrible shape. I'll never achieve my goals." You lose your motivation to train because you assume that you'll do poorly in class or rehearsal.

When you expect to dance poorly, you spend time worrying about possible mistakes and therefore get nervous before performances. This anxiety hurts your confidence because it makes you feel tense and physically uncomfortable, and there's no way that you can dance well when you're uptight. The negative self-talk and anxiety also cause negative emotions. You feel frustrated, angry, and helpless, all of which hurt your confidence even more and cause you to dance even worse. In addition, this swirl of negativity hurts your focus. You concentrate on the negatives rather than on things that will help you train and perform well.

Altogether, this cluster of factors—negative thoughts, anxiety, negative emotions, and poor focus—can cause you to make various mistakes. You may forget the choreography, get out of sync with your partner, or completely miss steps. Indeed, every part of your training and performing becomes more difficult, and your mind and body are more vulnerable to injury. If you're thinking negatively, caught in a vicious cycle, feeling nervous or depressed or frustrated, unable to focus, and in pain, you don't feel motivated to train, and you have little chance of dancing well.

Your confidence can be hurt by anything that counters your belief in your ability or suggests that this belief is unfounded. For example, confidence can be hurt by technical breakdowns, artistic miscalculations, costume or shoe malfunctions, a bad class or rehearsal, a partner's miscues, or a poor performance. These and other setbacks can lead you to question whether you're as capable as you thought you were.

Confidence can also be undercut by unrealistic expectations. Be sure that your confidence is reasonable. In other words, is your confidence consistent with your actual ability? If not, then you may have unrealistic expectations. If you're a perfectionist—as many dancers are—then you're particularly vulnerable to losing confidence because overly high expectations set you up for failure. If unreasonable expectations lead you to be overly critical of your performances, you may believe that you didn't dance as well as you should have, when in fact you may have performed well in terms of more reasonable expectations.

Another factor that can hurt a dancer's confidence is lack of experience or skill. For example, if you're new to a particular style of dance, you may not even have the experience to adequately judge how well you should dance. Indeed, dancers often consider a performance to be poor when in reality they are just grappling with the challenges of learning a new technique, style, or piece. In such situations, you may simply lack the experience to dance as well as you would like at this point. As a result, if you don't adjust your expectations to be consistent with your experience, you may suffer a decline in confidence.

Your confidence can also be affected by the pressure of performing in front of an audience, which can be a nerve-racking experience if you're not accustomed to it. Therefore, in addition to practicing particular dance skills, you also need to perform in front of a live audience as often as possible in order to build your confidence about being onstage. This experience helps you develop the ability to connect with your audience through eye contact and allow them to feel your energy without letting their gaze distract or intimidate you and thereby undermine your performance.

Complete the Confidence Inventory worksheet in the web resource to evaluate your confidence level and determine where you need to focus in order to build your confidence.

Progression of Confidence

What makes tap dancer Savion Glover and ballerina Wendy Whelan such fantastic performers? Of course, they each possess tremendous physical ability, technical skill, and artistry. But something else is distinctive about them and

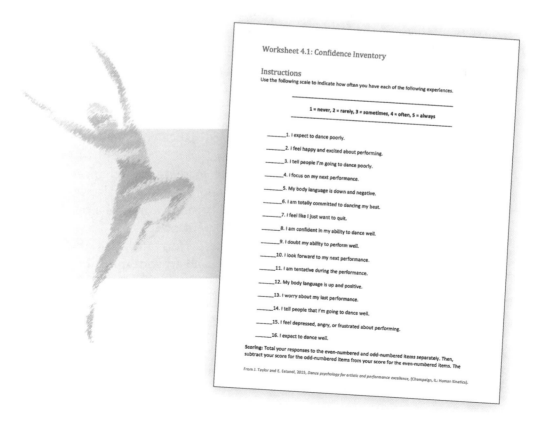

Worksheet 4.1: Confidence Inventory

Instructions
Use the following scale to indicate how often you have each of the following experiences.

1 = never, 2 = rarely, 3 = sometimes, 4 = often, 5 = always

_____ 1. I expect to dance poorly.

_____ 2. I feel happy and excited about performing.

_____ 3. I tell people I'm going to dance poorly.

_____ 4. I focus on my next performance.

_____ 5. My body language is down and negative.

_____ 6. I am totally committed to dancing my best.

_____ 7. I feel like I just want to quit.

_____ 8. I am confident in my ability to dance well.

_____ 9. I doubt my ability to perform well.

_____ 10. I look forward to my next performance.

_____ 11. I am tentative during the performance.

_____ 12. My body language is up and positive.

_____ 13. I worry about my last performance.

_____ 14. I tell people that I'm going to dance well.

_____ 15. I feel depressed, angry, or frustrated about performing.

_____ 16. I expect to dance well.

Scoring: Total your responses to the even-numbered and odd-numbered items separately. Then, subtract your score for the odd-numbered items from your score for the even-numbered items. The

From J. Taylor and E. Estanol, 2015, *Dance psychology for artistic and performance excellence,* (Champaign, IL: Human Kinetics).

other top dancers—their unwavering belief in their ability to succeed—and this quality is valuable at any level. Whether you're a professional, a college dancer, a committed community performer, or a competitive amateur dancer, you can benefit from developing strong and resilient confidence that enables you to dance at your highest level and achieve your performance goals.

Prime confidence in particular requires developing a deep, lasting, and resilient belief in your ability to achieve your dance goals. With prime confidence, you have faith in yourself as a dancer, and it keeps you positive, motivated, intense, focused, and emotionally in control. As a result, you can remain confident when you're tired, sick, or injured and even when you're having a poor rehearsal or bad performance.

Prime confidence also allows you to respect the challenges you face without feeling intimidated. Indeed, it encourages you to seek out challenging choreography, difficult pieces, and varied styles of dance. With prime confidence, you can view such challenges not as threats to avoid but as opportunities to demonstrate your capabilities. As a result, prime confidence enables you to dance consistently at your highest level.

Prime confidence is a belief, not a certainty, that you can achieve your goals. It's the confidence that if you're well trained, well rehearsed, and mentally prepared—and if you execute the choreography—you will succeed. Prime confidence means having faith in your ability and preparation, which allows you to stay focused on the positive experience of training and performing. When you're confident and expect to succeed, you're more motivated to train hard and to persevere when you face challenges; as a result, your dancing improves.

We're often asked the following question: Do I become confident by succeeding, or do I succeed as a result of being confident? Yes and yes. You don't move from zero confidence to prime confidence in one big step. Rather, it's a building process, much like that of developing physical fitness or technical proficiency. Confidence leads to success, which reinforces your confidence, which in turn leads to more success.

For example, imagine that you would like to dance your way onto the popular television show *So You Think You Can Dance* but are only 40 percent confident that you can do so. In order to increase your chances, you work on your strength, flexibility, technique, and artistry. You also use the confidence-building techniques described in this chapter, and as a result of all of this work your confidence increases to 60 percent.

You are now able to enjoy better training and performances, all of which helps you improve your conditioning, technique, and artistic expression. Your continued hard work and ongoing progress raise your confidence to 80 percent, which enables you to perform well in the early rounds of the competition. These results increase your confidence to nearly 100 percent, which enables you to achieve your goal of being selected for the show.

The following sections present five strategies that you can use to build a solid foundation of confidence. These approaches enable you to create a good environment for gaining confidence steadily and progressively. They also require that you take active steps to develop your confidence in all parts of your dance training. As a result, your confidence emerges in classes, rehearsals, and performances.

1. Preparation Breeds Confidence

The foundation of confidence is preparation. If you believe that you've done everything you can to dance your best—put in the hours conditioning your body, improving your technique, expanding your artistry, and developing your mind—then you feel confident in your ability to achieve your performance goals. If you've developed these areas as fully as you can, you have faith as you stand backstage, just before you go on, that you're as ready as you can be.

Preparation also offers you the opportunity to establish trust in your capabilities. As you overcome the many physical, technical, artistic, and mental challenges of training, you begin to believe that you can achieve your goals. Developing this trust depends in part on recognizing your efforts. To do so, pause at the end of every class or rehearsal to reflect on what you have accomplished—for example, meeting specific class goals or mustering the determination, effort, focus, and intensity required to complete a difficult workout. Note how this training session has taken you one step closer to your goals. Boost your confidence by acknowledging the progress you're making. See and feel yourself gaining strength, improving your technique, and developing your artistry.

2. Mental Skills Reinforce Confidence

You can use mental skills to maintain and strengthen your confidence. These mental skills are tools that you can pull out of your dance toolbox when you face challenges in training or performance. Such challenges can derive from either external or internal forces.

External challenges, for example, can range from mastering a particular style of dance or piece of choreography to handling issues with your costume or shoes. You can face these challenges constructively by using mental skills to remain motivated, focused, relaxed, and upbeat. Internal challenges can also take various forms, such as fatigue and loss of focus. When your body is tired, you can use mental skills to encourage yourself to keep going to the end of a performance. In addition, if you get distracted, you can use mental tools to push the distractions away and refocus on your performance. Knowing that you have the tools necessary to fix any difficulties with which you will be faced will help you overcome these challenges and enable you to maintain confidence in your ability to dance your best.

In short, these mental skills give you the tools you need in order to maintain control when you face either external or internal challenges. Here are some common mental skills for your dance toolbox that are discussed in this book:

- Goal setting to bolster motivation (see chapter 8)
- Intensity control to stay relaxed (see chapter 5)
- Key words to maintain focus and avoid distractions (see chapter 6)
- Emotional control to stay calm when things aren't going well during a performance (see chapter 7)

3. Adversity Ingrains Confidence

It is not enough merely to be confident in your ability to reach the finals of a nationwide competition or land a position in a coveted dance company. You also need to develop a belief that you can overcome the challenges and adversity involved in such an undertaking—for example, long hours in rehearsal, continuous criticism and correction of your technique, changing partners and choreographers, intense soreness in every muscle group, blisters, ingrown toenails, injuries, slippery stage floors, and cold theaters. When faced with these or other kinds of adversity, your biggest challenge is to maintain your confidence.

Anyone can be confident when things go well; what really counts is remaining confident when things go poorly! This is what prime dance is all about, and the primary way to gain this type of confidence is to expose yourself to adversity during your training. We all love to dance when we're well rested and relaxed, when we have comfortable well-worn shoes, when we know our partner well, and when we're dancing in our preferred style. In contrast, when conditions are less than ideal, we may be tempted to give less than total effort or to shorten or even skip a class or rehearsal.

The reality, however, is that performing conditions are rarely ideal. Fortunately, training and rehearsing under adverse conditions allows you to prepare yourself to respond positively to adversity during a performance, whether the challenge involves a wardrobe or shoe malfunction, being out of sync with your partner, a forgotten piece of choreography, a slippery stage, or music played too fast or too slow. Training in tough conditions helps you feel more familiar and comfortable with such challenges. As a result, when you face adversity during a performance, you can remain confident, give your best effort, and dance at your highest level.

Your response to adversity often dictates not only how you handle a given situation but also whether you move into a vicious cycle or an upward spiral. For example, if you make a mistake and aren't prepared for adversity, the anxiety generated by the error may cause you to lose confidence and focus, which in turn leads to more mistakes and plunges you into a vicious cycle of negativity and poor performance. On the other hand, if you come upon a challenge during a performance and have trained to handle adversity, you can stay positive and motivated, thus triggering an upward spiral in which you maintain your confidence and focus, thereby helping you continue to perform at a high level.

Though you probably enjoy taking classes and rehearsing in ideal settings—for example, a warm well-lit studio with a grippy floor—training in adverse conditions gives you several benefits. For one thing, it allows you to feel tough, resilient, confident, and inspired during your classes and rehearsals. It also gives you a chance to practice responding positively to conditions that you may face during a performance or competition. More specifically, this valuable experience helps you deal with adversity related to fitness, technique, artistry, and other performance-related factors more effectively when they arise during a performance.

As a result, when you face adverse conditions in a performance or competition, you won't be shocked, dismayed, or defeated by them. Instead, you'll say, "Been there, done that, no big deal," because you possess the confidence and the tools to overcome the adversity and deliver a great overall performance.

4. Support Bolsters Confidence

Whether you train with a dance team at school, attend a privately owned dance studio, or dance with a company, the social aspects of dance can play a big role in maintaining and building your confidence. This support can bolster your confidence in multiple ways. First, training with other dancers who are positive and motivated is contagious. If you spend time with people who are upbeat and passionate, it's hard not to feel the same way. You may also receive positive feedback from your instructor, choreographer, and fellow dancers: "Great work!" "Nice effort today."

Support for your dance involvement may also come from people outside of the dance community. In particular, support from your family is key, especially if you have significant family responsibilities (e.g., raising children). It can be challenging to find time to train without sacrificing other parts of your life, and this is even more difficult if you are preparing for a longer performance or competitive season. In the face of such challenges, receiving support and encouragement as you pursue your dance goals can build your confidence and reduce your stress. It is also helpful to receive similar support from friends, who must be forgiving when you periodically prioritize your training over social activities.

These kinds of support are particularly important after a difficult class or rehearsal, a low point in your training, or a bad performance. Support from other dancers can act as a lifeline that saves you from the potentially confidence crushing effect of such episodes. Indeed, just a few well-chosen words, a pat on the back, or a hug (from a teacher, choreographer, director, dance coach, fellow dancer, or family member) can help break out of a funk, put the poor performance in perspective, safeguard your confidence, and get back on track.

Remember also that support is a two-way street. Just as you receive encouragement from supporters, both within and outside of the dance world, you can also give support to others when the opportunity arises.

5. Success Validates Confidence

All of your efforts to build your confidence are geared toward helping you achieve success in your dance career. You may envision success as delivering great performances or reaching another dance goal. Whatever your vision, success starts in your daily training. As you participate in class, stretch, strength-train, or do Pilates or yoga, you achieve small victories that slowly but steadily bolster your confidence. Over time, you develop the confidence to achieve a big success, such as earning a coveted role or delivering a fantastic performance.

Because big successes don't come often, the smaller incremental gains are also crucial to strengthening and maintaining your confidence. To gain the benefits of little successes, recognize them when they occur. After every class or rehearsal, acknowledge the small victories that you've won. Reflect on the fact that you've worked diligently and achieved your day's training goals.

Confidence is key to a successful performance.

"I feel like I'm really inside the dancing. What clicked? Just having the opportunity to do difficult roles, and realizing that I can do them, is a big part of it. The more you get out onstage and do them, the more comfortable you become."

April Daly, Joffrey Ballet

These small victories generate positive emotions, such as inspiration, pride, excitement, satisfaction, and happiness; as a result, they root your confidence more deeply in your psyche. Combining your belief in your ability with powerful, positive emotions makes your confidence stronger and more resilient. You develop this resilience by making many small deposits in your "confidence bank." When you build a large confidence balance, you can make withdrawals on challenging rehearsal or performance days.

Training success also rewards your efforts—all that hard work really pays off— thus encouraging you to continue striving to achieve your dance goals. Ultimately, the small victories set the stage for a big success that fully validates the confidence that you have so patiently developed.

Developing Confidence

Confidence is a skill, and, as with technical skills, you can develop it through practice and experience. This parallel also has a downside; as with technical skills, it is possible to develop *poor* confidence skills. Specifically, if you consistently take a negative stance and do not believe in yourself, you may become very skilled at being negative, which hurts your confidence and your ability to perform your best.

For example, if you develop the bad technical habit of lifting your hip when you do a leg extension, you actually become skilled at lifting your hip when you extend your leg. That bad habit then shows itself during rehearsals and performances, where it causes you to lose your balance and disrupts your line. The same holds true for confidence. If you become skilled at being negative, that bad habit shows itself in your performances, where it hurts your confidence and undermines your dancing.

You can change bad confidence habits by retraining your thinking. If you purposefully and regularly practice good confidence skills, you can replace your negative old habits with positive new ones. The following sections give you specific strategies for replacing bad habits with effective confidence skills.

Practicing Positive Self-Talk

Positive self-talk is another powerful tool that you can use to maintain and strengthen your confidence. What you say to yourself at key points—at the barre, on the mat, during a difficult lift, before a turn, or at the start of a difficult sequence of choreography—affects what you think, how you feel, and how you dance. Whether positive or negative, your self-talk affects your attitude and therefore also helps determine the quality of your effort and perseverance in both your training and your performances.

Despite the value of positive self-talk, negativity is common in the dance world. Negative self-talk involves thinking or saying something that reflects a lack of confidence or a defeatist attitude—for example, "I'm going to dance badly today," "I stink," or "I can't deal with these conditions." Such comments are heard regularly in classes and rehearsals, and they can suck the life and the love right out of training and performing. If you say this sort of thing to yourself, you're convincing yourself that you have little chance to dance well. A negative attitude undercuts your efforts, decreases your motivation, reduces your focus, and generates negative emotions.

In contrast, if you use positive self-talk—for example, "I can deal with these conditions" or "my artistry will shine through"—your attitude translates into prime confidence, intensity, focus, and helpful emotions and thereby contributes to great performance. Positive self-talk increases your motivation to work hard because it helps you believe that your efforts will be rewarded. As a result, you're more likely to be relaxed and focused and to believe that you can handle anything that is thrown at you by the choreographer or the performance conditions. Your positive self-talk is also both reflected in and increased by feelings of excitement and joy.

In addition, positive self-talk gives you a powerful mental tool for handling fatigue by keeping your mind strong and your body moving smoothly for a flawless performance even when you're tired. As your body wears down toward the end of a rehearsal or performance, it communicates to your mind that it has had enough: "I get the point! You can stop now." In such moments, you can use positive self-talk to help your mind persuade your body to keep going. Indeed, positive self-talk can take you from barely getting off the ground to leaping through the air. It allows you to tap into that final reserve at the end of your performance when you must finish strong. If you say, "Keep going—this is what I've worked for, and I will not give up," then your body listens and responds.

Training Your Brain

At first glance, positive self-talk may seem like a simple strategy—you just replace your negative self-talk with positive statements. The challenge, however, lies in overcoming poor self-talk habits that are ingrained. Fortunately, just as you can retrain yourself to overcome bad dance techniques, you can also learn to retrain your brain and engage in positive self-talk. To begin retraining your self-talk, look at the situations in which you tend to become negative—for example, when you're about to go onstage. Then think of a positive statement you can say to yourself in order to continue feeling strong and confident, such as "I'm going to dance my best tonight."

To go deeper, figure out why you become negative in certain situations. Common reasons include fatigue, frustration, lack of preparation, and poor performance. In addition, many dancers find that a wave of negativity can be set off by a "hot button"—a situation that elicits a strong, immediate emotional reaction that is usually related to unfulfilled needs, rejection, pain, or fear from the past. Therefore, identifying these situations is an essential step in changing your self-talk.

Once you identify your hot buttons, monitor what you say to yourself in those moments. We've found that when hot buttons get pushed, dancers tend to rely on favorite negative self-talk: "I'm terrible." "I'm such a loser." "I don't even look like a dancer." "What's the point of even trying?" Changing this kind of self-talk requires that you realize *specifically* what you say, where you say it, and how bad it is for you. Most of the dancers we've worked with find patterns in the situations in which they use negative self-talk, in the causes of their negativity, and in the specific self-talk they use. To identify your patterns, use the Know Your Self-Talk worksheet in the web resource.

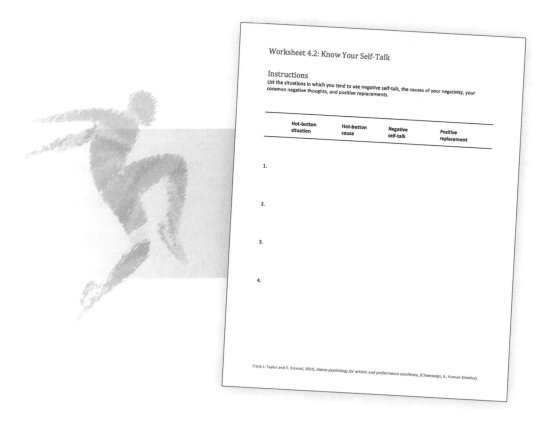

Worksheet 4.2: Know Your Self-Talk

Instructions

List the situations in which you tend to use negative self-talk, the causes of your negativity, your common negative thoughts, and positive replacements.

Hot-button situation	Hot-button cause	Negative self-talk	Positive replacement
1.			
2.			
3.			
4.			

From J. Taylor and E. Estanol, 2015, *Dance psychology for artistic and performance excellence*, (Champaign, IL: Human Kinetics).

Once you've identified your patterns, decide what positive self-talk you'll use to replace your habitual negative self-talk. The positive self-talk should be encouraging, but it must also be realistic. For example, if you say "I love being out there" when you really don't, or "I'm feeling so strong" even when you're not, you'll find it difficult to believe your own words. Therefore, your positive self-talk works better if you acknowledge the hot button while putting a positive yet realistic spin on it: "If I keep working hard, good things will happen." "Keep pushing through—you're almost there." "You can do this." By putting this new tool in your toolbox, you give yourself a way to change your self-talk and respond positively.

This change takes time, and ingraining your positive self-talk depends on your ongoing commitment to the process. If you're very skilled at negative self-talk, you'll have to constantly remind yourself to be positive. The first step is to realize when a hot-button situation is approaching, thus enabling yourself to focus on what to say when it happens. In the beginning, you may sometimes slip back into your established negative ways. Accept these slips as part of the process and return to being positive. With time and persistence, you'll make a gradual shift away from negativity and toward positive self-talk. Eventually, the day will come when you realize that you've just gone through one of your hot-button situations and stayed positive!

Balancing the Scales

When we work with dancers, we ask them to keep track of the positive and negative statements they make during classes, rehearsals, and performances. In most cases, the negatives far outnumber the positives. In an ideal world, of course, you would eliminate all negatives and express only positives. In the real world, however, if you care about dance at all, you may sometimes go to the "dark side" and think negatively.

To deal with this reality constructively, you can retrain your self-talk by first learning to balance the scales. The immediate goal is simply to increase the positives. If you're negative when you perform poorly, be positive when you do well. If you beat yourself up over a bad rehearsal or performance, pat yourself on the back for a good one. When you make a nice effort, say "nice effort" to yourself. When you do something well, give yourself a "job well done."

Once you've balanced the scales by increasing your positives, your next goal is to tip the scales in the positive direction by reducing the negatives. Ask why you're so hard on yourself when you dance poorly. Acknowledge the fact that for dancers at all levels, the road to success involves facing difficulties and learning lessons. In fact, these challenging times form an integral part of the learning process, but you benefit from them only if you look at them in a positive light.

This step of tipping the scales toward the positive is critical. Recent research has found that negative experiences—including negative self-talk, negative body language, and negative emotions—carry more weight than positive experiences.

In fact, it takes twelve positive experiences to balance one negative experience. Think about what this means for your everyday practice of dance: For every negative expression you make about yourself, whether it involves saying something negative or merely screaming in frustration, you must express yourself positively twelve times in order to counteract that one negative.

Your final goal is to tip the scales heavily in the positive direction. Sure, you're going to say negative things periodically; that's just part of being human and being a dancer. You get tired, sick, and injured. You get frustrated, angry, or depressed. Your choreographer yells at you for missing a step. The conditions for a rehearsal get the better of you. And the list goes on. But as long as most of your self-talk is positive, you put yourself in a good place to *stay* positive and be confident about your dancing.

Reinforcing With Positive Key Words

Another useful way to develop your confidence is to use key words that remind you to be positive. Make a list of words that help you feel positive and optimistic, then put the list somewhere that you'll see it regularly—for example, your locker, the mirror where you prepare for performances, your bedroom, or your refrigerator. When you look at a key word, say it to yourself. Every time you see it, it sinks in further, and eventually you truly believe it.

Using Negative Thinking in Positive Ways

Though we emphasize being positive at all times, we also realize that it can be challenging to do so. This awareness was brought home powerfully for Jim during his work with a youth dance company. Early in the season, he constantly exhorted the dancers to avoid negativity and be positive instead. Partway through the season, however, several of the dancers approached Jim and said that sometimes things really do stink and that during these times they couldn't just be positive. At this point, Jim realized that negative thinking is almost inevitable when a person doesn't dance well.

At the same time, negative thinking might be motivating if it impelled a dancer to *want* to improve. Faced with this seeming paradox, Jim thought about how dancers might use negative thinking in a positive way. Eventually, he recognized an important distinction that determines whether negative thinking helps or hurts a person's performance efforts.

That distinction separates two types of negative thinking—give-up and fire-up—and you can use it to help you handle negative thinking constructively. The give-up kind of negative thinking involves feelings of loss, despair, and helplessness—for example, "I'm terrible" or "I give up." In this type of thinking, you dwell on past mistakes and failures, thus undercutting your motivation and confidence and distracting your focus away from giving your best effort. Your intensity also drops because you're surrendering and accepting defeat. There is never a place in dance for give-up negative thinking!

In contrast, fire-up negative thinking involves feelings both of anger and of being psyched up: "I'm doing so badly—I hate dancing this way!" In this frame of mind, you purposefully look to do better in the future because you hate performing poorly. In other words, fire-up negative thinking *increases* your motivation to fight forward; your intensity goes up, and you're bursting with energy. In this way, you can use fire-up negative thinking as a positive tool for turning your performance around.

Therefore, if you have to be negative, frame the negativity as fire-up negative thinking. Remember, however, that negative thinking and negative emotions take a lot of energy that could be put to better use in your training and performances. So don't use it for too long.

Recognizing Strengths and Weaknesses

Many dancers have a difficult time seeing their strengths. Part of the reason is that dance often involves social comparison, and there is always someone who is stronger or more artistic or who does better turns, leaps, or extensions (a reality that is magnified by the mirror). You may pale in comparison in your own mind.

At the same time, regardless of how you stack up against someone else, you possess strengths that you can rely on to achieve your goals. However, they will help you only if you acknowledge them. Take a close look at what you bring to dance and identify your strengths and abilities. Doing so bolsters your confidence as you realize that you possess qualities that you can use to perform well. Commit to developing your strengths even further so that they exert an even greater positive effect on your performances. As you solidify your awareness of your strengths, you gain even more confidence that helps you achieve your goals.

> *"Compromise is crucial to longevity. Confidence must be tempered with caution, and a sense of abandon secured by knowledge of the body's weaknesses. I've finally begun to embrace these self-evident truths. I try to be prudent but not timid when taking risks, and to keep negative thoughts at bay."*
>
> Sascha Radetsky, soloist for American Ballet Theatre,
> former principal for Dutch National Ballet

Knowing your strengths, though, is only half the battle. It's just important to acknowledge aspects of your dance that hold you back. Though admitting these areas may feel like a blow to your ego, it's an essential part of building your confidence and achieving your dance goals. When you know what you need to work on, you can take steps to improve those areas and turn them into strengths.

For example, if you're not a very good turner, you can strengthen your outer rotators and practice turning. If you make turning a priority in your training, your confidence rises along with your improved technique and artistry. The amount of time and effort that you put into addressing weaker areas of your dance determines whether you merely minimize their limiting effect on your performance or actually turn them into strengths. Either way, you can enjoy much more confidence in these formerly underdeveloped areas.

Maintaining Positive Body Language

In working with professional dancers, we've noticed that they carry themselves in a certain way. They move and walk with confidence, and another way to develop your confidence is to learn to "walk the walk." The way in which you carry yourself does affect what you think and how you feel. If your body is down, your thoughts and feelings are down. If your body is up, your thoughts and feelings are up. It's hard to feel down when your body is up. Positive body language involves keeping your head high, your chin up, your eyes forward, your shoulders back, your arms swinging, and a bounce in your step. You look and move like a winner.

Being Optimistic

Optimists are upbeat people. They tend to see the glass not as half empty but as half full. Perhaps unsurprisingly, optimism also relates to dance success; the more optimistic a person is, the better she or he performs. When optimists are faced with a challenge, they tend to be confident and positive. They see difficulties—for example, performing

Confidence will carry you to new heights.
Photo courtesy www.sallaz.com

a new dance style, learning difficult choreography, or having to dance on their "bad side"—as opportunities to push themselves, gain experience, and improve as a dancer.

Furthermore, even when things don't go well, optimists are able to see difficulties as challenges to pursue rather than threats to avoid. Optimists also tend to persevere. The phrase "give up" is simply not part of their vocabulary, and they bounce back after a poor performance. Because optimists believe that things will turn out well, they maintain their effort and stay positive, relaxed, and focused. This state of mind sustains them through the worst of times. Their hopefulness also encourages them to challenge themselves and get out of their comfort zone. Though they may not always succeed, they are willing, for example, to try new dance styles, new partners, and new choreography. Similarly, they are willing to take a higher-level class and push themselves by working among more talented dancers.

You may be thinking, "Sure, it would be great to be an optimist, but I wasn't born that way, and everyone knows that you either have it or you don't." Wrong! Though some people do seem to be born optimists, optimism can also be learned. It just takes practice. You can become more optimistic by using the many confidence-building strategies we discuss in this chapter to slowly move your attitude in an optimistic direction.

This is not to say that it's easy to become more optimistic. After all, pessimism provides protective value: If you don't get your hopes up, you can't be so terribly disappointed when things don't go well; instead, the poor outcome simply confirms your expectation. But the downside of pessimism is that you may never free yourself to take a risk or face a new challenge. It also means that you can never perform to the very best of your ability or experience the joy of having given it your all. Therefore, being a pessimist is safe and comfortable—but ultimately frustrating and unsatisfying.

To become more optimistic, you have to take a leap of faith. This leap means saying, "To heck with it. I'm just going to give it everything I've got and see what happens. If things don't work out, I can live with that." Your past experiences and basic beliefs may not support your leap, but you're going to jump anyway. The great thing about taking this leap of faith is, if you're at all prepared to achieve your goals, you will probably succeed. The success then affirms your leap and makes your next one easier and less scary. As you take more leaps of faith, you become increasingly hopeful and optimistic that good things are coming. Before you know it, you look at every challenging situation and believe that you will overcome it and achieve your goals.

To begin developing your own positive self-talk, check out the dancer's litany shown in figure 4.2. Then put together your own dancer's litany emphasizing statements that are important to you.

Figure 4.2 **Dancer's Litany**

I love to dance.

I am a great dancer.

I always think and talk positively.

I expect to feel pressure, and that's okay, because I know how to handle it.

I am confident, relaxed, and focused when I dance.

I always work my hardest in class and rehearsal.

I will be the best dancer I can be.

I dance joyfully and effortlessly.

Confidence Challenge

The real test of confidence lies in how you respond when things don't go your way; in fact, this type of crucible is what we call the Confidence Challenge. It's easy to stay confident when you're healthy and rested and the conditions are ideal. Inevitably, however, you will also experience down periods and face adversity. When things get difficult, consistently successful dancers maintain their confidence; as a result, they can persevere rather than give up, and they know that over time their performance will come around.

Dancers with prime confidence not only maintain their confidence but also actively seek out ways to return to their optimal level. All dancers go through periods in which they don't perform well; the key is to get out of the rut quickly. Fortunately, you can develop the mental skills needed in order to meet the Confidence Challenge. You can learn to respond positively to such challenges by exposing yourself to demanding situations and difficult conditions—both in training and in performance—and practicing your positive responses.

Mastering the Confidence Challenge is a multifaceted process. First, you develop the attitude that demanding situations are not threats to be avoided but challenges to be sought out. When you're confronted with a Confidence Challenge, approach it as an opportunity to become a better dancer. Choose to believe that experiencing challenges is a necessary part of becoming the best dancer you can be. Accept the reality that these experiences will be uncomfortable due to their difficulty and unfamiliarity. And recognize the fact that as you expose yourself to more challenges, you will find them less threatening and more comfortable.

Fortified with this perspective, seek out every possible challenge in training, performance, and competition. In addition, be sure that you're well-prepared to meet the challenges you choose. Beyond a positive attitude, of course, you also need the appropriate physical fitness, technique, artistry, and mental skills. As you engage difficulties, stay positive and motivated. Focus on what you need to do to overcome the challenge rather than on how difficult it may be. Accept the fact that you may struggle as you begin to face a new challenge. View these experiences as opportunities to learn lessons that you can use when faced with similar challenges in the future. Finally—and most important—never, ever give up!

It's one thing to be confident in your ability as a dancer. It's a much more important thing to be confident in yourself as a person. Yet we have observed that many dancers struggle with their belief in their personal capabilities. Are you positive and confident in other aspects of your life—for example, in your relationships, at school or work, and in your avocations? If not, then you can use the same techniques presented in this chapter to strengthen your belief in yourself as a person.

ENCORE

- Confidence is the most important mental contributor to success in dance.
- Dancers can experience either a vicious cycle of diminishing confidence or an upward spiral of increasing confidence.
- Dancers can lose confidence due to technical breakdowns, costume malfunctions, a bad class or rehearsal, a partner's miscues, a poor performance, unrealistic expectations, or the stress of performing in front of an audience.
- Prime confidence consists of a deep, lasting, and resilient belief in your ability to achieve your dance goals.
- Confidence is a skill that you can develop with practice.
- You can build confidence through a progression involving rigorous preparation, the knowledge that you possess the mental skills to overcome challenges, the recognition that you have in fact overcome adversity before, the feeling of being supported by others, and the experience of success.
- You can improve your confidence by becoming aware of your negative self-talk, replacing it with positive self-talk, using positive body language, and responding positively to the challenges that you face as a dancer.

Center Stage: Cary

Being Your Best Ally, Not Your Worst Enemy

Cary, a 23-year-old jazz dancer, was his own worst enemy—not only in dance but also in most parts of his life. He often expected the worst, and unsurprisingly that's what usually happened. In rehearsals and performances, Cary's mind would turn against him, and he would dwell on a mistake rather than focus on dancing well for the remainder of the performance.

One day, Cary attended a talk on dance psychology sponsored by his local studio. The speaker explained the importance of confidence and said that even if a person is negative, he or she can turn things around and become more positive. Tired of his own negativity, Cary decided to give the speaker's ideas a try, though, characteristically, he didn't expect them to work.

Over his next week of training, Cary paid attention both to his self-talk and to what he said to others. After each class and rehearsal, he wrote down the negative and positive things he remembered saying. Even Cary was shocked to see in writing how negative he was. In a week's worth of training, he recalled thinking or saying 97 negative things and only 4 positive ones.

Cary then wrote down some positive things he *could* say to himself when he began to go to the dark side. Over the next few weeks, he committed himself to being more positive, but it was a real struggle. After the first week, his positive-to-negative ratio remained quite low—21 to 76—but it still marked an improvement, and it gave Cary hope. After a month, he finally turned the corner by making more positive statements than negative ones (44 to 21). This was not a stellar ratio, but he was heading in the right direction, and a month later his ratio was up to 76 to 10.

Soon thereafter, for the first time in quite a while, Cary felt excited about opening night. Through the early part of the performance, he felt good and experienced little negativity. About a third of the way through, he missed a beat and got a little behind in the choreography. As usual, negatives began to pop up, but he immediately countered them with positive self-talk. For the first time ever in a dance performance, Cary was able to recover from a mistake and finish without any other major mistakes. This was his best performance ever; just as important, he enjoyed himself immensely.

References

Bandura, A. (1977). Self-efficacy: Toward a unifying theory of behavioral change. *Psychological Review, 84,* 91–215.

Bandura, A. (1986). *Social foundations of thought and action.* Englewood Cliffs, NJ: Prentice Hall.

Bandura, A., & Adams, N.E. (1977). Analysis of self-efficacy theory of behavioral change. *Cognitive Therapy and Research, 1,* 287–308.

Bandura, A., & Cervone, D. (1983). Self-evaluative and self-efficacy mechanisms governing the motivational effects of goal systems. *Journal of Personality and Social Psychology, 45,* 1017–1028.

Banes, S. (1980). *Terpsichore in sneakers: Post-modern dance.* Boston: Houghton Mifflin.

Bennett, J.G., & Pravitz, J.E. (1987). *Profile of a winner: Advanced mental training for athletes.* Ithaca, NY: Sport Science International.

Brawley, L.R. (1984). Attributions as social cognitions: Contemporary perspectives in sport. In W.F. Straub & J.M. Williams (Eds.), *Cognitive sport psychology* (pp. 212–230). Lansing, NY: Sport Science Associates.

Bunker, L., & Williams, J.M. (2010). Cognitive techniques for improving performance and building confidence. In J.M. Williams (Ed.), *Applied sport psychology: Personal growth to peak performance* (pp. 235–255). Palo Alto, CA: Mayfield.

Cautela, J.R., & Wisocki, P.A. (1977). Thought-stoppage procedure: Description, application, and learning theory interpretations. *Psychological Record, 27,* 255–264.

Cunningham, M. (1951). The function of a technique for dance. In W. Sorell (Ed.), *The dance has many faces* (pp. 250–251). New York: World.

Deci, E., & Ryan, R. (Eds.). (2002). *Handbook of self-determination research.* Rochester, NY: University of Rochester Press.

Ellis, A. (1962). *Reason and emotion in psychotherapy.* New York: Lyle Stuart.

Estanol, E. (2004). *Effects of a psychological skills training program on self-confidence, anxiety, and performance in university ballet dancers.* Master's thesis, Willard Marriott Library, University of Utah.

Feltz, D.L., & Albrecht, R.R. (1985). The influence of self-efficacy on approach/avoidance of a high-avoidance task. In J.H. Humphrey & L. Vander Velden (Eds.), *Current research in the psychology/sociology of sport* (Vol. 1) (pp. 274–291). Princeton, NJ: Princeton Book.

Feltz, D.L., & Riessinger, C.A. (1990). Effects of in vivo emotive imagery and performance feedback on self-efficacy and muscular endurance. *Journal of Sport and Exercise Psychology, 12,* 132–143.

Ford, J. (n.d.). How to identify hot buttons. www.ehow.com/how_4543541_identify-hot-buttons.html.

Gauron, E.F. (1984). *Mental training for peak performance.* Lansing, NY: Sport Science Associates.

Gere, D. (1992, August). Mikko Nissinen: Strength regained, confidence restored. *Dance, 8,* 32–37.

Gould, D., Dieffenbach, K., & Moffet, A. (2002). Psychological characteristics and their development in Olympic champions. *Journal of Applied Sport Psychology, 14*(3), 172–204.

Greenspan, M.J., & Feltz, D.L. (1989). Psychological interventions with athletes in competitive situations: A review. *The Sport Psychologist, 3,* 219–236.

Hamilton, L.H. (1998). Advice for dancers: Emotional counsel and practical strategies. San Francisco: Jossey-Bass.

Hanrahan, S.J. (1996). Dancers' perceptions of psychological skills. *Revista de Psicologia del Deporte, 5*(2), 19–27.

Hanrahan, S.J. (2005). On stage: Mental skills training for dancers. In M.B. Andersen (Ed.), *Sport psychology in practice* (pp. 109–127). Champaign, IL: Human Kinetics.

Hefferon, K.M., & Ollis, S. (2006). "Just clicks": An interpretive phenomenological analysis of professional dancers' experience of flow. *Research in Dance Education, 7*(2), 141–159.

Humphrey, D. (1951). *The art of making dances.* New York: Grove Press.

Lee, C. (1982). Self-efficacy as a predictor of performance in competitive gymnastics. *Journal of Sport Psychology, 4,* 405–409.

Leland, E.I. (1983). *Relationship between self-efficacy and other factors to pre-competitive anxiety in basketball players.* Unpublished manuscript.

May, J.R. (1977). A psychophysiological study of self and externally regulated phobic thoughts. *Behavior Therapy, 8,* 849–861.

Moore, W.E., & Stevenson, J.R. (1991). Understanding trust in the performance of complex automatic sport skills. *The Sport Psychologist, 5,* 281–289.

Radetsky, S. (2012, April). Breaking free. *Dance Magazine.* www.dancemagazine.com/issues/April-2012/Breaking-Free.

Rushall, B.S. (1986). The content of competition thinking. In W.F. Straub & J.M. Williams (Eds.), *Cognitive sport psychology* (pp. 51–62). Lansing, NY: Sport Science Associates.

Rushall, B.S., Hall, M., Roux, L., Sasseville, J., & Rushall, A.C. (1988). Effects of three types of thought content instructions on skiing performance. *The Sport Psychologist, 2,* 283–287.

Schunk, B. (1984a). Enhancing self-efficacy and achievement through rewards and goals: Motivational and informational effects. *Journal of Educational Research, 78,* 29–34.

Schunk, B. (1984b). Self-efficacy perspective on achievement behavior. *Educational Psychologist, 19,* 48–58.

Taylor, J., & Schneider, T. (2005). *The triathlete's guide to mental training.* Boulder, CO: Velopress.

Taylor, J., & Taylor, C. (1987, January–February). The mental attitude: Self-confidence. *Dance Teacher Now,* 16–17.

Tharp, T. (1992). *Push comes to shove.* New York: Bantam.

Vealey, R.S. (1986). Conceptualization of sport-confidence and competitive orientation: Preliminary investigation and instrument development. *Journal of Sport Psychology, 8,* 221–246.

Weinberg, R.S. (1984). Mental preparation strategies. In J.M. Silva III & R.S. Weinberg (Eds.), *Psychological foundations of sport* (pp. 145–156). Champaign, IL: Human Kinetics.

Weinberg, R.S., Gould, D., Yukelson, D., & Jackson, A. (1981). The effects of pre-existing and manipulated self-efficacy on a competitive muscular endurance task. *Journal of Sport Psychology, 3,* 345–354.

Weinberg, R.S., Grove, R., & Jackson, A. (1992). Strategies for building self-efficacy in tennis players: A comparative analysis of Australian and American coaches. *The Sport Psychologist, 6,* 3–13.

Weinberg, R.S., & Jackson, A. (1990). Building self-efficacy in tennis players: A coach's perspective. *Journal of Applied Sport Psychology, 2,* 164–174.

Weiss, H. (2009, September). April Daly. *Dance Magazine.* www.dancemagazine.com/issues/september-2009/April-Daly.

Weiss, M.R., Weise, D.M., & Klint, K.A. (1989). Head over heels with success: The relationship between self-efficacy and performance in competitive youth gymnastics. *Journal of Sport and Exercise Psychology, 11,* 444–451.

Ziegler, S.G. (1987). Effects of stimulus cuing on the acquisition of groundstrokes by beginning tennis players. *Journal of Applied Behavioral Analysis, 20,* 405–411.

CHAPTER 5

Intensity

"The appearance of intensity may come from their devotion to what they are doing. It can give the look of being highly involved in the moment, that urgency that doing something precisely in the largest possible way can provoke."

Merce Cunningham

Portions of this chapter are reprinted from J. Taylor, 2001, *Prime Golf: Triumph of the Mental Game*.

Whether or not you're conscious of it, your intensity exerts enormous influence on both your training and your performance. Intensity is a multifaceted phenomenon. It encompasses the sensation of calm that envelops you as you wait in the wings, the excitement and exhilaration you feel as you take your place in the darkness before the curtain opens, and the raw nerves of anxiety and fear that you feel before a major audition.

Pre-performance intensity has a complex and conflicting nature, and it can either help or hurt your ability to dance your best. It can feel either positive and invigorating or negative and paralyzing. Even more confusing, unpleasant intensity is sometimes necessary for achieving your goals, and intensity that feels good doesn't always translate into a great dance.

Intensity is one of the most important contributors to dance immediately before you go onstage. It is so important because even complete mental preparation won't help you if your body is not physiologically capable of doing what it needs to do for you to dance your best. Beyond all of your other preparation, intensity sets the tone for the motivation, confidence, focus, and emotions that you carry onto the stage. It may also affect how readily you can access the mental skills that you have developed in training and that you need to use in your performances and competitions.

Intensity consists of two major components: physiological and perceptual. First, intensity is the amount of physiological activity you experience in your body, including your heart rate, blood flow, respiration, and deployment of adrenaline. Are you calm or nervous? Relaxed or tense? Intensity lies on a continuum that ranges from very relaxed (e.g., sleeping) to incredibly intense (e.g., feeling sheer terror or excitement). Somewhere between these two extremes is the level of intensity at which you dance your best. This ideal level varies between dancers, styles of dance, and roles. Some dancers perform best when they're very relaxed, others when moderately intense, and still others when very intense.

The preferred level of intensity is also influenced by choreography. You may need higher intensity, for example, when performing pieces that are fast or edgy or involve a strong character. In contrast, you may need lower intensity for pieces that are slower, lyrical, or more emotionally expressive. And a role in a production may require you to use different levels of intensity in order to maximize your physicality and virtuosity in different parts.

It may also be necessary for you to modulate your intensity in relation to the physical demands of a performance. Because intensity involves energy that needs to be conserved—much like gasoline in an automobile's fuel tank—longer performances call for lower intensity. If you burn too much fuel early on, you run out of gas before the show is over. Therefore, you must determine the level of intensity at which you can dance best in the relevant choreographic pieces, then adjust that calculation in light of your available energy output in order to last through the performance.

The second major component of intensity involves your *perception* of intensity. Do you perceive it positively or negatively? Does it feel comfortable or distressing? Two dancers can feel the same thing physiologically yet interpret those physical sensations in very different ways. For example, one may view the intensity as excitement that aids performance, whereas the other sees it as anxiety that hurts performance.

Both the physical experience of intensity and the perception of intensity are affected by several mental factors, including your confidence, your emotions, and your focus. If you lack confidence, feel frustrated, and focus on beating your competitors rather than on performing your best, you may see your intensity as a negative factor. In contrast, if you're confident, positive, happy, excited, and focused on doing your best, you can view your intensity positively.

This dynamic also works in the other direction; that is, your intensity influences your confidence, focus, and emotions. For example, if you're optimally intense, you're likely to be more confident, focus well, and experience positive emotions. In contrast, if you're really nervous, you're likely to lose confidence, be more easily distracted, and feel fear.

Signs of Over- and Under-Intensity

Different levels of intensity produce a wide array of physical and mental symptoms that can help you recognize when your intensity is too high or too low. These signs are usually obvious, but you may not notice them if you've become accustomed to them. In addition, even if you do notice them, you may not realize that they indicate a problem. Once you learn to recognize these signs, you can identify times when you're not dancing at your ideal intensity and then take steps to reach your ideal level.

Over-Intensity

The most common signs of over-intensity are muscle tension and breathing difficulty. Many dancers say that when they're too intense they feel tension in their neck, shoulders, and legs. This tension hinders performance. For example, if your neck and shoulders are tense during a fast jumping sequence, then your muscles shorten and you can't be as fast, flowing, or explosive. Similarly, if your torso is tense, your artistry and fluidity suffer. If the tension affects your legs, it compromises your ability to execute high extensions and smooth transitions.

Many dancers also report that when they feel nervous their breathing becomes short and choppy. This restriction in breathing is a natural reaction to stress, but it limits the intake of oxygen, which is crucial in dance. Constrained breathing means that your body doesn't work efficiently, your muscles are more likely to cramp, and you tire more quickly. The quality of your breathing also tends to be reflected in the smoothness of your movements. If your breathing is long and smooth, you can lengthen your lines and suspend your turns and jumps. However, if your breathing is abrupt and choppy, your movements are jerky and uncomfortable, and everything feels hard.

Over-intensity can also manifest in other technical effects. For one thing, when you're overly intense you may exhibit poor posture and stiff movement. Muscle tension also causes your shoulders and center of gravity to rise. In addition, over-intensity can disrupt your coordination and technical thinking, thus leading to technical or choreographic errors throughout a performance.

Over-intensity can even hurt you mentally. Anxiety lowers confidence and creates doubt about your ability: "If I'm nervous, I must not be prepared for this performance." In addition, the physical and mental discomfort associated with over-intensity may produce negative emotions, such as frustration, anger, and despair. These mental effects—anxiety, doubt, and negative emotions—disrupt your focus by drawing your attention away from dancing your best and onto the bad feelings instead.

Under-Intensity

Though it is less common, you may also experience under-intensity before or during a performance. The most frequent symptoms of under-intensity are low energy and lethargy. In this state, you lack the energy and oomph that you need in order to give your best effort. Under-intensity is less uncomfortable than over-intensity, but it can hurt your performance just as much because it deprives you of multiple physical requirements—including sufficient heart rate, respiration, blood flow, and adrenaline—for dancing your best.

On the mental side, under-intensity undermines your confidence, motivation, and focus. As a result, you lack faith in your ability to succeed; indeed, you may not feel like being out there at all. This lack of interest causes you to be easily distracted and to have difficulty staying focused on your performance. It may also cause you to make careless mistakes, thus resulting in a lackluster performance.

Choreographers and directors may interpret these effects as indicating apathy on your part, which may make them less likely to cast you in their pieces or give you opportunities to dance in more challenging roles. Under-intensity may also send a message to your teacher, choreographer, or director that you don't want to continue dancing, which could lead them to decide not to renew your contract.

Complete the Intensity Inventory worksheet in the web resource to identify your current level of intensity and determine whether or not this level is working for you.

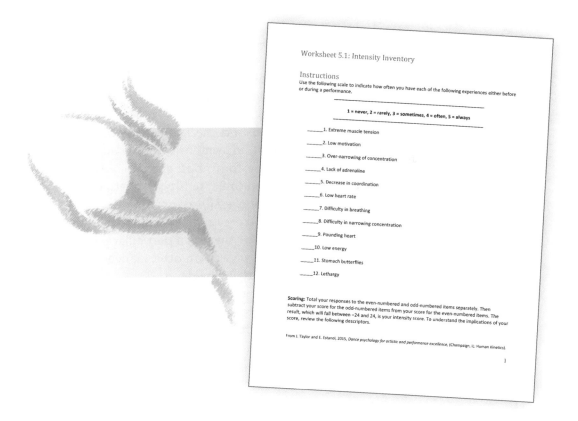

Worksheet 5.1: Intensity Inventory

Instructions
Use the following scale to indicate how often you have each of the following experiences either before or during a performance.

1 = never, 2 = rarely, 3 = sometimes, 4 = often, 5 = always

_____ 1. Extreme muscle tension

_____ 2. Low motivation

_____ 3. Over-narrowing of concentration

_____ 4. Lack of adrenaline

_____ 5. Decrease in coordination

_____ 6. Low heart rate

_____ 7. Difficulty in breathing

_____ 8. Difficulty in narrowing concentration

_____ 9. Pounding heart

_____ 10. Low energy

_____ 11. Stomach butterflies

_____ 12. Lethargy

Scoring: Total your responses to the even-numbered and odd-numbered items separately. Then subtract your score for the odd-numbered items from your score for the even-numbered items. The result, which will fall between −24 and 24, is your intensity score. To understand the implications of your score, review the following descriptors.

From J. Taylor and E. Estanol, 2015, Dance psychology for artistic and performance excellence, (Champaign, IL: Human Kinetics).

1

Developing Prime Intensity

Prime intensity involves two components: First, it is the ideal amount of phys-iological activity necessary for you to dance your best. Second, it is the level of intensity that you *perceive* as most positive and beneficial to your training and performance. As discussed earlier, no certain level of intensity is ideal for everyone; therefore, your goal is to discover the level of intensity that enables you to dance at *your* highest level.

Within this overall goal, you can pursue several objectives in developing prime intensity. First, define your prime intensity, then recognize the signs of over-intensity and under-intensity. Next, identify performance situations—such as being late, replacing a hurt dancer at the last minute, or adapting to choreographic changes—in which your intensity goes up or down. Finally, use psych-up and psych-down techniques (described a bit later in the chapter) to reach and maintain prime intensity throughout your performances.

You can learn to adjust your intensity in much the same way that you use a thermostat to maintain the most comfortable temperature in your home. Because you're sensitive to changes in temperature, you notice when your house is too warm or too cold. When the temperature becomes uncomfort-able, you adjust the thermostat to a more comfortable level. Similarly, intensity is your internal temperature, which also needs to be adjusted periodically. You can learn to be sensitive to indications that your intensity is no longer comfortable—in other words, that it's not allowing you to dance well. You can then use certain intensity-control techniques as a sort of thermostat to raise or lower your intensity to its prime level.

The ultimate goal of prime intensity is to find the fine line of optimal intensity that lies between over-intensity and under-intensity. Prime intensity is the physiological level at which your body performs best and you are most comfortable. Therefore, the closer you get to prime intensity, the better your body performs and the better you dance. Successful dancers understand exactly where that line of prime intensity is, and they can "tightrope-walk" on it, thereby maximizing what their bodies can give them in a particular performance. They're also able to stay on that line longer than other dancers can, which enables them to perform at a consistently higher level.

This ability extends to their careers in the long term. Dancers are most likely to get injured when they perform with inadequate levels of intensity. Too much intensity makes muscles tight and therefore more prone to pulls, sprains, and tears. Too little intensity makes a dancer sloppy in both focus and technique, thus increasing the risk of injuries such as a twisted ankle or torn knee ligament.

> *"I began to discriminate between fear and excitement. The two, though very close, are completely different. Fear is negative excitement, choking your imagination. Real excitement produces an energy that overcomes apprehension and makes you want to close in on your goal."*
>
> Twyla Tharp

To identify your prime intensity, use the Intensity Identification worksheet in the web resource. Think back to several performances in which you danced well. What was your level of intensity in these performances? Were you relaxed, energized, or really fired up? Remember the thoughts, emotions, and physical sensations you experienced during these performances. Were you positive or negative, happy or angry, at ease or tensed up? Next, think back to several times when you were disappointed in how you danced. Again, recall your level of intensity and remember the thoughts, emotions, and physical sensations you experienced.

Now review these recollections. In doing so, most dancers find a distinct pattern. When you dance well, you tend to do so with a particular level of intensity. This is your prime intensity. When you dance well, you also tend to experience certain thoughts, emotions, and physical sensations. In contrast, when you do worse than expected, you probably experience a very different

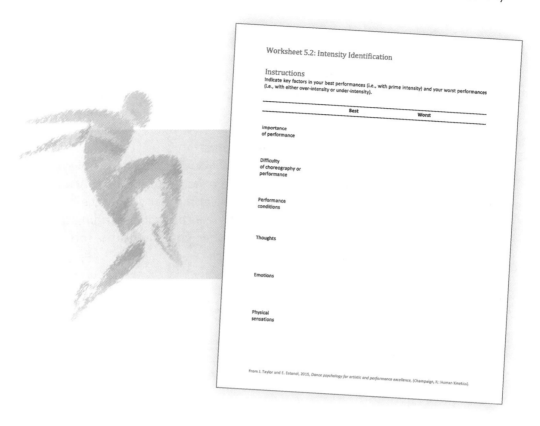

level of intensity—either higher or lower than your prime intensity—and a different set of thoughts, emotions, and physical sensations.

You can develop further understanding of your prime intensity by experimenting with different levels of intensity in class and observing how each level affects your performance. If you find it difficult to remember your thoughts, emotions, and physical sensations, record them in a journal before and after each class, along with notes about how you danced during that class. Include descriptions of how the session felt to you, as well as feedback from teachers, choreographers, and directors. This well-rounded information helps you develop an accurate perception of the quality of your dance.

Here is a good exercise you can use in your dance rehearsals to help you identify your prime intensity. Let's say you're rehearsing an upcoming role from top to bottom (if you're doing different pieces in a show, then say you're rehearsing all of the pieces back to back, with a few minutes between pieces for costume changes). During the first run-through, emphasize low intensity. Before you begin, take several slow, deep breaths; relax your muscles; and focus on calm thoughts (e.g., "easy does it," "cool and calm"). Throughout this run-through, focus on keeping your body relaxed and calm.

During the second run-through, focus on experiencing moderate intensity. Before the set, take a few deep but more forceful breaths, move around the studio, and focus on more energetic thoughts (e.g., "let's go," "pick it up"). During this run-through, adopt a more vigorous mind-set and focus on putting more effort and energy into your movements.

In the final run-through, use high intensity. Before you start, take several deep, forceful breaths with special emphasis on a hard and aggressive exhalation; move around very actively (or jog in place) before the start; and repeat intense self-talk statements (e.g., "fire it up," "get after it") with energy and force. During the run-through, maintain an aggressive mind-set and focus on putting everything you have into your movements.

Continue this exercise for several days so that you can see clearly how your intensity influences your performance. As with the Intensity Identification worksheet, you will probably see a pattern indicating that you dance better at one of the three levels of intensity. You can use this understanding both before and during performances to recognize when your intensity is too high or too low and then adjust it to your prime level.

Reducing Over-Intensity

During our work with dancers, we have identified three factors that can greatly increase intensity in a way that causes a vicious cycle of negativity: unfamiliarity with the situation, unexpected events, and a focus on the uncontrollable. If you address these factors proactively, you can reduce your chance of experiencing over-intensity before or during a performance.

One of the best ways to deal with an unfamiliar situation is simply to become familiar with it. This approach is most relevant to getting comfortable with a performance venue—the dressing rooms, the wings, the lighting arrangements, and the seating configuration. If you're unfamiliar with a venue in which you're auditioning, performing, or competing, you can get the lay of the land either by visiting it ahead of time or by arriving early enough to spend the first 15 to 30 minutes getting acquainted with the environment. If you're unable to use either of these options, ask instructors, choreographers, or fellow dancers who have performed at the venue to describe it for you so that you can prepare yourself mentally.

The best way to deal with unexpected events is to purposefully take an attitude of expecting the unexpected. Think through the things that could go wrong, thus increasing your anxiety, and make plans to deal with them. For example, you might pack extra pairs of shoes, tights, and even underwear.

You can also take this approach with choreography. For example, when Elena choreographs difficult sequences or lifts, she often helps her dancers generate alternate plans to use if, say, they fail to fully complete a lift. These planned alternatives enable dancers to maintain their composure when the unexpected happens and continue their performance at a high level. Table 5.1 presents examples of things that can go wrong; feel free to add your own possibilities.

If you're like most dancers, you want to believe that you can control everything. In reality, however, in dance as in life, many things are outside of

TABLE 5.1   **Expecting the Unexpected**

UNEXPECTED DEVELOPMENT	RESPONSE PLAN
Late arrival to performance site	Use shortened pre-performance routine.
Forgotten clothing or accessory	Pack extra supplies and gear.
Worn-out dance slippers	Pack a backup pair of slippers that is properly broken in.
No rehearsal space	Plan an alternative physical warm-up routine.
Poor floor surface	Stay relaxed, focused, and warm.
Change in schedule	Repeat pre-performance routine or do a shortened version of it.
Role change	Stay calm and run through role change mentally and physically.
Missed lift or step	Do planned alternative choreography or improvise and catch up in the next phrase.

your control—for example, the venue, the choreographer, and other dancers. Accepting this fact reduces your chance of experiencing over-intensity when confronted by events that are beyond your control.

In fact, the only thing you can truly control is yourself. Trying to control anything outside of yourself results in anxiety and frustration. Therefore, if you attend to yourself, you feel more confident, relaxed, and focused; as a result, you are better able to adapt to situations outside of your control. Table 5.2 distinguishes between factors that are controllable and others that are uncontrollable.

TABLE 5.2   **What's in Your Control?**

CONTROLLABLE	UNCONTROLLABLE
Your behavior	Others' attitudes, thoughts, emotions, motivation, and behavior
Your physical condition	
Your motivation and effort	Other dancers' performances
Your attitude	Choreography
Your thoughts	Music
Your emotions	Lighting
Your preparation	The performance space
Your performance	The stage set
	Last-minute changes

Do *not* worry about things over which you have no control! Focus on things that you *can* control.

Before and during performances, it's natural for your intensity to increase and even for you to feel nervous. To dance your best, take active steps to modulate your intensity to its prime level. You can lower your intensity by using the following psych-down techniques.

Breathing Deeply

When you experience over-intensity, your breathing is one of the first things that's disrupted. It becomes short and choppy, and you don't get as much oxygen as your body needs. You can regain control of your breathing by focusing on taking slow, deep breaths.

Deep breathing provides several benefits. Most important, it ensures that you get enough oxygen for your body to function. It also enables you to relax, feel better, and develop a greater sense of control. This increased comfort allows you to more readily let go of negative thoughts and reestablish your confidence. It also helps you shed negative emotions, such as frustration and despair. Finally, focusing on your breathing takes your mind off of things that interfere with your performance and puts it back onto factors that enable you to dance well. Deep breathing can be especially valuable when the pre-performance atmosphere is frenetic.

> *"You spend all day going, "Make sure you do this, make sure you make that correction, make sure you make this change there." And then right before the show you go, "Don't think about any of that."*
>
> Andrew Veyette, principal dancer, New York City Ballet

In addition, if you're performing several pieces—and therefore running from the stage to the dressing room and back to the stage—deep breathing helps you reduce your intensity and speeds your recovery from exertion. Heading into a transition, your heart rate is often high and your adrenaline flowing. As you approach the stage, take several deep breaths to settle your intensity and help you refocus on your place at the beginning of the next section or piece. These deep breaths ensure that your body is more relaxed and comfortable; as a result, your movements are more fluid, and you're better able to focus on your dancing.

Relaxing Your Muscles

The most common sign of over-intensity is muscle tension. Before a performance, muscle tension is usually caused by pre-performance anxiety, which most often manifests itself in the neck and shoulders. Pre-performance muscle tension causes discomfort precisely at a time when you're trying to feel calm and confident. In addition, once you begin dancing, it inhibits the flow and smoothness of your movements and, therefore, the grace with which you perform your role. Muscle tension can also impair your accuracy, speed, and sharpness of movements and generally make you feel that you have less control over your body.

For these reasons, if you develop the ability to prevent and relieve muscle tension before and during performances, you can help your body stay relaxed and perform well. As with deep breathing, muscle relaxation is beneficial because it allows you to regain control of your body and feel more physically comfortable. It also offers the same mental and emotional advantages provided by deep breathing.

You can practice muscle relaxation in two ways: passive and active. In passive relaxation, you can imagine tension as a liquid that fills your muscles, thus creating physical and mental discomfort. If you imagine this liquid muscle tension draining from your body, you feel more relaxed.

To practice passive relaxation before a performance, close your eyes and follow the procedure described in figure 5.1. Take your time, focus on your

Figure 5.1   **Passive Relaxation**

Imagine that there are drain plugs on the bottom of your feet. When you open them, all the tension will drain out of your body, and you will become very, very relaxed. Take a slow, deep breath.

Now, open those plugs. Feel the tension begin to drain out of your body—down from the top of your head, past your forehead and your face. You're becoming more and more relaxed. The tension drains out of your jaw and down past your neck. Now your face and neck are warm, relaxed, and comfortable. Take a slow, deep breath.

The tension continues to drain out of your upper body, out of your upper arms and shoulders, and past your hands and forearms. Now your hands, arms and shoulders are warm, relaxed, and comfortable. Take a slow, deep breath.

The tension continues to drain out of your upper body, past your chest and upper back, down past your stomach and lower back. Your upper body is becoming more and more relaxed. There is no more tension left in your upper body. Now your entire upper body is warm, relaxed, and comfortable. Take a slow, deep breath.

The tension continues to drain out of your lower body, down past your buttocks, past your thighs, and past your knees. Your lower body is becoming more and more relaxed. The tension drains out of your calves. There is almost no tension left in your body, and the last bit of tension drains past your ankles, the balls of your feet, and your toes.

Now do a brief survey of your body from head to toe to ensure that no tension remains in your body. Your entire body is warm, relaxed, and comfortable. Replace the drain plugs so that no tension can get back in. Take a slow, deep breath. Feel the calm and relaxation envelop you. Enjoy that feeling and remember what it feels like to be completely relaxed.

breathing and your muscles, feel the tension leave your body, and, at the end, focus on your overall state of physical relaxation and mental calmness. You can also use passive relaxation during a performance, particularly during breaks or as you stand behind the wings, which is a time when dancers often feel tension in the neck and shoulders. If you focus on allowing the tension to drain out of any tight muscles, you enable yourself to maintain a relaxed position and stay comfortable to the end of the performance. You will probably want to practice this laying down on the floor or on a mat initially. Once you have imagined it in your body, you can do it sitting down or even standing up.

If your body is extremely tense and passive relaxation is insufficient to relax your muscles, you can use active relaxation. For instance, you may find it difficult to relax your muscles when your intensity is too high and your muscles are tight due to fatigue or pain. In such cases, instead of trying to relax your muscles, do just the opposite—that is, tighten them even more, *then* release them. This approach works because of something called the opponent-principle process in our muscles: After being tightened, our muscles rebound back past that level of tension to a more relaxed state.

For example, before a performance or competition, your level of muscle tension might be an 8 on a 10-point scale, where 1 means totally relaxed and 10 means very tense. This is a problem, of course, if you perform your best at a muscle tension level of 4. Paradoxically, you can address the problem by further tightening your muscles—up to a level of 10—thus eliciting the natural reaction in your muscles to rebound back past 8 toward a more relaxed level. In this way, making your muscles more tense essentially causes them to become more relaxed.

Active relaxation involves tightening and relaxing four major muscle groups: face and neck, arms and shoulders, chest and back, and buttocks and legs. It can also be individualized to focus on specific trouble spots. To perform the active relaxation technique itself, use the procedure described in figure 5.2. As you do active relaxation, focus on the difference between tension and relaxation. Notice that you are in fact able to induce a greater feeling of relaxation, and at the end of the exercise focus on your overall state of physical relaxation and mental calmness.

You can use active relaxation as a preventive measure to help you stay relaxed before the start of a performance. It also gives you a powerful tool for resolving muscle tension that builds up during long performances or amidst the mounting pressure of a competition. Relaxing tight muscle groups during breaks can help you recognize built-up tension, counteract the physical effects of pressure, and maintain your form and pace until the curtain falls.

Another way to counteract muscle tension is by shaking out your limbs periodically before you go on stage. Tension can cause your center of gravity to rise, particularly when it results from over-intensity or from holding the same position for a long time (e.g., being in the corps and having to remain

Figure 5.2 Active Relaxation

We're going to start with you taking several deep breaths until you find a nice, comfortable pace for your breath . . . in . . . and out . . . in . . . and out. We will begin tightening and relaxing the muscles in your body systematically and progressively to allow your body to fully let go of tension.

We will start by focusing on your feet . . . Tense the muscles in your feet by scrunching your toes toward your shoes or the floor . . . first only at about 50 percent of the possible total tension . . . Notice how this feels . . . then increase the tension to 80 percent . . . Notice the difference in how your feet feel as the tension increases . . . Now take it to full tension, 100 percent . . . Gather all of the tension and, with a deep exhale, let go completely and relax your feet . . . Notice the difference in how your feet feel when they are tense versus relaxed . . .

Now let's repeat the process with your feet . . . Tense at 50 percent . . . 80 percent . . . full tension . . . Get them as tight as you can, then exhale and release the tension and fully relax your feet . . . again focusing on the feeling of relaxation when your muscles are completely relaxed.

We will now move up your body . . . Focus your attention on your calves, and we will repeat the process . . . While maintaining the relaxation in your feet . . . engage your calves at 50 percent . . . Take them to 80 percent . . . and full tension . . . Relax and release . . . Feel your calves becoming supple . . .

Move up to your legs . . . tensing your quadriceps, hamstrings, and inner thighs . . . Tense them at 50 percent and notice how this feels . . . Take it to 80 percent and really notice the tension . . . Take them up to 100 percent, full tension . . . then exhale and release, fully allowing your legs to let go of all of the tension . . . Notice the difference between being tense and being relaxed . . . Repeat with your glutes . . . 50 percent . . . 80 percent . . . full tension . . . and completely let go as you exhale.

Continue to take deep breaths as you repeat with your abdominal muscles . . . 50 percent . . . 80 percent . . . full tension . . . Now exhale and let go, noticing the difference in how these muscles feel.

Now move to your hands and arms by making a fist and bringing your forearms closer to your biceps . . . Tense at 50 percent . . . 80 percent . . . full tension . . . Exhale and release your arms completely, focusing on feeling the difference, the tingling, and the complete relaxation.

Now we'll move to your neck and shoulders . . . Tighten by bringing your shoulders toward your ears . . . Begin at 50 percent of full tension . . . Notice how this feels, so that you can relax even when they are not so tight . . . Increase to 80 percent . . . full tension . . . and exhale and completely relax and release . . . Notice the difference . . . (If you like, repeat the process for this area.)

Finally, we will move to your face . . . Scrunch your face, trying to bring your facial muscles toward your nose . . . at 50 percent . . . 80 percent . . . and full tension . . . Relax and let go.

Now address every muscle in your body. Be sure that every muscle is as tight as you can get it. Tight . . . loose. Feel the relaxation. Take a slow, deep breath. Once again with your entire body: tight . . . loose . . . Every muscle in your body is warm and relaxed. Feel the difference between the states of tension and relaxation in your entire body. Take a slow, deep breath.

Now go through a mental checklist to ensure that every muscle is relaxed: your feet, calves, thighs, buttocks, stomach, back, chest, arms, shoulders, neck, and face. Every muscle in your body is completely relaxed.

still for a while). When this happens, you may lose both power and grace, and your movements may be choppy and lack elegance and flow. To help your body settle back down, and thereby improve your comfort and performance, make it a practice to periodically raise and lower your shoulders, swing your arms, and shake out your hands.

Shifting Your Focus

Over-intensity before a performance often results from focusing on the performance's outcome. If you're worried about the result—for example, winning a competition, earning a coveted role, or receiving a company contract—you're bound to get nervous because the prospect of failing feels threatening. To reduce the anxiety caused by an outcome focus, redirect your focus to the process. A process focus takes your mind off of the concerns that cause your over-intensity, such as the result of your performance. It directs your thoughts instead to factors that enable you to dance your best; therefore, it calms you, builds your confidence, and gives you a greater sense of control over your performance.

Ask yourself, "What do I need to do right now to perform my best?" This focus on process might include attending to your technique, to your artistry, or to mental skills, such as positive thinking (see chapter 4) and the psych-down strategies described in this chapter. You can shift your focus to your breathing or to muscle relaxation, each of which takes your mind off of the outcome and directly relaxes your body.

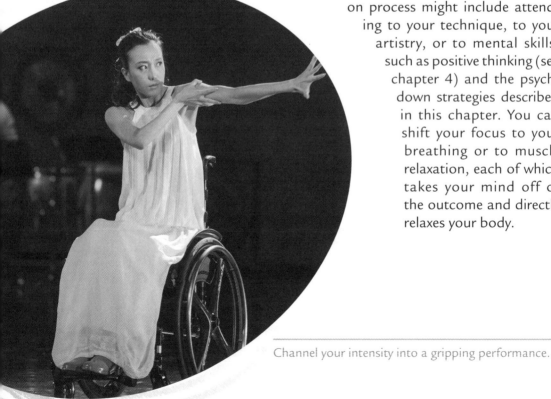

Channel your intensity into a gripping performance.

Using Key Words

When dancers become overly intense, they tend to focus on their discomfort rather than step back and do something to calm down. However, you don't have to fall into this trap. Instead, you can use key words to remind yourself of what you need to do with your intensity in order to dance well (see the Intensity Key Words worksheet in the web resource).

Intensity key words can be used in three ways. First, you can use them before a performance, audition, or exam to keep yourself settled and calm before you go on. Second, you can use them proactively in situations where you expect to feel anxious—for example, when you're about to go on stage for a solo. Third, you can use them reactively when you become nervous during a performance. We recommend that you write one or two key words on a piece of tape and place it in your locker or on your dressing room mirror, where it will remind you frequently of what you want to focus on to stay relaxed.

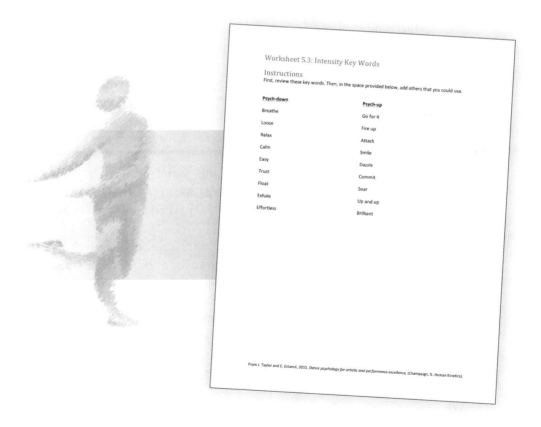

Worksheet 5.3: Intensity Key Words

Instructions

First, review these key words. Then, in the space provided below, add others that you could use.

Psych-down

Breathe

Loose

Relax

Calm

Easy

Trust

Float

Exhale

Effortless

Psych-up

Go for it

Fire up

Attack

Smile

Dazzle

Commit

Soar

Up and up

Brilliant

From J. Taylor and E. Estanol, 2015, *Dance psychology for artistic and performance excellence*, (Champaign, IL: Human Kinetics).

Listening to Music

Music is one of the most popular tools you can use to control your intensity before a performance. We all know that music affects us profoundly in both the physical and the emotional realms. Indeed, music can evoke happiness, sadness, inspiration, and anger; it can also excite or relax you. For these reasons, many professional dancers can be seen wearing earbuds as they prepare for a performance. Sometimes they listen to the music to which they will dance. At other times, they listen to music that helps them feel calm and comfortable.

Music exerts a direct physiological effect on you. For example, calming music slows your breathing and relaxes your muscles; put simply, it helps you feel good. It also affects you mentally by helping you feel confident and motivated and by generating positive emotions, such as joy and contentment. In addition, calming music takes your mind off of aspects of the performance that may cause you to feel doubt or anxiety. The overall sensation of listening to relaxing music is a generalized sense of peace and well-being.

Smiling

This last technique for lowering intensity is one of the strangest—and most effective—we've ever come across. Its power was driven home to Jim a few years ago when he worked with a professional dancer who was having a particularly bad dress rehearsal. She was performing poorly, and the choreographer was frustrated. The dancer approached Jim during a break, feeling angry and with her body in knots, and asked Jim what she could do.

Jim didn't have a ready answer, but he could see a huge frown in her face. He told her to smile. She said, "I don't want to smile." Again, Jim told her to smile. She said she was not happy and didn't want to smile. Yet again, Jim told her to smile. This time, just to get him off of her back, she smiled. Jim told her to hold the smile, and to his astonishment the next two minutes brought a physical and emotional transformation.

As the dancer stood there with the smile on her face, the tension drained out of her body. Her breathing slowed and deepened, and her tense posture softened. Soon she looked more relaxed and felt better, and the smile that had started out as forced became natural. She returned to her rehearsal with a vastly different mind-set and different emotions, and these changes showed in her dancing for the remainder of the rehearsal. Her movements were more fluid and graceful, the overall quality of her dancing improved, and her rehearsal—which had been on a very bad path—turned out to be very beneficial to her.

This dancer's response to Jim's suggestion was so dramatic that he wanted to learn how such a change could occur. He examined the research related to smiling and learned two things. First, as we grow up, we become conditioned to the positive effects of smiling. In other words, we learn that when we're smiling, we're happy and life is good. Second, research also shows that smiling releases brain chemicals, called endorphins, that exert a physiological relaxation effect. Fortunately, for most dancers, smiling is part of what we're expected to do while performing. As a result, it may be the easiest and most natural way to remain relaxed, engaged, and able to fully enjoy yourself while dancing.

> *"I close my eyes and take deep breaths to lower my heart rate; it's relaxing. I can get into my own zone for a while."*
>
> Emily Ramirez, BalletMet Columbus

Remedying Under-Intensity

Intensity letdowns are less common than over-intensity, but they can still reduce the quality of your dance. They can occur for any of various reasons. For example, you may experience a physical letdown if you successfully dance a very demanding piece and feel relieved to have gotten through it. If, on the other hand, you dance poorly, you may experience a physical and emotional letdown.

In either case, your body no longer has the necessary blood flow, oxygen, and adrenaline to maximize your strength and stamina. In addition, you lose confidence, motivation, and focus. Inevitably, this physical and psychological letdown deteriorates the quality of your dancing. You can address this problem by using psych-up techniques to raise your intensity to your prime level.

Breathe Intensely

Just as deep breathing can reduce intensity, intense breathing can increase it. If you find your intensity dropping—for example, as you fatigue toward the end of a long piece—use several hard exhalations to take your body and mind to a more intense level. Intense breathing gets more oxygen into your system, increases your blood flow and your adrenaline, and generally energizes you. Mentally, intense breathing creates a more focused attitude and increases feelings of assertiveness.

Move Your Body

Intensity is, most basically, physiological activity; therefore, the most direct way to increase intensity is to take physical action. In other words, move: Walk or run around, jump up and down, do leaps and turns—anything to get your body going. Moving your body increases your heart rate, respiration, blood flow, and adrenaline. It lets you shake off lethargy and experience more energy, which is particularly important for high-energy performances and times when you feel sluggish or overly tired. Moving also helps you feel more motivated, confident, and focused.

Use High-Energy Self-Talk and Body Language

One of the main causes of drops in intensity is letdown thinking—for example, "this is no big deal" or "I just don't have it today." Such thoughts undercut your performance, but you can replace them with high-energy self-talk: "Keep your energy up," "finish strong," and "stay pumped." High-energy self-talk increases your intensity and helps you regain your motivation, confidence, and focus. In particular, when you're tired and hurting during a long performance, you can use an internal monologue of high-energy self-talk to carry yourself through the tough parts to the end of the show.

When you need to psych yourself up, augment your high-energy self-talk with appropriate body language—for example, pumping your fist or slapping your thigh. The combination of words and actions increases your intensity and fires you up. Some dancers even do grand battements, pirouettes, or big leaps to stay pumped up.

Use Key Words

Just as you can use key words to lower your intensity, you can also use them to counter letdowns and psych yourself up (see the Intensity Key Words worksheet). Saying intensity key words such as "I'm pumped" and "strong" with conviction and energy can raise your intensity, generate positive thoughts and emotions, and help you dance your best.

Listen to Music

In addition to the benefits of music described earlier, music can also be used to raise your intensity and get you psyched up and motivated. High-energy music—whether classical, rock, hip-hop, or country—can raise your heart rate, increase your respiration, and trigger the release of adrenaline. The overall effects of listening to high-energy music include higher levels of inspiration, motivation, confidence, excitement, and energy.

As you know, over-intensity—in the form of anxiety, stress, and worry—can permeate not just dance but every aspect of your life, including relationships, school, and work. Though you can't escape the stresses of life outside of dance, you can make them more manageable by using the same intensity-control techniques described in this chapter for handling dance-related stress. Applying these performance strategies to your overall life allows you to handle everyday stressors in a healthy manner.

Many dancers find that using these techniques away from dance—for example, at bedtime or right before a school exam—allows them to reduce their tension and worry and therefore function better. To see these benefits in your own life, practice deep breathing, relax your muscles, and use the other strategies presented here to lower your stress level and feel better every day. You will not only dance better but also improve your health and well-being.

ENCORE

- Your intensity immediately before you go on stage is one of the most important contributors to your dancing.

- Intensity involves both the amount of physiological activity you experience and whether you perceive that activity as positive or negative.

- Signs of over-intensity include tight muscles, short and choppy breathing, loss of coordination, and feelings of stress.

- Signs of under-intensity include low energy, lethargy, lack of motivation or confidence, and difficulty in focusing.

- Prime intensity is the level of physiological activity that helps you dance your best and that you perceive as most beneficial to your performance.

- Your intensity goals include knowing your prime level of intensity, recognizing signs of over-intensity and under-intensity, identifying dance situations in which your intensity is either too high or too low, and using psych-up or psych-down techniques to reach your prime intensity.

- You can determine your prime intensity by considering performances in which you danced well versus those in which you danced poorly and noting patterns in your intensity at those times.

- Psych-down techniques include deep breathing, muscle relaxation, focusing on process, using appropriate intensity key words to remind yourself to lower your intensity, and listening to music that calms you.

- Psych-up techniques include intense breathing, moving your body, using high-energy self-talk and body language, and energizing yourself with appropriate intensity key words and music.

Staying Cool, Calm, and Collected on Stage

Stacy was always a nervous wreck before her performances. She was 27 years old and had been performing professionally for almost a decade, but performing never got any easier. Stacy loved to take classes and rehearse, but for a few days before every performance she felt a knot in her stomach and had trouble sleeping. Her husband finally encouraged her to see a dance psychologist to find a solution.

In working with the psychologist, Stacy learned that the cause of her anxiety was her attitude toward performance. Specifically, she tended to think constantly about the mistakes she might make and agonize over who might be in the audience and what they might say. The psychologist helped her see that she could change her attitude in a way that would enable her to relax, enjoy herself, and dance her best.

With her next performance approaching, Stacy decided to put what she had learned into action. She focused on getting totally prepared for her role. She spent extra time rehearsing the role technically and artistically, getting her costumes and shoes ready, organizing her hair and makeup supplies, and reviewing the choreography in her mind. She noticed that keeping busy with performance-related preparations made her feel more relaxed and in control. She also made time to close her eyes, take a few deep breaths, smile, and think about how excited she felt about the opportunity she had been given.

Each evening, after she got home from rehearsal, Stacy put on some relaxing music, lay down, and followed the deep breathing and muscle relaxation exercises that she had learned from her dance psychologist. She also pictured herself feeling relaxed before the curtain went up and beautifully dancing various parts of the role with artistry and precision. After these sessions, Stacy always felt better. In bed at night, she repeated the breathing and relaxation exercises and found that she was falling asleep much more quickly.

As opening night approached, Stacy felt more relaxed than usual. During her early-morning preparations, she continued to focus on breathing deeply, staying relaxed, and getting her body warmed up and her mind focused on the enjoyment of moving her body to the music. On opening night, once her performance got under way, she settled in and felt confident, relaxed, and focused. She delivered a great performance, and, most important, felt comfortable and enjoyed herself immensely.

References

Bacon, S.J. (1974). Arousal and the range of cue utilization. *Journal of Experimental Psychology, 102,* 81–87.

Bandura, A., & Simon, K.M. (1977). The role of proximal intentions in self-regulation of refractory behavior. *Cognitive Therapy and Research, 1,* 177–193.

Banes, S. (1980). *Terpsichore in sneakers: Post-modern dance.* Boston: Houghton Mifflin.

Beck, A. (1976). *Cognitive therapy and emotional disorders.* New York: International University Press.

Bennett, J.G., & Pravitz, J.E. (1987). *Profile of a winner: Advanced mental training for athletes.* Ithaca, NY: Sport Science International.

Berstein, D., & Borkovec, T. (1973). *Progressive relaxation training: A manual for the helping profession.* Champaign, IL: Research Press.

Brawley, L.R. (1984). Attributions as social cognitions: Contemporary perspectives in sport. In W.F. Straub & J.M. Williams (Eds.), *Cognitive sport psychology* (pp. 212–230). Lansing, NY: Sport Science Associates.

Carver, C.S., & Scheier, M.F. (1982). *Attention and self-regulation: A control theory approach to human behavior.* New York: Springer-Verlag.

Caudill, D., Weinberg, R., & Jackson, A. (1983). Psyching-up and track athletes. A preliminary investigation. *Journal of Sport Psychology, 5,* 231–235.

Csikszentmihalyi, M. (1975). *Beyond boredom and anxiety.* San Francisco: Jossey-Bass.

Csikszentmihalyi, M. (1990). *Flow: The psychology of optimal experience.* New York: Harper & Row.

Easterbrook, J.A. (1959). The effect of emotion on cue utilization and the organization of behavior. *Psychological Review, 66,* 183–201.

Elko, P.K., & Ostrow, A.C. (1991). Effects of a rational-emotive education program on heightened anxiety levels of female collegiate gymnasts. *The Sport Psychologist, 5,* 235–255.

Estanol, E. (2004). *Effects of a psychological skills training program on self-confidence, anxiety, and performance in university ballet dancers.* Master's thesis, Willard Marriott Library, University of Utah.

Gelatt, R. (1980). *Nijinsky: The film.* New York: Ballantine.

Gould, D., Dieffenbach, K., & Moffet, A. (2002). Psychological characteristics and their development in Olympic champions. *Journal of Applied Sport Psychology, 14*(3), 172–204.

Gould, D., Horn, T., & Spreemann, J. (1983). Sources of stress in junior elite wrestlers. *Journal of Sport Psychology, 5,* 159–171.

Greenspan, M.J., & Feltz, D.L. (1989). Psychological interventions with athletes in competitive situations: A review. *The Sport Psychologist, 3,* 219–236.

Hanin, Y.L. (1980). A study of anxiety in sports. In W.F. Straub (Ed.), *Sport psychology: An analysis of athlete behavior* (pp. 236–249). Ithaca, NY: Mouvement.

Hanrahan, S.J. (2005). On stage: Mental skills training for dancers. In M.B. Andersen (Ed.), *Sport Psychology in practice* (pp. 109–127). Champaign, IL: Human Kinetics.

Harris, D.V. (2010). Relaxation and energizing techniques for regulation of arousal. In J.M. Williams (Ed.), *Applied sport psychology: Personal growth to peak performance* (pp. 185–207). Palo Alto, CA: Mayfield.

Harris, D.V., & Harris, B.L. (1984). *The athlete's guide to sports psychology: Mental skills for physical people.* New York: Leisure Press.

Helin, P. (1987). Mental and psychophysiological tension at professional ballet dancers' performances and rehearsals. *Dance Teacher Now, 21,* 7–14.

Jacobson, E. (1938). *Progressive relaxation.* Chicago: University of Chicago Press.

Kamata, A., Tenenbaum, G., Hanin, Y. (2002). Individual zone of optimal functioning (IZOF): A probabilistic conceptualization. *Journal of Sport & Exercise Psychology, 24*, 189–208.

Kanfer, F.H., & Karoly, P. (1972). Self-control: A behavioristic excursion into the lion's den. *Behavior Therapy, 3*, 398–416.

Kirschenbaum, D.S., Wittrock, D.A., Smith, R.J., & Monson, W. (1984). Criticism inoculation training: Concept in search of strategy. *Journal of Sport Psychology, 6*, 77–93.

Kroll, W. (1979). The stress of high-performance athletes. In P. Klavora & J.V. Daniel (Eds.), *Coach, athlete, and the sport psychologist* (pp. 211–219). Toronto: University of Toronto.

Landers, D.M. (1978). Motivation and performance: The role of arousal and attentional factors. In W.F. Straub (Ed.), *Sport psychology: An analysis of athlete behavior* (pp. 91–103). Ithaca, NY: Mouvement.

Landers, D.M., & Boutcher, S.H. (2010). Arousal–performance relationships. In J.M. Williams (Ed.), *Applied sport psychology: Personal growth to peak performance* (pp. 163–184). Palo Alto, CA: Mayfield.

Leith, G. (1972). The relationship between intelligence, personality, and creativity under two conditions of stress. *British Journal of Educational Psychology, 42*, 240–247.

Leland, E.I. (1983). *Relationship between self-efficacy and other factors to pre-competitive anxiety in basketball players*. Unpublished manuscript.

Manley, M., & Wilson, V.E. (1980). Anxiety, creativity, and dance performance. *Dance Research Journal, 12*, 11–22.

Martens, R., Burton, D., Vealey, R., Bump, L., & Smith, D. (1983). *The development of the Competitive State Anxiety Inventory-2* (CSAI-2). Unpublished manuscript.

Meichenbaum, D. (1977*). Cognitive behavior modification: An integrative approach*. New York: Plenum.

Meyers, A.W., Schleser, R.A., Cooke, C.J., & Cuvillier, C. (1979). Cognitive contributions to the development of gymnastic skills. *Cognitive Therapy and Research, 3*, 75–85.

Neiss, R. (1988). Reconceptualizing arousal: Psychological states in motor performance. *Psychological Bulletin, 103*, 345–366.

Oxendine, J.B. (1970). Emotional arousal and motor performance. *Quest, 13*, 23–32.

Parker, S.J. (Executive Producer). (2013). Principals [Online video series episode]. In *City Ballet*. New York: AOL On Originals. http://on.aol.com/show/cityballet-517887470/episode/517996964.

Quested, E., Bosch, J.A., Burns, V.E., Cummings, J., Ntoumanis, N., & Duda, J.L. (2011). Basic psychological need satisfaction, stress-related appraisals, and dancers' cortisol and anxiety responses. *Journal of Sport and Exercise Psychology, 33*, 828–846.

Silva, J.M., & Hardy, C.J. (1984). Precompetitive affect and athletic performance. In W.F. Straub & J.M. Williams (Eds.), *Cognitive sport psychology* (pp. 79–88). Lansing, NY: Sport Science Associates.

Sonstroem, R.J. (1984). An overview of anxiety in sport. In J.M. Silva III & R.S. Weinberg (Eds.), *Psychological foundations of sport* (pp. 104–117). Champaign, IL: Human Kinetics.

Speilberger, C.D. (1972). *Anxiety: Current trends in theory and research* (Vol. 1). New York: Academic.

Taylor, J., & Schneider, T. (2005). *The triathlete's guide to mental training*. Boulder, CO: Velopress.

Walker, I., & Nordin-Bates, S.M. (2010). Performance anxiety experiences of professional ballet dancers: The importance of control. *Journal of Dance Medicine & Science, 14*(4), 134–145.

Weinberg, R.S. (1984). Mental preparation strategies. In J.M. Silva III & R.S. Weinberg (Eds.), *Psychological foundations of sport* (pp. 145–156). Champaign, IL: Human Kinetics.

Weinberg, R.S. (1988). *The mental advantage: Developing your psychological skills in tennis*. Champaign, IL: Leisure Press.

Weinberg, R.S. (1990). Anxiety and motor performance: Where to from here? *Anxiety Research, 2*, 227–242.

CHAPTER

Focus

"When I dance I am really meditating rather than performing for an audience. I am completely absorbed by the music and the steps I choose to respond to the music."

Agnes de Mille

Focus is one of the most misunderstood mental factors in dance. Most dancers think of focus as concentrating on one thing for a long time. But focusing in dance is much more complex. Dance requires you to focus on many things all at once over a time period ranging from 10 minutes to 3 hours. Therefore, your ability to focus effectively often dictates your success in your performance.

To help you understand focus and how it affects your performance, let's define a few key terms. First, your attentional field consists of everything you *could* focus on, whether inside of you (e.g., thoughts, emotions, and physical responses) or outside of you (e.g., sights and sounds). The ability to attend to internal and external cues in your attentional field is what we refer to as focus itself. Prime focus in particular involves focusing only on the cues in your attentional field that help you dance well. Therefore, it requires the ability to adjust your focus as needed, both internally and externally, during your dance performance. By necessity, of course, it also involves blocking out the many potential distractions in your attentional field.

In contrast, poor focus involves attending precisely to those internal or external distractions—that is, the cues that can hurt your performance. Examples of internal distractions include negative thoughts, anxiety, unpleasant emotions, muscle fatigue, and pain. Examples of external distractions include other dancers, the backstage crew, the audience, the lighting, and costume and technical mishaps.

Whether internal or external, distractions can pull your attention away from prime focus in one of two ways: by interfering or by simply being irrelevant. Interfering distractions, of course, hurt your performance directly. Examples include negative thoughts, injuries, and costume malfunctions. Irrelevant distractions, on the other hand, don't directly interfere with your efforts, but they still distract you from effective focus. Examples include conversations among the backstage crew, thoughts about what you might have for dinner, and an overdue project at school or work.

Achieving prime focus can be particularly challenging when positive focus cues and distractions are one and the same thing. Suppose, for example, that during a particular piece involving the corps, you need to focus on the dancers with whom you are partnering in order to avoid collisions and ensure that you are all in unison. At the same time, if you become distracted by your fellow dancers—for instance, if another dancer makes a misstep—you may lose focus on important cues, such as your technique, the music, and the ways in which you need to interact with other dancers or with the scenery. A variety of strategies will be discussed later in this chapter to help you strike this balance.

Thinking Versus Focusing

Focusing differs from thinking. This distinction affects not only your ability to concentrate on important aspects of your dance performance but also your motivation, confidence, intensity, and emotions. For its part, thinking can be judgmental and critical. Therefore, if you make a mistake when you're in thinking mode, your awareness of that error can turn into criticism and negativity, thus hurting your confidence and your dancing and perhaps even causing you to feel bad about yourself as a dancer.

You can tell whether you're thinking or focusing by examining your emotional reactions when you're faced with a difficult situation, such as a demanding dance master or several missteps in a row. If you're thinking, you're likely to react with strong negative emotions because the obstacle blocks your path to your goals. You may feel any number of negative emotions, ranging from annoyance and irritation to frustration, anger, and despair. This emotional reaction can lead to "paralysis by analysis," a state in which you think so much about mistakes that you're frozen by uncertainty and indecision.

Focusing, on the other hand, simply involves attending to internal or external cues. This process is objective and detached from judgment or criticism. If you make a mistake in this mode, you simply accept it and focus on correcting it in the future. Because excessive thinking doesn't come into play, you don't feel upset or get distracted by judging the miscue or blaming yourself. As a result, you can correct the error quickly. In focusing mode, then, you're able to simply use the mistake as information to correct a problem and perform better in the future.

Focus Cues for Dance

Dance makes considerable demands on your ability to focus. Unlike artistic endeavors that involve only a few important cues or require only a short attention span, dance can confront you with dozens of essential cues over the course of hours (see figure 6.1). You can better adapt to these demands by recognizing the many cues that you focus on during training and performance. If you understand the diverse cues to which you must attend, you can be more aware of them, see how they affect your performance, and take steps to focus on performance-relevant cues while avoiding distractions.

Figure 6.1   Performance-Relevant Focus Cues

Costume changes

Shoes

Floor surface and conditions

Temperature

Props

Scenery

Music

Fellow dancers

Timing and speed

Entrances and exits

Transitions

Time

Key focus areas for performance include preparing yourself physically, mentally, and logistically. Preparation involves a wide variety of factors: warming up and stretching; perhaps running through key steps or sections of your role; making last-minute adjustments to costumes; and communicating as needed with any partners, other dancers, or the choreographer. It also includes getting your make-up and hair ready and securing your costume and shoes, as well as setting up any supplies you may need backstage (e.g., water, snacks, hair spray, bobby pins, and costume changes).

When you're about to go onstage, you must focus on refreshing your make-up, checking your costume, settling your nerves, ensuring that your body is at prime intensity, and reviewing your choreography. As you wait behind the wings for your entrance, focus on your breathing and reassure yourself with positive affirmations. Then smile as you step into the spotlight!

As you move onto the stage and begin your performance, another set of cues becomes important. Focusing on the music enables you to attend to tempo, timing, choreography, and placement. If you've practiced using the music as your cue in rehearsals, your mind can focus on your artistry, expression, and interpretation of your role. You must also be attuned to other dancers onstage in order to avoid collisions and move in harmony with them according to the choreography.

As you exit the stage and wait for your next entrance, focus on recovering from your exertion by relaxing your muscles or taking a drink of water. If you have little time for the transition, simply focus on taking a few breaths, moving quickly to your next entrance, and engaging with your next choreography. If you're dancing in a long ballet with multiple costume changes, focus on quickly getting to the dressing room, changing, redoing your make-up, and returning to the stage.

Identifying Your Focus Style

Our work with dancers makes clear how important it is to identify your focus style—that is, your preference for paying attention to certain cues. In other words, you may well be more comfortable focusing on some cues and avoiding others. If so, this dominant style influences all aspects of your dance. It surfaces most noticeably when you're faced with challenging conditions in training or performance, such as difficult choreography, quick costume changes, or the call to stand in for a just-injured fellow dancer and learn the new role 10 minutes before the show.

The two types of focus style are internal and external. To help you identify your style, use the Focus Inventory worksheet in the web resource.

Internal Focus Style

Dancers with an internal focus style perform best when they're totally and consistently focused on themselves, whether before or during a class, rehearsal,

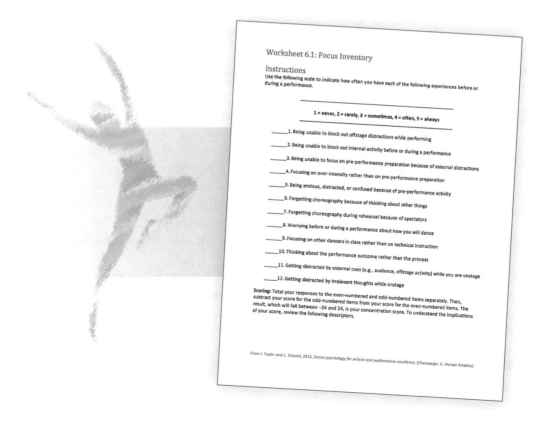

Worksheet 6.1: Focus Inventory

Instructions
Use the following scale to indicate how often you have each of the following experiences before or during a performance.

1 = never, 2 = rarely, 3 = sometimes, 4 = often, 5 = always

_____ 1. Being unable to block out offstage distractions while performing

_____ 2. Being unable to block out internal activity before or during a performance

_____ 3. Being unable to focus on pre-performance preparation because of external distractions

_____ 4. Focusing on over-intensity rather than on pre-performance preparation

_____ 5. Being anxious, distracted, or confused because of pre-performance activity

_____ 6. Forgetting choreography because of thinking about other things

_____ 7. Forgetting choreography during rehearsal because of spectators

_____ 8. Worrying before or during a performance about how you will dance

_____ 9. Focusing on other dancers in class rather than on technical instruction

_____ 10. Thinking about the performance outcome rather than the process

_____ 11. Getting distracted by external cues (e.g., audience, offstage activity) while you are onstage

_____ 12. Getting distracted by irrelevant thoughts while onstage

Scoring: Total your responses to the even-numbered and odd-numbered items separately. Then, subtract your score for the odd-numbered items from your score for the even-numbered items. The result, which will fall between −24 and 24, is your concentration score. To understand the implications of your score, review the following descriptors.

From J. Taylor and E. Estanol, 2015, *Dance psychology for artistic and performance excellence*, (Champaign, IL: Human Kinetics).

or performance. They keep their focus narrow—only on their movement, choreography, or music. These dancers are easily distracted by activity in their immediate surroundings.

If internally focused dancers broaden their focus and take their mind off of themselves—for example, if they talk about nondance topics with their partner during a rehearsal—they may become distracted, and the quality of their dance may decline. At performances, they like to be left alone before the curtain goes up, and they tend to disengage from conversation with other dancers. They can also get distracted by their own thoughts, doubts, and fears. Therefore, they need to ensure that their internal focus stays on cues that help them prepare and dance their best.

Dancers with an internal focus may possess exquisite technique and seemingly unshakable focus and balance, yet at the same time struggle with artistry and with connecting their performance externally to their audience. For this reason, they may be overlooked for roles that they are qualified to perform. Dance does require the ability to shift focus, and dancers with an internal focus must learn to perform outward—toward their audience—and to switch their focus from internal to external quickly, depending on the choreography or the role they are dancing.

External Focus Style

Dancers with an external focus style perform best when they broaden their focus and keep their mind off of dance per se. They focus on dance only just before beginning a rehearsal or performance. When their focus turns too much inward, these dancers have a tendency to think too much and become negative and critical; this overly narrow focus causes them to lose confidence and experience over-intensity. Therefore, for these dancers, it is essential to shift their focus away from dance until just before they begin rehearsing or performing. Even during a performance, dancers with an external focus can be seen talking with other dancers during transitions, behind the wings, and just prior to entering the stage.

Even so, these dancers get into trouble if they broaden their focus so much that they become distracted by external pressures that increase their fears or doubts (e.g., who is in the audience evaluating their performance). Therefore, they benefit from learning how to focus narrowly on performance-relevant cues—such as the music or their partner—that keep them in the zone where their focus enables them to dance their best.

The external focus style runs counter to beliefs held by many dancers, ballet masters, and choreographers. Many people think that if a dancer is not totally focused on training or performance at every moment, then she or he is not serious about dance. In reality, however, dancers with an external focus style perform best when they keep their focus wide and avoid thinking too much or becoming too serious.

"You don't want to be in your head thinking: Oh there's that really hard step coming up that I've had to practice 20 times and I still don't really feel confident in. You know, you have to get into a meditative state when you're just within the music."

Megan Fairchild, principal, New York City Ballet

Girded by this understanding of focus styles, you can now identify your own focus style. Do you get easily distracted and need to keep your mind constantly on dance in order to perform well? Or do you think too much and need to keep your mind off of dance until it's time to train or perform?

Recall past performances when you've danced well. Were you totally focused on dance, or did you keep your mind off of dance beforehand? Alternately, perhaps you've learned to strike a balance, focusing internally but keeping your focus broad enough that you don't fall into worry. Or maybe you prefer to focus externally but can still switch to an internal cue when you need to refocus onstage. In addition, recall past rehearsals and performances when you've danced poorly. Were you thinking too much, or were you distracted by things going on around you?

As with most dancers, you can probably identify a pattern in which you tend to perform your best when you focus in one way and perform poorly when you focus in another way. For some dancers, however, recalling these experiences proves to be more confusing than clarifying. In such cases, we've found that the following questions help quickly identify one's focus style. If you find yourself in this group, think of what you focus on when you arrive at a class or rehearsal:

1. Are you focused on finding your choreographer or partner, noticing details of the dance space, or finding the bathroom?

2. Do you scan the scene to figure out the studio's layout and where the dancers are gathering while also noticing the studio's atmosphere and feel?

3. When you walk into the studio, are you keenly aware of your thoughts and feelings and any sensations of hunger or cold or heat? Are you aware of your breath, your heart rate, or a tune in your head?

4. Do you get consumed by one thought, worry, or sensation (e.g., hunger or needing to use the bathroom) and therefore arrive at the studio either lost in your head or trying to satisfy one sensation?

If the first item in the list describes you, then you have an external focus style that is particularly sensitive to details. If you identify with the second item, then you have an external focus style that is more directed toward the big picture. Identifying with the third item indicates that you have an internal focus style that picks up many psychological, emotional, and physical cues. And the fourth item describes an internal focus style with a tendency to dwell on one thing at a time.

Understanding your focus style is essential for managing it effectively. This process involves knowing how you focus best and then actively using your focus in a way that is consistent with your preferred style. The ability to manage your focus style is most important in difficult rehearsals and performance situations. Otherwise, when you're under pressure or faced with adversity, you may revert to a focus style that interferes with rather than helps your dancing.

For example, if you perform best with an external focus style, you may find yourself turning your focus inward when things aren't going well. This response backfires if you think too much and become negative and critical, which in turn causes your performance to suffer. Or perhaps you simply become unable to switch your focus to the necessary cues when the performance demands it, thereby leaving yourself prone to mistakes.

When you start to lose your prime focus style under pressure, first recognize that you're moving away from it and then take steps to redirect your focus to the style that works best for you. For example, if you realize that you're focusing too internally, actively direct your focus outward by taking your mind off of dance and directing it onto the audience or other dancers.

Narrow, internal focus can help dancers perfect movements in practice.

Cultivating Focus Flexibility

The demands of dance require considerable flexibility in your focus. During a dance performance, you must attend to many diverse cues, both internal and external. Therefore, adhering rigidly to one focus style limits your ability to attend to all necessary cues. To avoid this pitfall, work to understand your focus style, recognize helpful and harmful cues, and be flexible in where you direct your focus. This approach enables you to use your focus to enhance your classes, rehearsals, and performances.

Jim has developed a useful tool for understanding your focus style and developing control of your focus. Imagine your focus as a variable-beam flashlight—that is, one whose beam can be adjusted either to illuminate a wide area or to brighten a narrow area. In this conception, your mental focus is like a beam that you project to illuminate or highlight certain focus cues.

If you have an internal focus style, you want to shine your beam only on necessary performance-related cues. To accomplish this goal, you narrow your beam to keep your eyes fixed on what you're required to do for your particular role, and you avoid talking to others. This tight-beam focus enables you to block out unnecessary external distractions.

However, you must also recognize when you need to broaden your beam in order to avoid making mistakes. For example, if you're too focused on yourself, you may dance out of sync with the rest of the corps; you may even crash into other dancers. Therefore, as you focus on important dance cues, you must notice when to make your beam either narrower (if you're dancing alone) or a little wider (to include dance partners, other dancers, or scenery). But you never widen it so much as to get distracted by thoughts such as who is in the audience, what you'll do after the show, or whether you'll get the next lead role.

In contrast, if you have an external focus style, you want to widen your beam when you're not rehearsing or performing in order to take your mind off of dance. Yet you also need to narrow your beam shortly before you begin a rehearsal or performance. Moreover, if you have an external focus style, your goal is to direct your focus off of dance except when it is absolutely necessary to focus on it. To do this, you widen your beam by looking around or talking with other dancers as you get ready for a performance and during longer breaks and costume changes. Doing so keeps you from shifting inward and thinking too much.

However, when it's time to refocus on your dancing, you narrow your beam enough to focus specifically on something that helps you perform well. To facilitate this process, you can identify other dancers who have a similar focus style and therefore feel comfortable talking about nondance topics before going onstage. At the same time, you should respect dancers who have an internal focus style and refrain from talking to them.

To review, then, there are times when, regardless of your focus style, you need to either narrow or widen your beam in order to meet the demands of the class, rehearsal, performance, or competition.

Here's a good exercise to help you get a better feel for how to use your variable-beam focus. The next time you're getting ready for a class or rehearsal, first widen your focus to take in the big picture of the class, which might include the entire dance space or the dancers as a whole. Next, narrow your focus to individual dancers or specific details of the studio. Then turn your focus inward to get a general sense of your thoughts, emotions, and physical sensations. Finally, direct your focus onto details of your internal world; for example, notice your heartbeat and breathing.

One important part of improving your focus involves identifying which cues help or hurt your dancing. When you know what to focus on—and what to avoid focusing on—you are better positioned to attend to performance-relevant cues and ignore performance-irrelevant cues (see the worksheet titled Performance-Relevant Versus Performance-Irrelevant Cues in the web resource).

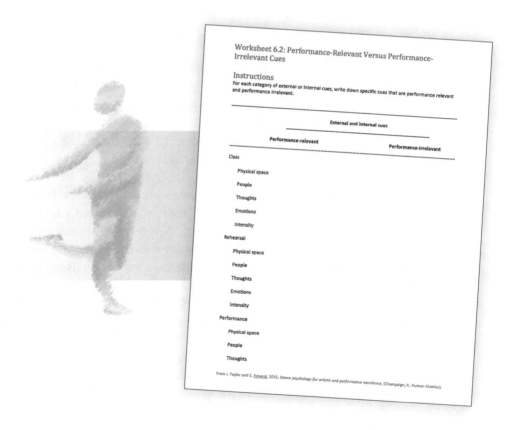

Worksheet 6.2: Performance-Relevant Versus Performance-Irrelevant Cues

Instructions
For each category of external or internal cues, write down specific cues that are performance relevant and performance irrelevant.

External and internal cues

	Performance-relevant	Performance-irrelevant
Class		
Physical space		
People		
Thoughts		
Emotions		
Intensity		
Rehearsal		
Physical space		
People		
Thoughts		
Emotions		
Intensity		
Performance		
Physical space		
People		
Thoughts		

From J. Taylor and E. Estanol, 2015, *Dance psychology for artistic and performance excellence.* (Champaign, IL: Human Kinetics).

Developing Focus Control

Developing focus control is essential to ensuring that your focus style helps rather than hurts your performance. This process involves several steps. Having identified your focus style and recognized the internal and external cues that help and hurt your performance, you can now use focus-control strategies to adjust your focus internally and externally as needed.

We humans obtain most of our information about the world through our eyes. Therefore, the most direct way to control your focus is to control your eyes. To this end, you can think of your eyes themselves as variable flashlights whose beams you can either widen or narrow. For example, if you want to minimize external distractions during a class, rehearsal, or performance, you can narrow your field of vision by focusing on the steps, the area of the stage where you're performing, or the people around you, while using a fuzzier focus in your peripheral vision. However, we recommend against completely blocking out the periphery. Indeed, the fast pace of dance requires you to allow some broader cues to enter your field of vision in case you need to swerve, skip, or jump at the last moment in order to save your performance.

For example, it is not uncommon for dancers to lose parts of their costume or hairpiece, for scenery to come undone, or for a dancer to make a mistake and appear where he or she is not supposed to be. The solution is to strike a balance by keeping a fuzzy focus on the periphery that allows you to adapt quickly to mishaps while also focusing clearly on the task at hand. You also must remember to direct some of your focus toward the audience, sharing your performance and expressing your feelings as you connect with the audience through your eyes, smile, and gestures.

If, on the other hand, you find that you're thinking too much, widen your focus beam by taking a big-picture perspective on what is happening in front of you and clarifying which cues you need to focus on in the next part of your role. Looking around in this way distracts you from your thoughts, clears your mind, and enables you to narrow your variable beam onto your current performance situation.

Using Focus Key Words

Using focus key words is a simple way to maintain or regain your focus during a class, rehearsal, or performance. Focus key words are brief, descriptive reminders of what you need to focus on in order to dance well. Their value comes from your ability to refer to them quickly and easily when you need to focus on something that helps your performance.

This accessibility is particularly important when you're struggling with distractions or feeling tired toward the end of a performance. In these situations, you can get so wrapped up in the difficulties that you forget to focus on cues that help you overcome the challenges. To maintain your focus through a tough period, repeat key words that help you attend to something constructive. Your focus key words can refer to factors that are physical (e.g., "breath" or "lift"), technical (e.g., "head up" or "point feet"), artistic (e.g., "smile" or "smooth"), or mental (e.g., "strong" or "quick").

Focus key words are most effective when you create them in advance. For example, you might develop two or three key words for challenging parts of a particular dance piece or performance. Pre-performance key words might include "calm" and "easy." Key words for turning might include "up," "spot," and "up, up, up." Key words for jumps might include "attack," "soar," and "power." Transition key words might include "settle" and "breathe."

You can increase the power of your key words to help you focus by using them during classes and rehearsals, particularly in situations in which you get distracted. Practicing the use of your key words during training ingrains them in your mind; then, when similar challenges arise during a performance, you can readily turn to them to help you maintain or regain your focus. Post your focus key words in your locker or on your dressing room mirror so that you see them often. These tangible reminders make doubly sure that you remember to focus on important things during performances (see the Performance-Relevant Key Words worksheet in the web resource).

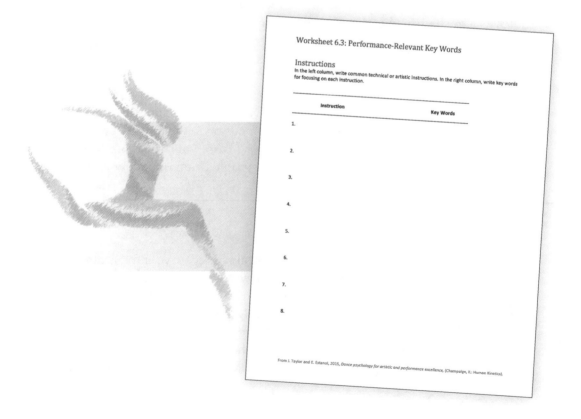

Worksheet 6.3: Performance-Relevant Key Words

Instructions
In the left column, write common technical or artistic instructions. In the right column, write key words for focusing on each instruction.

Instruction	Key Words
1.	
2.	
3.	
4.	
5.	
6.	
7.	
8.	

Relaxing Your Body, Focusing Your Mind

Research has shown that when a person's intensity moves above prime level, the person may narrow his or her focus too much and therefore find it difficult to attend to all relevant cues. This finding is especially important in dance, which requires you to focus on many things in order to perform well. The good news is that because of this relationship between intensity and focus, you can improve your focus by relaxing your body.

Use the psych-down techniques described in chapter 5 to keep your body relaxed, to prevent your focus from becoming too narrow, and to stay flexible in your breadth of focus. Relaxing yourself also removes some common distractions associated with anxiety—for example, breathing difficulty, racing heart, and muscle tension. Feeling at ease also reduces distracting worries and enables you to focus on all of the things that are necessary for you to dance your best.

Outcome Versus Process

Perhaps the greatest obstacle to achieving prime focus is the adoption of an outcome focus before or during a performance or competition. An outcome focus involves attending to the possible results of the performance or competition—for example, dancing well or poorly, winning or losing, getting positive or negative reviews, garnering or failing to garner a contract, and receiving a favorable or unfavorable reaction from the audience after the curtain falls. Many dancers believe that focusing on the outcome increases their chance of achieving a desired result. In reality, however, an outcome focus hurts performance and makes you less likely to achieve your dance goals.

In fact, every time you shift from a process focus to an outcome focus, your performance declines. This drop in performance occurs for several reasons. First, you no longer focus on things that help you dance well—for example, music, technique, and artistry. Second, because dance moves so fast, failing to be mentally present in the moment causes both your technique and your artistry to suffer. Third, an outcome focus causes your intensity to move away from its prime level, either getting too high because you feel nervous or getting too low because you're thinking about what you'll do after the performance.

The critical point here is that the outcome appears only after the process has taken place—that is, when the performance or competition is over. Therefore, in a certain sense, the outcome is unrelated to the process of the performance. In fact, an outcome focus usually produces the opposite of the outcome you want, which of course is a great performance and the achievement of your dance goals.

The way to achieve these desired results is to focus instead on the process of the performance—again, on factors such as technique, pace, and artistry.

In order to stay focused on the process, here is a valuable question to ask yourself: "What do I need to do *now*?" If you're answering this question, you're focusing on the things that help you dance your best.

> *"I spent hours processing emotional and physical pain, gaining awareness that things are temporary and passing. Performing this work requires great reserves of mental concentration. It is exceedingly challenging in terms of duration and stamina. I'm glad I took the initiative to make space for this mental training."*
>
> Katherine Fisher, producer, director, dancer, and choreographer

Four Ps of Focus

You have no influence over many aspects of dance—for example, fellow dancers, the temperature in the theater, and the condition of the stage floor. Focusing on these uncontrollable factors distracts you from focusing on things you can control and therefore detracts from your efforts to dance your best. In fact, the only thing you can control in your dancing is yourself—or, more specifically, personal factors such as your attitude, thoughts, emotions, intensity, effort, technique, hydration, and nutrition. If you focus on useful areas that you can control, then you know that you're doing everything possible to achieve your goals.

Here's a general rule that you can follow to help yourself identify the areas to focus on in your dance. This rule lays out what we refer to as the four Ps: positivity, process, present, and progress. The first P, positivity, involves focusing on positive factors that help your performance and avoiding negative factors that hurt it. Remember the saying, "What we focus on is what grows." Focus on your confidence and positive feelings so that they increase rather than decrease right before you go onstage.

The second P, process, involves focusing on what you need to *do* before and during the performance. You may even narrow this area of focus enough to address specific aspects of your role. It does not, however, involve attending to what might happen at the end of the performance.

The third P, present, involves focusing on what you can do at *this* moment of your performance. It does not involve focusing on either the past (which cannot be controlled) or the future (which can be controlled, in whatever degree is possible, only by influencing the present).

The last P is progress. Dancers often compare themselves with other dancers when they should focus instead on their own improvement. What's

Center Stage: Zach

Increasing Focus, Decreasing Distractions

Zach, a 14-year-old, had wanted to be a professional tap dancer ever since seeing Gregory Hines dance six years earlier. Zach had trained incredibly hard from age 11 onward, and he had recently been rewarded with an invitation to join a prestigious ballet school.

Once he started ballet, however, he had trouble focusing for extended periods of time, and he felt that his distractibility was slowing his development. He often forgot his choreography and missed a few steps before he could refocus. During long pieces, his mind sometimes wandered, causing him to make a mistake or exhibit sloppy technique. He experienced the same focusing problems in school, and testing indicated that he had a mild attentional impairment.

After reading an article written by Elena in a dance magazine, Zach told his parents that he wanted to work with her to help him focus better in his dance. In their first session, Elena told him that focusing problems are common among dancers and he could use specific techniques to improve his focus. Elena suggested that he start by simplifying his space in the dressing room and talking less with his fellow dancers. These changes reduced Zach's potential distractions and enabled him to focus better on his own preparations.

In addition, Elena helped Zach learn to use mental imagery of himself dancing, which helped him identify important focus cues and gave him practice at focusing for longer periods of time. She also prompted Zach to choose key words to repeat to himself during classes and rehearsals; as he began using these key words, he found that his mind wandered much less than in the past.

After working with Elena for six weeks, Zach noticed that he was less distracted during rehearsals and that his focus had improved greatly during performances. He regularly used imagery just before going onstage. Then, if he lost focus during a piece, he regained it quickly by repeating his key words or humming the rhythms of the music. For the first time in his career, Zach was able to focus and dance consistently well through an entire piece!

important is that you see yourself progressing toward the goals that you want to achieve. You have a better chance of achieving those goals if you focus on your own progress.

Developing your power to focus offers great benefits not only for your dancing but also for your life as a whole. Specifically, you will be well rewarded if you identify your focus style, understand prime focus, and develop your ability to achieve it. Recognizing your focus style may also help you reduce relationship tensions that can arise when others feel either that you're not paying attention to them or that you're too inwardly focused and therefore missing cues outside of yourself.

In addition, training yourself to narrow or widen your focus according to the situation helps you avoid falling prey to doubt, worry, and anxiety. Indeed, our experience of any given situation is often made either better or worse by what we choose to focus on. Therefore, if you use the techniques described in this chapter to train yourself to focus effectively, you will feel more confident and relaxed in all aspects of your life.

ENCORE

- Focus involves the ability to attend to factors that help you dance your best and avoid distractions that hurt your dance.

- Dance confronts you with considerable focus demands of various kinds, such as pre-performance preparations, choreography, music, costumes, other dancers, and props.

- One's focus style can be either internal or external. An internal focus style involves wanting to stay completely focused on your dance rather than looking around or talking to others. An external focus style means deliberately not thinking about the performance until you have to do so just before you dance.

- You can think of your focus as a variable-beam flashlight that you can adjust to be narrower or wider depending on the specific demands of a given situation.

- You can use several strategies to control your focus: controlling your eyes to avoid distractions, repeating focus key words that remind you of what you want to focus on, relaxing your body to facilitate good mental focus, focusing on the process rather than the outcome, and paying attention to the four Ps (positivity, process, present, and progress).

References

Bennett, J.G., & Pravitz, J.E. (1987). *Profile of a winner: Advanced mental training for athletes.* Ithaca, NY: Sport Science International.

Boutcher, S.H., & Crews, D.J. (1987). The effect of a preshot attentional routine on a well-learned skill. *International Journal of Sport Psychology, 18,* 30–39.

Bunker, L., & Williams, J.M. (2010). Cognitive techniques for improving performance and building confidence. In J.M. Williams (Ed.) *Applied sport psychology: Personal growth to peak performance* (pp. 235–255). Palo Alto, CA: Mayfield.

Carman, J. (2005, September). The silent majority: Surviving and thriving in the corps the ballet. *Dance Magazine.* www.dancemagazine.com/issues/September-2005/The-Silent-Majority-Surviving-and-Thriving-in-the-Corps-de-Ballet.

Carver, C.S., & Scheier, M.F. (1982). *Attention and self-regulation: A control theory approach to human behavior.* New York: Springer-Verlag.

Csikszentmihalyi, M. (1975). *Beyond boredom and anxiety.* San Francisco: Jossey-Bass.

Csikszentmihalyi, M. (1990). *Flow: The psychology of optimal experience.* New York: Harper & Row.

De Mille, R. (1981). *Put your mother on the ceiling.* Santa Barbara: Ross-Erickson.

Easterbrook, J.A. (1959). The effect of emotion on cue utilization and the organization of behavior. *Psychological Review, 66,* 183–201.

Edwards, J. (2012, September). Technique my Way: Katherine Fisher—Improving stamina in body and mind. *Dance Magazine.* www.dancemagazine.com/issues/September-2012/Technique-My-Way-Katherine-Fisher.

Egeth, H., & Bevan, W. (1973). Attention. In B.B. Wolman (Ed.), *Handbook of general psychology* (pp. 395–418). Englewood Cliffs, NJ: Prentice Hall.

Gauron, E.F. (1984). *Mental training for peak performance.* Lansing, NY: Sport Science Associates.

Graham, M. (1974). A modern dancer's primer for action. In S.J. Cohen (Ed.), *Dance as a theatre art: Source readings in dance history from 1581 to the present* (pp. 135–142). New York: Dodd, Mead.

Greenspan, M.J., & Feltz, D.L. (1989). Psychological interventions with athletes in competitive situations: A review. *The Sport Psychologist, 3,* 219–236.

Hanrahan, S. (2005). On stage: Mental skills training for dancers. In M.B. Andersen (Ed.), *Sport psychology in practice* (pp. 109–127). Champaign, IL: Human Kinetics.

Harris, D.V., & Harris, B.L. (1984). *The athlete's guide to sports psychology: Mental skills for physical people.* New York: Leisure Press.

Kamata, A., Tenenbaum, G., & Hanin, Y. (2002). Individual zone of optimal functioning (IZOF): A probabilistic conceptualization. *Journal of Sport & Exercise Psychology, 24,* 189–208.

Kroll, W. (1979). The stress of high performance athletes. In P. Klavora & J.V. Daniel (Eds.), *Coach, athlete, and the sport psychologist* (pp. 211–219). Toronto: University of Toronto.

Nideffer, R.M. (1976). Test of attentional and interpersonal style. *Journal of Personality and Social Psychology, 34,* 394–404.

Nideffer, R.M. (1979). The role of attention in optimal athletic performance. In P. Klavora & J.V. Daniel (Eds.), *Coach, athlete, and the sport psychologist* (pp. 99–112). Toronto: University of Toronto.

Nideffer, R.M. (2010). Concentration and attentional control training. In J.M. Williams (Ed.), *Applied sport psychology: Personal growth to peak performance* (pp. 257-269). Palo Alto, CA: Mayfield.

Nideffer, R.M., & Sharpe, R.C. (1978). *A.C.T., attention control training.* New York: Wyden Books.

Ravizza, K. (1983). Developing concentration skills for gymnastic performance. In L.-E. Unestahl (Ed.), *The mental aspects of gymnastics* (pp. 113-121). Orebro, Sweden: VEJE.

Schmid, A., & Peper, E. (2010). Techniques for training concentration. In J.M. Williams (Ed.), *Applied sport psychology: Personal growth to peak performance* (pp. 271-284). Palo Alto, CA: Mayfield.

Taylor, J., & Schneider, T. (2005). *The triathlete's guide to mental training.* Boulder, CO: Velopress.

Weinberg, R.S. (1984). Mental preparation strategies. In J.M. Silva III & R.S. Weinberg (Eds.), *Psychological foundations of sport* (pp. 145-156). Champaign, IL: Human Kinetics.

Zaichkowsky, L.D. (1984). Attentional styles. In W.F. Straub & J.M. Williams (Eds.), *Cognitive Sport Psychology* (pp. 140-150). Lansing, NY: Sport Science Associates.

CHAPTER 7

Emotions

"*When you go on that stage, there are so many people watching you. You just want to give them everything you have. You do what you feel.*"

Allison Holker, *So You Think You Can Dance* (season 2)

When many people reflect on dance, they think about the physicality and the artistry that dancers demonstrate so wonderfully. Yet based on Elena's own dance experience, as well as feedback from the many dancers with whom we have worked, the physical side of dance, though certainly challenging, is not the most demanding part. Instead, the consensus indicates that the most taxing aspects of dance are emotional.

During the course of your training and performing, you will experience the entire spectrum of emotions. You may feel exhilaration, pride, fulfillment, and contentment. You may also feel frustration, disappointment, and despair. You may feel many other emotions as well, and you may feel many of them at once. You may feel them regularly, or unpredictably, or with increasing force as you develop in your dance career and face the demands of more challenging roles or bigger companies.

These emotional highs and lows are normal and healthy parts of dance. In fact, emotions may be why you participate in the art form in the first place. Dance causes you to feel deeply, perhaps more deeply than you feel in other parts of your life. And when you feel emotions with such acuteness and power, you feel alive and vital. These powerful emotions enable you to express yourself more fully in your dance.

The downside of feeling emotions so strongly is that you don't feel only the positive ones. In fact, pleasant and unpleasant emotions are often opposite sides of the same coin, and you must be willing to feel the so-called bad emotions (e.g., anger and fear) if you want to experience the positive ones. Your goal, then, is not to avoid negative emotions—you can't. Rather, your goal must be to accept negative emotions, figure out what's causing them, resolve them, and replace them with positive emotions.

Causes of Negative Emotions

In dance as in life overall, emotions arise out of past experiences in the form of beliefs that you hold about yourself. Negative emotions associated with these beliefs are part of what is commonly known as the "baggage" that people carry from their process of growing up. This baggage can include low self-esteem, perfectionism, and fear of failure, and it can produce negative feelings such as anger, frustration, fear, and sadness. Baggage can also cause you to respond emotionally in unhealthy ways to current situations, thus sabotaging your pursuit of your dance goals.

Negative emotions can be provoked by unforeseen or unfortunate occurrences in your dance training and performance. One of the great lessons that dancers learn is that Murphy's Law rules: Whatever can go wrong will go wrong, and probably at the worst possible moment. This tendency creates obstacles, setbacks, and just plain bad luck that elicit many negative emotions.

For example, you may feel frustration when you have a costume tear or a zipper break. You may feel helplessness and despair when confronted with a cold theater, a slippery floor, or poor lighting. You may feel disappointment after a mistake-riddled performance. You may feel fear when faced with an injury. And you may feel any or all of these negative emotions if you're not making progress in your training or if you fail to win a desired role.

If you unwittingly allow such emotions to become habitual, then you may automatically respond negatively to a particular circumstance even when that response does more harm than good. For example, a dancer named Susan slipped and fell during three consecutive auditions. She was devastated by these unfortunate events and developed a belief that she was cursed. During subsequent auditions, she felt terrified of slipping, and this fear caused her to dance tentatively and without spirit.

Because Susan didn't dance as well as she could have in these auditions, she didn't earn roles that she coveted. Later, even after several successful auditions, she slipped again and felt so upset that she couldn't recover and finish the audition. Yet, throughout all of this turmoil, she never thought to check whether something in her shoes or the flooring might have caused her to slip. She simply attributed her falls to being cursed.

Our emotions are natural reactions to the ups and downs of life. When things go well, we feel happy, contented, and excited. When things go poorly, we feel frustrated, disappointed, and sad. When life is just plain going, we may feel bored and blasé. The key is to accept the normalcy of the emotional roller coaster and avoid being overcome by negative emotions.

Negative emotions can hurt your performance both physically and mentally. For one thing, they cause you to lose your prime intensity. When you feel frustration and anger, for example, your intensity may increase, thus leading to muscle tension and breathing difficulties. These effects may sap your energy and cause you to tire quickly. In contrast, when you experience disappointment and despair, your intensity drops sharply, and you no longer have the necessary physiological capacity—that is, the respiration, blood flow, and adrenaline—to dance well. Positive emotions, in contrast, affect your physiology in a much different way. When you're contented, for example, your body is calm and relaxed. When you're excited, your body is energized, which can help you stay focused on your goals and motivated in your training.

Negative emotions also hurt you mentally. In simple terms, a negative emotion is a response to a perceived threat—in this case, a threat that you will fail to achieve your dance goals. Your emotion is telling you that, deep down, you're not confident that you can be successful. As a result, your confidence declines, and you may feel doubt and uncertainty. In addition, because negative emotions are so strong, they may make it difficult for you to focus on what helps you dance your best. Negative emotions can also hurt your motivation to train and perform because they take the enjoyment out of those experiences. These various mental factors can also feed on each other, thereby creating a vicious cycle of decline. For example, a loss of confidence and a resulting increase in intensity can trigger frustration or sadness, which in turn can undercut you in other mental areas.

Here again, whereas negative emotions can cause various problems, positive emotions offer many mental benefits. They motivate you to pursue your dance goals because they reward your efforts with good feelings. They foster positive thinking, which builds confidence. They encourage you to stay focused by removing aspects of your performance that cause distractions such as negative thinking, doubt, and worry. And they reduce pain by releasing neurochemicals that act as an anesthetic (see chapter 13 for more on the relationship between emotions and pain).

"I understand now just how much a dancer can say without even opening her mouth. I am a quiet person, but when I dance I never feel shy. I have always felt the power I hold as a dancer to command attention without demanding it, to say something meaningful to anyone who watches closely. I love that dance rewards the viewer who looks for nuances, because it has rewarded me in that way for so long, and I know it always will."

Gavin Larsen, principal, Oregon Ballet Theatre

Interpreting Your Emotions

The emotions you experience can tell you a lot about yourself, both physically and mentally. In fact, your emotions may be the best measure of whether you've struck the proper balance between volume, intensity, and recovery in your dance training. When you have that balance, you feel happy, excited, and motivated. When you don't have it, you feel frustrated, irritable, and depressed, and your body tells you that changes are needed.

Because of the constant and intense demands that you place on your body in your dance training, you will experience considerable physical ups and downs. These experiences will range from feeling thoroughly energized to feeling completely spent. Moreover, your emotions will tend to parallel how you feel physically, and because of these fluctuations you may ride an emotional rollercoaster during your performance season.

When you're on this ride, your emotions can tell you a lot about your training intensity and your level of general life stress. When your intensity is too high, you're more likely to feel negative emotions, such as fear, frustration, anger, and melancholy. When you're anxious, you're more sensitive to negative emotions and more likely to feel them more acutely. You're also likely to feel negative emotions in your training and performances if you're experiencing stress away from dance.

Continued high-intensity training and life stress can make your immune system less effective. If your immune system can't adequately manage your training demands, your body may break down. You may feel ongoing fatigue, be unable to get enough sleep, and lack sufficient motivation and energy to train. You may get sick and be unable to shake it off. You may sustain minor injuries that don't seem to heal. With any of these developments, you feel negative emotions more frequently and more strongly.

Your emotions may also serve as an indicator of the quality of your nutritional intake. Particularly in longer or more intense periods of training or performance, a downward shift in your emotions can signal a nutritional crisis—for example, a drop in blood sugar, insufficient calorie intake, or dehydration. Therefore, it pays to remain cognizant of the connection between nutrition and emotion and to respond promptly to red flags in order to prevent further nutritional and emotional deterioration. Even when you feel like you're in an inescapable pit of despair, refueling you body can reduce your negative emotions and help you return to a positive emotional state and regain your optimal energy level.

Your emotions can also tell you a great deal about your state of mind. If, for example, you are very emotionally sensitive, easily frustrated, or frequently irritable, then you are not in a good mental place. To determine the cause of this emotionality, look at your motivation and confidence, your stress level, your relationships, and other important parts of your life. What is causing your emotions to be out of sorts?

The common theme throughout this discussion is the significant relationship between your physiology (e.g., intensity, fatigue, illness, injury, nutrition), your psychology (e.g., motivation, confidence, stress), and your emotions. If you're physically healthy and psychologically comfortable, your emotions are probably positive. If, however, you are struggling physically or psychologically, your emotions may be negative. Therefore, you can use your emotions as a litmus test to determine how you're doing physically and mentally and to identify times when you need to take action to get yourself back on track. Use the Positive and Negative Emotions worksheet in the web resource to examine your emotions and their impact on your health and your performance.

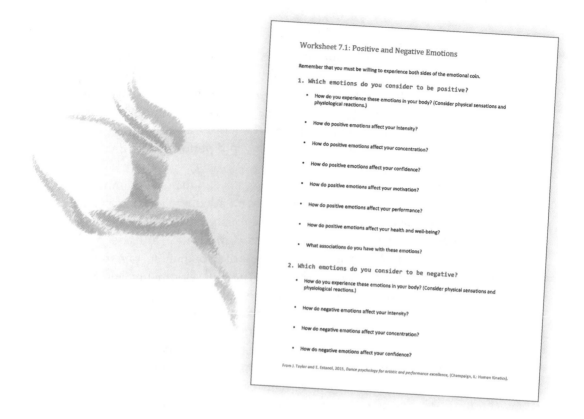

Worksheet 7.1: Positive and Negative Emotions

Remember that you must be willing to experience both sides of the emotional coin.

1. Which emotions do you consider to be positive?

- How do you experience these emotions in your body? (Consider physical sensations and physiological reactions.)

- How do positive emotions affect your intensity?

- How do positive emotions affect your concentration?

- How do positive emotions affect your confidence?

- How do positive emotions affect your motivation?

- How do positive emotions affect your performance?

- How do positive emotions affect your health and well-being?

- What associations do you have with these emotions?

2. Which emotions do you consider to be negative?

- How do you experience these emotions in your body? (Consider physical sensations and physiological reactions.)

- How do negative emotions affect your intensity?

- How do negative emotions affect your concentration?

- How do negative emotions affect your confidence?

From J. Taylor and E. Estanol, 2015, *Dance psychology for artistic and performance excellence*, (Champaign, IL: Human Kinetics).

Differentiating Emotional Reactions

At the heart of emotional reactions, there appears to lie a simple distinction between threat and challenge. Emotional threat can arise when you become overly invested in your dance (that is, when you enter the "too zone" discussed in chapter 1). In this state of mind, your self-esteem—how you feel about yourself as a person—becomes overly connected to how you dance in training and performances. Emotional threat can be associated with pressure that is either self-imposed or forced on you by others, such as family members or choreographers.

When you think this way, your self-esteem is on the line every time you train or perform. As a result, you're driven to avoid failure because you perceive it as a direct attack on your self-worth as a person. It's easy to see why someone who holds this belief can experience dance as emotionally threatening. To relieve the threat, the person may experience a fight-or-flight reaction.

In the fight response, you develop an extreme motivation to train. You may push yourself unmercifully in an effort to reach a level of fitness or artistry that ensures success and thereby reduces the emotional threat. However, you may push so hard that you overtrain or become injured or burned out. Thus, rather than alleviating the emotional threat, the fight response can lead to the very thing that is so threatening in the first place: failure.

Positive emotions heighten
your performance.

The flight
response, on
the other hand,
can lead to a loss of
motivation for training
and performing. Failing
to train properly leaves you
in bad physical condition and
perhaps technically unsound, which
causes you to have low expectations for success in your performances. Then, onstage, where the threat of failure is strong and immediate, the flight response may lead you to sabotage your efforts as you perform. Overall, being out of shape, quitting, or sabotaging yourself can seem like a way to protect your self-esteem because it gives you an excuse for failure.

In contrast to the dynamics of emotional threat, emotional challenge is associated with caring deeply about your dance but staying clear of the too zone. Instead, you enjoy the process of dance—the training, the camaraderie, and the roles—regardless of how you perform. You gain pleasure from all aspects of your training and see performance as an opportunity to find out what you're capable of. When you view dance as an emotional challenge, it is an experience that you can relish and seek out. You can strive to give your best effort, and you can accept the results when you don't dance up to your expectations.

Emotional challenge is expressed in the strong desire to push yourself beyond your perceived limits, to achieve your goals, and to grow as a dancer and a person. At the same time, you hold dance in perspective and maintain a healthy balance between dance and other parts of your life. Therefore, the emotional challenge stance is so highly motivating that you love facing the challenges presented by dance. Research has also shown that dancers who perceive emotional situations as challenges rather than as threats tend to experience a greater sense of getting their basic psychological needs met; in other words, they experience dance as more satisfying and enjoyable. Use the Examining Emotional Threats worksheet (in the web resource) to assess your own personal "too" and "flow" zones.

Surmounting Emotional Obstacles

You will experience many different emotions during training and performance: inspiration, irritation, pride, disappointment, frustration, joy, excitement, and sadness. Some of these emotions feel good, and others feel lousy. Some help you dance well, and others seem like anchors tied around your ankles or lead weights sitting on your shoulders.

Within this mix of feelings, four negative emotions are the most difficult to overcome, and they can not only keep you from achieving your dance goals but

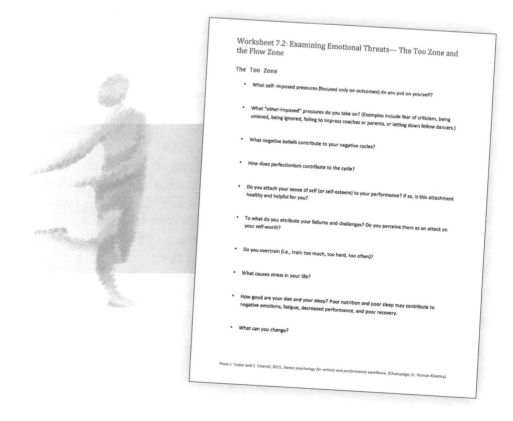

Worksheet 7.2: Examining Emotional Threats— The Too Zone and the Flow Zone

The Too Zone

- What self- imposed pressures (focused only on outcomes) do you put on yourself?

- What "other-imposed" pressures do you take on? (Examples include fear of criticism, being unloved, being ignored, failing to impress coaches or parents, or letting down fellow dancers.)

- What negative beliefs contribute to your negative cycles?

- How does perfectionism contribute to the cycle?

- Do you attach your sense of self (or self-esteem) to your performance? If so, is this attachment healthy and helpful for you?

- To what do you attribute your failures and challenges? Do you perceive them as an attack on your self-worth?

- Do you overtrain (i.e., train too much, too hard, too often)?

- What causes stress in your life?

- How good are your diet and your sleep? Poor nutrition and poor sleep may contribute to negative emotions, fatigue, decreased performance, and poor recovery.

- What can you change?

From J. Taylor and E. Estanol, 2015, *Dance psychology for artistic and performance excellence*, (Champaign, IL: Human Kinetics).

also suck the joy out of your efforts. These four emotions are fear, frustration, despair, and postperformance depression.

Fear

Dance can be scary. It presents dancers with many fear-provoking experiences that may carry harmful consequences, both in the immediate future and over the long term. These fears may involve the very real physical possibilities of pain and injury, as well as psychological concerns such as failure and rejection. Fear is usually uncomfortable and can be debilitating, both physically and emotionally; as a result, it can hurt your performances and detract from your experience of dance. However, by understanding and actively combating your fear, you can put yourself in a better position to dance your best and enjoy both your training and your performance efforts.

Fear can pose a powerful psychological obstacle to achieving your goals. Regardless of the source of your fear, it can create a cascade of deficits in psychological areas that are essential for success. Fear can reduce your motivation to train and perform because doing so is physically and psychologically uncomfortable. It can hurt your confidence if the fear involves the belief that some form of harm—physical, mental, or related to status—will result from your efforts.

This loss of motivation and confidence may cause you to become cautious, tentative, and unable to fully commit yourself. In addition, even when you try to commit, fear cripples your ability to focus. In fact, the emotional and physical experiences of fear can be so strong that you find it hard to focus on things that help your performance. Fear also strangles any enjoyment you may have in your dance participation and ultimately cripples your dancing.

> "I've learned that you cannot let fear overtake you . . . . Yes,
> you have to be sensible, but if you let fear cripple you, then you
> just move correctly and you don't dance anymore. Dancing is
> a combination of control and abandon, and you have to have
> that abandon to feel like you're dancing."
>
> Pat Catterson, choreographer and dancer

Fear may also be expressed profoundly in physical symptoms, including anxiety, muscle tension, shallow breathing, headache, stomachache, and loss of coordination. These symptoms can create tremendous discomfort individually or in combination. They can also burn energy that you need for long performances, stifle your artistry and physicality, and sabotage your technique. In short, the physical symptoms of fear interfere with your ability to dance your best.

Fear of Pain

Fear of pain is an unavoidable part of dance life. Perhaps most immediate is the fear of pain due to exertion in physically demanding classes, rehearsals, auditions, performances, and long performance seasons. Indeed, pain experienced during training is a normal part of dance, and all dancers know they will feel it at some point.

Granted, in a certain way, pain is sometimes rewarding as a sign of hard work toward achieving your goals. Nonetheless, you must also work to transcend your fear of pain, especially in situations—such as auditions, performances, and examinations—in which pushing yourself to the next level can make the difference between getting or losing a job or promotion. Pushing through this pain depends in part on acknowledging that it is temporary and affirming that your body will recover.

There is a point, however, at which pain can be so severe that you seriously fear it. This fear may cause you to slacken your efforts due to worry that you'll be unable to handle the pain and therefore won't make it to the end of class or rehearsal.

Fear of Injury

Fear of injury has a basis in reality. Though we don't know of any statistics to support this claim, Elena's dance experience and our work with dancers suggest that almost all committed dancers sustain at least one serious injury during their career. In addition, of course, dancers also face a steady parade of the muscle pulls, sprains, bruises, and blisters that are just part of dance life.

This reality derives from the fact that dance puts considerable demands on your body; moreover, these demands increase along with the level, frequency, and intensity of your dance. Indeed, it's rare for a dancer *not* to sustain an injury due to overuse, improper technique, or inadequate recovery. When an injury is serious (e.g., torn knee ligament) or recurrent (e.g., nagging hamstring pull), it can discourage you from pushing yourself harder and even cause you to feel fearful about continuing your training efforts.

Fear of injury typically rears its ugly head most prominently when a dancer is asked to learn a complex new skill or perform a new choreographic move or a partnering trick that involves being thrown in the air and trusting the partner to make the catch. Certainly, this fear makes sense. We all possess an inborn self-protective mechanism that says, "Uh-oh, be careful; that looks dangerous, and I could get seriously hurt."

If this type of fear arises, acknowledge how you feel and voice your concerns to your teacher, director, choreographer, or partner. You may benefit from receiving extra instruction, watching someone else perform the skill, or working with a spotter to ensure that if something goes wrong you will be caught and therefore avoid injury. At the same time, monitor your self-talk. Take a positive approach, trusting your partner, teacher, and choreographer to be there for you.

This process is important because if you never voice your concern, then you may attempt the skill while feeling fearful and tentative, which puts you at greater risk of injury. On the other hand, when you get some reassurance—as well as the opportunity to break down the step and practice it several times—you can build mastery, confidence, and comfort. As a result, you feel more comfortable and less fearful, which increases your likelihood of learning the skill and performing it well.

Fear of Failure

Beyond fears about physical injury, your ability to dance your best and enjoy the process can also be undercut by fears related to psychological aspects of the experience. As discussed earlier, one common form of such fear is the fear of failure, which can arise if you become overly invested in your dance efforts. Fear of failure is commonly thought of as involving a belief that failure will bring about a negative consequence—for example, disappointing others or losing their respect, feeling embarrassment or even shame, or failing to achieve one's goals.

Fear of failure exerts great power over many dancers because they connect how they dance to their expectations about whether they will be loved and valued—either by themselves or by others. In other words, their feelings about themselves are based on whether they succeed or fail to live up to dance-related expectations. Most dancers are motivated to succeed and to gain affirmation from themselves and praise from others. But those who fear failure are often driven to avoid failure and the criticism and negative impressions that they believe come with it. Their very self-esteem, therefore, is based on their ability to avoid failure and gain love, respect, and value by achieving success in dance. This fear of failure may be reinforced by an unhealthy level of perfectionism.

Fear is an essential human emotion that protects you when your physical or psychological well-being is threatened. Unfortunately, it can also arise in situations where it is neither required nor helpful. Regardless, however, your goal when you experience fear is not to banish it but to master it and remove it as an obstacle to your progress. Indeed, people often think of courage as the absence of fear, but true courage is the ability to perform in the face of fear.

Fears come in all shapes and sizes, and we recently conducted a survey to gain insight into the fears that are common among dancers. Some of these fears are rational; in other words, they focus on something that is worthy of fear—for example, landing the wrong way or being dropped by a partner. Other are irrational, such as worry about falling off of the stage (this fear is more common than you might think).

You grow as a performer by managing your fears.

Most fears felt by dancers involve something going wrong during a performance: being "off" either technically or artistically, missing an important technical section, falling out of a turn, forgetting the choreography, running into another dancer, missing an entrance, having a costume malfunction, or having a toe-shoe ribbon come undone. Other fears involve psychological injury, such as failing to earn a coveted role.

One characteristic shared by all of these fears is the fact that no matter how farfetched they may be, they are as real for you as you believe them to be. Nor do they just go away on their own. In fact, they can persist and become ingrained in your thinking and your emotions. To overcome fears, you must face them, address them, and put them behind you. Breaking free of fears liberates you to push yourself to your limits, enjoy your dance experiences, and achieve your goals.

The first step in mastering your fear is to understand it. Is the cause of your fear obvious—for example, being dropped by your partner during a lift with which the two of you have struggled? Or is its source more obscure—such as pre-performance anxiety that manifests as worry about impressing your parents, critics, or general audience? Once you identify your fear, familiarize yourself with it. When does it arise—that is, in what situations? What thoughts are associated with it? How does it make your body feel? What reduces it?

If you develop a clear understanding of your fear, you can directly address its cause in order to relieve it as quickly and easily as possible.

Our survey showed widespread agreement on the fears described in this section. Therefore, if you experience such fears in your dancing, you're not alone; in fact, your fears are probably also felt by many dancers around you. This shared experience tells you that your fear is normal, and this recognition can help you keep fear in perspective and prevent it from consuming you. Gaining perspective on fear helps you realize that it doesn't have to cripple you—that, in fact, you have the power to master it. You can gain further perspective on your fear, as well as insights for handling it, by talking with others about it.

Rational fears are best resolved by finding a solution to the cause of the fear. Doing so requires relevant information, experience, rehearsal time, and skills. For example, if you're afraid of being dropped by your partner during a difficult lift, you can reduce your fear by practicing it often and gaining comfort and familiarity with it. In other cases, you can remove the source of the fear, or prevent it from arising in the first place, by changing the situation that causes it. For instance, fear of a slippery stage might be relieved by walking and dancing on the stage before the performance or by modifying the concerning area with water or rosin.

Mastering irrational fears requires a different approach. Because irrational fears have no objective solution, you can neither solve the fear nor readily change the situation that causes it. Instead, you must counter the irrational *beliefs* that cause the fear; in other words, you must be rational about your irrationality. For example, if you fear falling off of the stage, you can remind yourself that you have never done so, nor have you ever heard of anyone doing so. You can also imagine yourself dancing close to the edge but not falling off. Even after this rational debunking, however, your irrational fear may linger or pop up again. If it does, accept it as normal, decide to put it out of your mind, and focus on tangible aspects of your dance.

Regardless of whether your fears are rational or irrational, you can use several practical techniques to help you overcome them (see the Managing Your Fears worksheet in the web resource). For one thing, you can gird yourself against your fears by using positive thinking focused on your strengths. You can also resist fear by focusing on things that help you deal with it—for example, proper technique and awareness of other dancers' positions on the stage. If you're focused on these or other process factors, you aren't focused on fear.

Because fear is expressed physically—for example, as muscle tension, increased heart rate, or shallow breathing—you can also reduce it by using the deep breathing and muscle relaxation techniques described in chapter 5. When you create a physical state that counters the sensations of fear, you feel less of it. Possibilities include picturing a relaxing scene, practicing muscle relaxation strategies, laughing and joking (which is sometimes the best strategy, because you can't be afraid and laugh at the same time), smiling, and simply focusing on your love of dance.

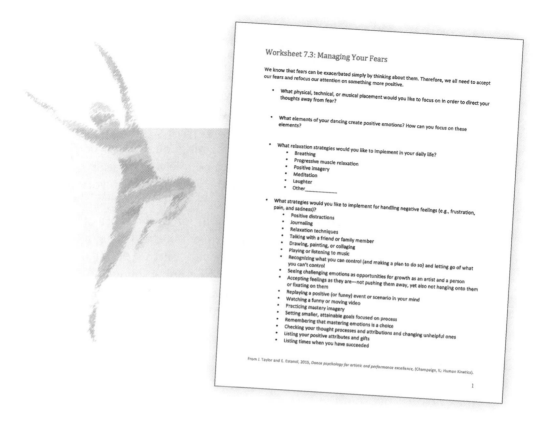

Worksheet 7.3: Managing Your Fears

We know that fears can be exacerbated simply by thinking about them. Therefore, we all need to accept our fears and refocus our attention on something more positive.

- What physical, technical, or musical placement would you like to focus on in order to direct your thoughts away from fear?

- What elements of your dancing create positive emotions? How can you focus on these elements?

- What relaxation strategies would you like to implement in your daily life?
  - Breathing
  - Progressive muscle relaxation
  - Positive imagery
  - Meditation
  - Laughter
  - Other_____

- What strategies would you like to implement for handling negative feelings (e.g., frustration, pain, and sadness)?
  - Positive distractions
  - Journaling
  - Relaxation techniques
  - Talking with a friend or family member
  - Drawing, painting, or collaging
  - Playing or listening to music
  - Recognizing what you can control (and making a plan to do so) and letting go of what you can't control
  - Seeing challenging emotions as opportunities for growth as an artist and a person
  - Accepting feelings as they are—not pushing them away, yet also not hanging onto them or fixating on them
  - Replaying a positive (or funny) event or scenario in your mind
  - Watching a funny or moving video
  - Practicing mastery imagery
  - Setting smaller, attainable goals focused on process
  - Remembering that mastering emotions is a choice
  - Checking your thought processes and attributions and changing unhelpful ones
  - Listing your positive attributes and gifts
  - Listing times when you have succeeded

From J. Taylor and E. Estanol, 2015, *Dance psychology for artistic and performance excellence*, (Champaign, IL: Human Kinetics).

1

These strategies distract you from fear, help you focus instead on something that reduces fear, and increase your sense of control over your fear. If the fear is irrational or can cause little real harm, one great way to get over it is simply to accept it and get on with what you're doing. In fact, we've found that the most fear-provoking response is just thinking about your fears, which rarely turn out as bad as you imagine. Finally, don't expect your fear to disappear overnight. Be patient and work on overcoming it. In fact, as you gain experience, confidence, and comfort, you often find that the fear fades on its own.

Frustration

Frustration may be your most significant emotional obstacle to achieving your dance goals. We've all experienced frustration when we're unable to do something as we pursue our goals. We feel stuck, get uptight, and have difficulty focusing. The best way to describe the feeling is this: AAARRGGHH!! It is a truly infuriating feeling.

But what exactly is frustration, and what causes it? Simply put, frustration arises when the path toward your goal is blocked. Most dancers and teachers think of frustration as a bad emotion, but it is more complex than that. Frustration is hardwired into us and provides tremendous adaptive value. Indeed, it starts out as a good emotion because it motivates us to remove the obstacle blocking our path. We try harder, and that extra effort frequently clears the path and enables us to continue pursuing our goals.

Unfortunately, if, despite our best efforts, we can't overcome a roadblock, then frustration can become a destructive emotion. In fact, if frustration isn't dealt with quickly, it can trigger what we refer to as a "negative emotional chain," in which frustration initiates a descent into a series of truly unhealthy emotions.

Unresolved frustration can morph into anger. Most dancers and teachers view anger as a bad emotion, but, like frustration, it has both positive and negative sides. Anger starts out being helpful because it is motivating. When you're angry, you want to go after whatever is causing your anger—for example, inability to master a new piece of choreography.

Unfortunately, for most dancers, anger swiftly becomes a harmful emotion. Feelings of anger resemble those of frustration with the volume turned up. Your body becomes tense, and if you're working on complex dance steps you lose your coordination and the quality of your performance declines. In addition, your focus narrows so much that you miss crucial cues that could help you dance your best. Anger also clouds your thinking, leaving you unable to think clearly or focus on finding a solution to the cause of your frustration.

Adversity is a normal and inevitable part of dance—for example, a costume malfunction or a mistake in choreography. Indeed, it is a rare performance in which nothing goes awry, and in the face of adversity dancers often feel frustrated. So, if everyone faces adversity in dance, what separates those who fall prey to frustration and perform poorly from those who rise above it and perform well? The answer lies in how one reacts to adversity. The most successful dancers are those who respond best to the challenges they face.

Responding positively to frustration can prevent stronger and more harmful negative emotions from arising. Therefore, your goal is to react positively to the first signs of frustration. This reaction starts with developing a positive attitude toward common causes of frustration in dance, such as missing a technical section, crashing into another dancer, finding the music to be either too fast or too slow, or experiencing a costume malfunction. Accept the fact that you will have such problems and that on some days things just won't go your way.

In addition, recognize that overcoming adversity on a challenging day can enable you to have a satisfying dance experience even as it teaches you valuable lessons, such as the benefits of staying positive, motivated, relaxed, and focused. Not only does it allow you to become a stronger dancer, but also it demonstrates to your teachers, choreographers, and directors that you are an adaptable dancer who can perform well even when things go wrong. This type of dancer is sought after by most directors and choreographers!

When you adopt this healthy attitude toward frustration, you position yourself to take practical steps to counter it when it occurs. First, learn to identify the situations in which frustration usually arises for you. Perhaps, for example, it occurs during classes when you're trying to master a new technique or during rehearsals when you're learning a new role. If you've felt frustrated in certain circumstances before, you're likely to do so again. However, if you can recognize the frustration as it approaches, then you can do something either to avoid it or to let it go when it arrives.

More specifically, if you recognize that frustration is just around the corner, you can find a solution to the problem that causes the frustration in the first place. For example, if you get frustrated in class when you make a mistake, then practice *not* stopping; instead, continue dancing, which trains you to recover more quickly during a performance. In fact, for this very reason, when Elena teaches dance, she always instruct her dancers to keep going when they make a mistake or forget a piece of choreography.

When faced with frustration, start by recognizing that you have been presented with an opportunity to be an emotional master rather than an emotional victim. As an emotional master, you can choose how you react to frustration in rehearsals, exams, auditions, and performances. In any given situation, the sooner you choose to take an emotional mastery approach in response to your frustration, the sooner you can feel better and dance your best. This may well require you to do some learning. Despite the fundamental role that frustration plays in your efforts to be your best, you probably haven't been shown how to deal with it in a constructive way. Your goal is to learn to stop the frustration immediately—before it takes hold of you and leads you toward anger and despair.

The first mistake that many dancers make when faced with frustration is to respond by simply increasing their effort. In other words, they do whatever they were already doing—but more and harder. Unfortunately, this response amounts to what some refer to as a kind of insanity: doing the same thing and expecting different results. Instead, when frustration arises, rather than just plowing ahead, do the opposite and step back from the situation that is causing your frustration. For example, if you just can't seem to get the hang of a new technical skill, set it aside and take a break. Stopping the activity creates emotional distance from the frustration, thus easing its grip on you.

During the break, do something fun and relaxing: Get a snack (hunger can lead to frustration), listen to music, or talk to friends. This step lessens the uncomfortable physical symptoms that come with frustration and generates positive emotions (e.g., happiness, excitement) that can counteract your feelings of frustration. Another powerful way to counter frustration is to do something at which you can succeed—for example, your favorite dance steps—thus feeding your confidence and generating positive emotions to replace the frustration.

Once you've broken the intense feelings of frustration, return to the challenging dance steps with a focus on understanding the problem. This is the final step: finding a solution. Though you may want to give yourself plenty of opportunity to identify the problem and find the solution for yourself, we encourage you to reach out to teachers, choreographers, and other dancers. Here's another helpful hint: Sometimes it's useful to break the problem down into smaller, more manageable problems.

Even when you use these strategies, there will be times when you can't immediately clear the obstacles blocking the path to your goals. When this is the case, it is futile to continue pursuing those goals, and doing so puts you at risk of an emotional descent. Sometimes the obstacles are simply too great to surmount on that day.

When you reach this point, you can either change your goals or choose to wait for another day. In the first option, you change your goals to ones that you can achieve in the short term. For example, suppose that you're frustrated because you're struggling with the end of a lengthy piece and, despite your best efforts, you just can't get the last few steps. In this case, if you continue to pursue the goal of mastering the entire piece, you will likely go quickly from frustration to anger to despair. However, if you shift your goals—say, to focus on practicing the piece up to the frustrating last steps—you can still experience some success and benefit from the rehearsal.

There are also going to be days, however, when you just can't make progress toward your goals. On these days, continuing to try without success only discourages you; therefore, it actually hurts your efforts in the long run. In this case, it may be wise to deliberately give up for now and choose to dance another day.

"It's going to be good, or it's not going to be good, and you just have to go out there and enjoy it regardless. Sure, things may not go perfectly, but change it up, in the moment. If you're off, do something different and sell it."

Robert Fairchild, principal, New York City Ballet

Despair

If you're not able to clear the obstacles of fear and frustration from your path, your emotions shift to the final stage of the negative emotional chain: despair. In our observation and experience, if you move from frustration to anger, any continued efforts that day will probably fail. In addition, in the bigger picture, if you experience the negative emotional chain on a regular basis—sinking repeatedly into despair—you will likely lose your motivation and become unwilling to make a sustained effort. With each descent down the negative emotional chain, you believe a little more deeply that your actions are ineffective, and over time you lose confidence in your ability to achieve your goals.

Despair is the most difficult emotion to deal with because it carries feelings of hopelessness and finality. When you feel despair, you've lost confidence in your ability to achieve your goals; as a result, your motivation to continue your efforts disappears. The physical attributes that enabled those efforts now decline, including your heart rate, respiration, and blood flow. When you experience despair, you also slow down and give up mentally. Despair is so emotionally painful because it leads you to cease your efforts and lose any chance of dancing your best and reaching your goals.

Despair results from the feeling that you have lost control of your performance. It can derive from physical causes—for example, if you sustain an injury, become dehydrated or undernourished, or experience considerable pain. It can also arise in response to performance conditions, such as a theater that is too cold or too hot, a soft stage floor, or poor lighting. And it can result from psychological changes, such as a loss of confidence following a poor performance, failure to earn a coveted role, or the stress of a serious injury that keeps you away from dance for a long time. In all cases of despair, you feel that you've lost the ability to pursue your goals and are unable to regain it.

Finding the resolve to overcome despair may be your greatest emotional challenge as a dancer. Mastering despair is difficult because you feel that you're at the very end of your rope and have little faith that you can recover. Even so, as with other emotions, mastering despair is a choice that you make. This choice is particularly hard because your despair itself arises from believing that you don't have a choice. We have found, however, that even in the worst situations, you can make changes to relieve the despair. You won't necessarily resolve the situation completely, but you can make changes that ease your despair and keep you going.

Overcoming despair starts with understanding its causes. We've found that despair always derives from a specific cause, and, generally speaking, any cause has a solution. Perhaps the most difficult part of taking this first step is that of stepping back from the situation far enough to consider it objectively. If you can briefly detach yourself from your despair, you can usually identify its cause.

Once you know what's causing your despair, make changes to resolve it. In some cases, you can address the cause directly; for instance, if you're overtrained and burned out, you can take a few days off to rest and rejuvenate. Some other causes of despair cannot be solved directly—for example, disappointment in failing to gain a long-sought role. In such cases, you may need to adjust your goals. Losing out on a role is disappointing, but it doesn't mean the end of your dance career. You can still benefit by continuing your effort, doing your best, and learning from the experience.

In fact, just getting back into the studio means that you have overcome adversity, gained mastery over your emotions, and decided to persist. Furthermore, it shows your classmates, colleagues, and directors that you are serious about your dance, that they can count on you, and that you will work your hardest regardless of which roles you play. This resilience is an important attribute, and directors look for it. Nobody wants to have a "drama queen" (or king) in their school or company.

When you despair, your mind sends a message to your body to do the same. You can counter this dynamic by creating physical changes that resist the unhelpful decline in intensity. To do so, use the psych-up techniques described in chapter 5, such as intense breathing, high-energy self-talk and body language, and intensity key words. These strategies produce a physical state that counters the feelings of letdown that accompany despair; they also spark positive emotions (e.g., pride, inspiration) that reinvigorate your motivation and confidence. It may also be helpful to watch videos of previous performances in which you succeeded; indeed, reminding yourself of your talents, skills, and abilities may even help you begin an upward spiral.

Postperformance Depression

Most every dancer who ever committed time and energy to training and performing knows this feeling. During training and the performance season, you're motivated, excited, and energized. As you approach opening night, emotions

Laughter and camaraderie are important parts of recovery.

run very high, and once you're performing you feel elated at accomplishing your goal. Immediately after the season, you may feel relief and excitement but also sadness. It may not hit you for a day or two, but when it does, you feel down, lethargic—sad.

The malaise may still be there after a week. You may even start to worry: "Why am I so down?" You can try to resist it by getting back to your training, but doing so may make it worse. You begin to wonder if it will ever go away. You have been struck by postperformance depression (PPD).

PPD is a common affliction that many dancers experience after a big performance or at the end of a performing season. These downturns are natural and, despite dancers' best efforts, usually unavoidable. Therefore, if you experience PPD, don't try to deny your feelings; in fact, PPD plays an essential role in your continued physical and mental health. Yet it can also be a source of uncertainty, concern, and just plain discomfort.

Any performance that means something to you requires a tremendous investment of your physical, psychological, and emotional resources. That investment causes you to put considerable time, energy, and effort into your training and to make substantial sacrifices in other parts of your life. In other words, your life becomes all about preparation for the big performance. This investment, and the conclusion of your efforts, can lead to PPD.

These down feelings are especially likely if you fail to achieve your performance goals. The lack of a payoff can create feelings of frustration, anger, and disappointment that exacerbate the normal and healthy PPD that you would otherwise experience. They can also make recovery from PPD slower and more difficult.

When the big performance or long season is over, PPD may occur for several reasons. First, your body has been performing at a high level for so long—initially in training and then in performance—that it needs a break. Because your body no longer needs to be up, it gears down. In fact, there is a physiological basis for most of this letdown type of depression (as distinguished from the kind that calls for anti-depressant medication). In a sense, the body takes a brief vacation in order to rest and rejuvenate. In turn, because our thoughts and emotions are fundamentally physiological, this physical downturn also expresses itself mentally in down thoughts and emotions.

In addition, this so-called depression includes a direct psychological and emotional component. For months, your life has had a certain purpose; you have directed your training, rehearsals, thoughts, and focus toward achieving a clearly defined objective. When that effort ends—whether in the form of a final class exam or a final curtain at the end of a performance season—the purpose that has guided you is gone. Along with that purpose, you also experience a short-term loss of a sizable part of your identity: the part that says, "I am a dancer." These losses may leave you feeling rudderless. It is common for dancers in this situation to ask certain basic questions: "Who am I?" "What now?" You may feel unmotivated, question your recent performance and ability, and feel uncertain about your future as a dancer.

Such an emotional letdown can be a powerful and uncomfortable part of PPD. After the emotional high—the excitement and joy—of your intense training and performance, the combination of the physiological decline and the psychological loss of purpose often leads to down emotions, such as sadness, listlessness, irritability, and general malaise. These emotions can range from mild to quite severe, depending on your personality, your experience with dancing, your coping skills, and your level of success in your just-completed performance or season. Dancers with PPD may also lose interest in other aspects of their lives, withdraw from activities they used to enjoy, feel sorry for themselves, and generally mope around, especially if they have performed below expectations or failed to win a sought-after role or promotion.

Given that some level of PPD is inevitable after big performances, the key question is not how to avoid it but how to get through it as fast as possible and use it to prepare for your next big performance or season. The first step is to accept that PPD is a normal and necessary part of dance. Therefore, allowing it to run its course while using it to your benefit helps you minimize both its severity and its duration. In fact, PPD plays a vital role in your recovery from big performances in much the same way that a rest day improves your fitness after an intense week of rehearsals or performances. Dancers with PPD often feel that it will never go away, and this perception may cause them to feel even more down. Part of the acceptance process involves acknowledging that these feelings are okay and will pass in time.

As an active, goal-directed person, you may be tempted to resist PPD by setting a new goal and returning to intense training before you're physically or psychologically ready. If you try this strategy, you may prolong the PPD. For one thing, you're more likely to get sick, because your immune system is not operating at its highest level. You may also get injured, because neither your body nor your mind is ready for renewed demands.

Instead, allow yourself to experience and naturally pass through the PPD. Be good to yourself. Ensure that you get extra rest and eat healthily. Get a regular massage, take yoga, and try not to overtax yourself. Enjoy being without a goal or direction. Revel in doing things you couldn't do when you were training and rehearsing intensely: having weekends free, going to sleep after 9 p.m., and eating foods that you may have resisted in order to be at your peak.

Use this time also as an opportunity to reconnect with loved ones and with things that you love doing (e.g., camping, hiking, biking, or swimming) but have sacrificed for the sake of your intense dance schedule. You might also explore other areas in which you can develop mastery, such as learning a new language, reading an intriguing book, or exploring new places and cultures. This is a time for emotional, physical, and mental refueling.

This period of indulgence gives your body the rest it craves and your spirit the lift it needs. It allows your mind and body to rejuvenate more quickly and enables you to return sooner to your usual high-energy self. It also gives you meaningful sources of validation that help you generate positive emotions to counteract your malaise and feel good about yourself despite the absence of reinforcement from dancing.

Finally, do things that you enjoy simply for the experience—no goals, no purpose. This state of simply being, rather than doing, helps you keep your dance in perspective, feel joy in your participation, and maintain some degree of balance in your life despite your investment in dance. In addition, it makes certain that when you do return to training, you participate for positive, healthy, and life-enriching reasons. It also ensures that you're physically, psychologically, and emotionally ready to meet the challenge of pursuing the new goals you set for yourself.

Mastering Your Emotions

Our response to emotional situations is at least partially hardwired into us at birth. For example, some of us are more sensitive, others more volatile, and still others more stoic. At the same time, genetics alone is not destiny; in other words, you don't have to be at the mercy of your emotions. Some people believe that they have little control over their emotions. If their emotions hurt them, they believe that they just have to accept it because they can't do anything about it. Such individuals are emotional victims. You are capable, however, of gaining control of your emotions and becoming an emotional master.

Gaining mastery over your emotions poses a considerable challenge because they are deeply ingrained by both your genetics and your experiences. To change your emotions, you have to start by believing that change is possible. Emotions involve making a choice that is simple but not easy. The choice is simple because if you have the options of feeling bad and dancing poorly or feeling good and dancing well, you certainly want to choose the second option. Even so, the choice is not easy if, like most people, you carry baggage and habits that pull you down an negative emotional path. The power of choice starts with developing awareness of times when your baggage and habits rear their head. You can then choose a positive response that leads to good feelings and successful performance.

Changing your emotions may require you to examine your baggage—for example, low self-esteem, perfectionism, or fear of failure. If the emotions are strong and interfere not only with your dance but also other aspects of your life, you might consider seeking help from a qualified counselor or psychologist. Such guidance can assist you in better understanding and letting go of your baggage and learning new emotional responses that better serve you in both dance and life.

Emotional mastery begins with recognizing the negative emotional reactions that hurt your efforts. When you start to feel negative emotions in training or performance, notice what you feel—for instance, frustration, anger, or despair.

Next, identify the situations that cause these feelings, such as seeing someone you viewed as a lesser dancer get a role that you wanted. Then consider what might be the underlying cause of your emotions, such as feeling weak or inadequate.

Emotions that interfere with dance performance often derive from poor emotional habits that can be retrained in much the same way as you retrain poor dance techniques. To continue the process of emotional mastery, specify alternative reactions to situations that commonly trigger your negative emotions. For example, instead of saying, "My pirouettes are so sloppy," and feeling frustrated when you can't get them right, try saying, "Focus and be strong," in order to generate pride in your efforts and inspiration in working toward your goals. This positive emotional response not only helps you let go of the initial negative emotion. It also motivates you to maintain your effort and intensity, generates positive emotions that give you more confidence, and allows you to focus on factors that help you raise the level of your dance performance.

Because your baggage and habits are ingrained, it takes time to gain emotional mastery and instill positive emotional reactions. However, with practice and the realization that you feel and perform better with positive emotional responses, you can retrain your emotions and develop positive emotional skills that help you achieve your goals.

Fostering Positive Emotions

Although this chapter focuses on negative emotions and how to overcome them, it is equally important for you to learn to experience and express positive emotions. Whereas negative emotions warn you when a problem may be arising, positive emotions show you what to seek and look forward to. Indeed, positive emotions—enthusiasm, inspiration, pride, satisfaction, and joy—are both the emotional goals that you should strive for and the emotional rewards for your efforts.

Experiencing and learning from positive emotions can also help you gain emotional mastery. You have daily opportunities to create, express, and share the positive emotions that you feel, particularly in training and performance. There are no rules or techniques for benefiting from positive emotions. You learn about them by allowing yourself to experience and express them. When you're excited about a great rehearsal, focus on your excitement and let it engulf you. When you're inspired by someone else's performance, tell that person and allow yourself to feel the inspiration deeply. When you're filled with joy from a great class, share it with your teacher and bask in its warmth.

The more you acknowledge and experience your positive emotions, the more readily accessible they are for you when you feel down. If you suspect that sharing your positive feelings with dance friends or colleagues may engender feelings of jealousy or envy, then share them with your nondance friends, with family members, or in a journal. Taking time to validate your positive feelings and experiences enables you to access them when you need them the most.

Center Stage: Gloria
Denying Fear the Power to Rule Your Dance

Gloria, 19 years old, was a demi-soloist in a collegiate performing company. She had been working very hard, and her director gave her an opportunity to dance a principal role in the second cast. Initially, Gloria felt very excited about the role, but her excitement quickly turned to panic on the first day of rehearsal. Not only was the ballet incredibly challenging; it also included many overhead thrown lifts for the principal role. Gloria was fearful of thrown lifts and immediately felt the fear grip her body: Her muscles stiffened, her throat closed, her heart pounded, and her breathing shortened.

In spite of this visceral reaction, Gloria was determined not to be defeated by her fear. That evening, she used the web to research ways of overcoming fear and put together a plan for conquering her fear and dancing her the best. In particular, she read that when faced with an irrational fear, a person can choose how to react, and she made a conscious and committed decision to face her fear rather than allowing it to intimidate her.

To carry out her decision, Gloria took several steps. First, she obtained a copy of the rehearsal video so that she could watch it over and over again. As she watched the dancer in the video, she visualized herself doing the lifts. She also confided in her partner that she was scared to be thrown in the air. Her partner was very supportive and reassured her that he wouldn't drop her.

In addition, Gloria learned that the physical symptoms of her fear were the most difficult part to overcome because they were so powerful and immediate. To address this challenge, she began to practice breathing and relaxation exercises before her rehearsals in order to train her body to be more relaxed. She also used mental tools—positive self-talk and focusing techniques—to help her overcome the twinges of fear that she still felt.

After several weeks of preparation, Gloria performed the full lift and, despite feeling a little nervous, did it well. She improved with each subsequent attempt until she and her partner could execute the lift flawlessly. She was amazed at how easy it felt, and she gained immense confidence from mastering not only the lift but also her fear. Over time, the lift became a favorite move that she looked forward to and performed beautifully.

ENCORE

- The emotional aspects of dance are the most demanding.

- A strong relationship exists between your emotions and your body.

- Negative emotions in dance may be caused by the baggage that dancers carry from their childhood, by unexpected occurrences, and by the natural ups and downs of dance.

- Negative emotions can hurt you both physically and mentally.

- Emotional reactions to the demands of dance can be categorized as either threatening (to be avoided) or challenging (to be pursued).

- The four most common emotional obstacles in dance include fear (of pain, injury, and failure), frustration, despair, and postperformance depression.

- Postperformance depression consists of physical and emotional letdown and is common after a big performance or a performance season.

- You can actively foster positive emotions to help you minimize your emotional lows and maximize the emotional highs that dance is all about.

References

Bacon, S.J. (1974). Arousal and the range of cue utilization. *Journal of Experimental Psychology, 102,* 81–87.

Bandura, A. (1977). Self-efficacy: Toward a unifying theory of behavioral change. *Psychological Review, 84,* 191–215.

Bandura, A. (1986). *Social foundations of thought and action.* Englewood Cliffs, NJ: Prentice Hall.

Bandura, A., & Simon, K.M. (1977). The role of proximal intentions in self-regulation of refractory behavior. *Cognitive Therapy and Research, 1,* 177–193.

Banes, S. (1980). *Terpsichore in sneakers: Post-modern dance.* Boston: Houghton Mifflin.

Beck, A. (1976). *Cognitive therapy and emotional disorders.* New York: International University Press.

Boud, D., Keogh, R., & Walker, D. (1985). *Reflection: Turning experience into learning.* New York: Routledge.

Brawley, L.R. (1984). Attributions as social cognitions: Contemporary perspectives in sport. In W.F. Straub & J.M. Williams (Eds.), *Cognitive sport psychology* (pp. 212–230). Lansing, NY: Sport Science Associates.

Buckroyd, J. (1995). The provision of psychological care for dancers. *Performing Arts Medicine News, 3,* 1.

Buckroyd, J. (2000). *The student dancer: Emotional aspects of the teaching and learning of dance.* London: Dance Books.

Carver, C.S., & Scheier, M.F. (1982). *Attention and self-regulation: A control theory approach to human behavior.* New York: Springer-Verlag.

Caudill, D., Weinberg, R., & Jackson, A. (1983). Psyching-up and track athletes. A preliminary investigation. *Journal of Sport Psychology, 5*, 231–235.

Easterbrook, J.A. (1959). The effect of emotion on cue utilization and the organization of behavior. *Psychological Review, 66*, 183–201.

Ellis, A. (1962). *Reason and emotion in psychotherapy*. New York: Lyle Stuart.

Estanol, E., Shepherd, C., & MacDonald, T. (2013). Mental skills as protective attributes against eating disorder risk in dancers. *Journal of Applied Sport Psychology, 25*(2), 209–222.

Gould, D., Horn, T., & Spreemann, J. (1983). Sources of stress in junior elite wrestlers. *Journal of Sport Psychology, 5*, 159–171.

Graham, M. (1974). A modern dancer's primer for action. In S.J. Cohen (Ed.), *Dance as a theatre art: Source readings in dance history from 1581 to the present* (pp. 135–142). New York: Dodd, Mead.

Hamilton, L.H. (1998). *Advice for dancers: Emotional counsel and practical strategies*. San Francisco: Jossey-Bass.

Hanin, Y.L. (1980). A study of anxiety in sports. In W.F. Straub (Ed.), *Sport psychology: An analysis of athlete behavior* (pp. 236–249). Ithaca, NY: Mouvement.

Hanin, Y.L. (1989). Interpersonal and intergroup anxiety: Conceptual and methodological issues. In C.D. Speilberger & D. Hackfort (Eds.), *Anxiety in sports: An international perspective* (pp. 19–28). Washington, DC: Hemisphere.

Helin, P. (1987). Mental and psychophysiological tension at professional ballet dancers' performances and rehearsals. *Dance Teacher Now, 21*, 7–14.

Kanfer, F.H., & Karoly, P. (1972). Self-control: A behavioristic excursion into the lion's den. *Behavior Therapy, 3*, 398–416.

Kroll, W. (1979). The stress of high-performance athletes. In P. Klavora & J.V. Daniel (Eds.), *Coach, athlete, and the sport psychologist* (pp. 211–219). Toronto: University of Toronto.

Lang, P. (1977). Imagery in therapy: An information processing analysis of fear. *Behavior Therapy, 8*, 862–886.

Larsen, G. (2009, September). Why I Dance. *Dance Magazine*. www.dancemagazine.com/issues/september-2009/Why-I-Dance.

Manley, M., & Wilson, V.E. (1980). Anxiety, creativity, and dance performance. *Dance Research Journal, 12*, 11–22. Lansing, NY: Sport Science Associates.

McGuire, K. (2012, July). Listening to your body. *Dance Magazine*. www.dancemagazine.com/issues/July-2012/Listening-to-Your-Body.

Montee, K. (1992, October). Miami City Ballet: Moving fast. *Dance, 10*, 43–45.

Parker, S.J. (Executive Producer). (2013). Principals [Online video series episode]. In *City Ballet*. New York: AOL On Originals. http://on.aol.com/show/cityballet-517887470/episode/517996964.

Quested, E., & Duda, J.L. (2010). Exploring the social-environmental determinants of well- and ill-being in dancers: A test of basic needs theory. *Journal of Sport & Exercise Psychology, 32*(1), 39–60.

Scanlan, T.K., Stein, G.L., & Ravizza, K. (1989). An in-depth study of former elite figure skaters: Sources of enjoyment. *Journal of Sport and Exercise Psychology, 11*, 65–83.

Schacter, S., & Singer, J.E. (1962). Cognitive, social, and physiological determinants of emotional state. *Psychological Review, 69*, 379–399.

Sonstroem, R.J. (1984). An overview of anxiety in sport. In J.M. Silva III & R.S. Weinberg (Eds.), *Psychological foundations of sport* (pp. 104–117). Champaign, IL: Human Kinetics.

Stodelle, E. (1984). *Deep song: The dance story of Martha Graham*. New York: Schirmer.

Taylor, J., & Schneider, T. (2005). *The triathlete's guide to mental training*. Boulder, CO: Velopress.

Walker, I., & Nordin-Bates, S.M. (2010). Performance anxiety experiences of professional ballet dancers: The importance of control. *Journal of Dance Medicine & Science*, *14*(4), 134–145.

Wallach, M.A., & Kogan, N. (1965). A new look at the creativity–intelligence distinction. In P. Vernon (Ed.), *Creativity* (pp. 235–256). Baltimore: Penguin Education.

White-McGuire, B. (2009, October). Why I dance. *Dance Magazine*. www.dancemagazine.com/issues/October-2009/Why-I-Dance.

Zajonc, R.B. (1985). Emotion and facial efference: A theory reclaimed. *Science, 228*, 15–21.

PART III

PRIME DANCE TOOLS

This part of the book goes beyond the foundational information provided in part I and the practical strategies provided in part II. This third part introduces you to four powerful tools to enhance your mental preparation as you pursue the experience of prime dance.

Chapter 8 explains the value of setting a variety of tangible goals for dancing your best. It describes the most effective way to set goals and highlights key goals that you should establish in all aspects of your dance training. This chapter also guides you through the process of developing an organized goal-setting program that helps you achieve your dance dreams.

Chapter 9 introduces you to the most powerful mental tool for enhancing your technical and artistic dance experience: imagery. This chapter shows you how seeing and feeling yourself dance in your mind's eye can help you make remarkable gains in all aspects of your dance. It also gives you an assessment tool for evaluating your imagery skill and identifying how you can train to improve it. In addition, it helps you develop an organized and structured imagery program that enables you to use imagery to its greatest benefit.

Chapter 10 describes an essential tool—the use of routines—that helps you develop prime dance by preparing thoroughly for classes, rehearsals, and performances. This chapter makes crystal clear why every professional dancer we know uses a well-organized routine before dancing. The chapter details where routines can best be deployed—namely, in classes, before performances, and during transitions. It also covers the nuts and bolts of routines and lists the key elements of an effective routine. Finally, it guides you in preparing routines that best meet your own needs.

Chapter 11 pulls together the strategies and tools presented in parts II and III and shows you how to incorporate them into a mental training program that is organized, comprehensive, and individualized. Specifically, it guides you through the four phases of building an individualized mental training program: design, implementation, maintenance, and evaluation. A sample program is also provided.

CHAPTER

Goal Setting

"Everything I've done has allowed me to be here. I set realistic goals and stayed focused on them."

David Zurak, professional dancer and actor

*M*otivation is not enough to make you the best dancer you can be. Motivation without goals is like wanting to get somewhere without knowing where to go. Goals act as the road map to your desired destination. They also increase your commitment and motivation, identify deliberate steps toward your dance aspirations, and allow you to track your progress. The key role that goal setting plays in realizing your vision is captured in the prime dance goal formula:

motivation + goals = progress

Types of Goal

In order to maximize the value of goal setting to you as a dancer, you should set seven types of goal. The first three types—long-term, yearly, and performance—can be categorized as outcome oriented because they describe specific results that you want to achieve.

- Long-term goals represent what you ultimately want to achieve in dance, such as earn a college scholarship or dance professionally.

- Yearly goals indicate what you want to achieve in the next 12 months— for example, earning a desired role or progressing from corps member to soloist.

- Performance goals specify *how* you want to dance in particular productions during the coming season.

These outcome-oriented goals are important because they provide the destinations for your goal-setting program. Once you set your outcome goals, place them in the distance to mark what you ultimately want to achieve. Remembering these goals motivates you when your training gets difficult and you start to wonder whether your efforts are worth it. On the other hand, some dancers become so focused on their outcome goals that those goals interfere with the dancer's effort to achieve them. Obsession with achieving certain results can keep them from focusing on what they need to do in order to reach their goals. It also takes the fun out of training and performance.

Thus there is a danger in focusing exclusively on your outcome goals. Indeed, most outcome goals are not entirely within your control, and putting too much emphasis on them not only increases the pressure you feel to achieve them, but also the disappointment you experience if they go unmet. For example, imagine that you are seeking a promotion or a coveted role. Even though you understand that you need to do certain things in order to be considered, the decision ultimately rests in the hands of the choreographer or director.

We address this reality not to discourage you but to help you take a healthy perspective on the investment that you make on your outcome goals. We also raise the issue in order to emphasize the fact that the way to achieve your outcome goals is to focus primarily on another set of goals—your *process* goals—which are entirely up to you. Process goals include both training and lifestyle goals.

- Training goals identify what you need to do in your physical, technical, and mental training in order to achieve your outcome goals.
- Lifestyle goals indicate what you need to do in your general lifestyle in order to reach your outcome goals—for example, healthy sleep and diet, effective participation in work or school, and satisfying relationships.

As you well know, dancing isn't just about the act of dancing (e.g., taking classes, rehearsing, and performing) or even the tangible results of your hard work (e.g., winning a desired role or acceptance into a dance school or company). There is more to dancing than just, well, dancing. You need a reason to dance and to get something out it. That's where two experiential, or process, types of goals—fulfillment goals and feeling goals—come into play. These goals emphasize the personal benefits that you gain from dance.

- Fulfillment goals specify what you want to get out of your dance experiences, such as improved health and fitness, enjoyment, challenge, friendships, or progress toward a college degree or a career in dance.
- Feeling goals represent how you want to feel during or about dance performance—for example, "I want to dance with ease," "I want to feel strong and graceful," or "I want to have a great time during the performance."

When you focus on your experiential (process) goals, you give yourself a reason to dance and to experience the deeply personal rewards of dancing. These goals encourage you to pursue your process goals, which in turn ensure that you do what needs to be done to reach your outcome goals. Your emphasis on the experiential and process aspects of your dance makes pursuing your outcome goals more manageable, enables you to focus on the enjoyment of dance, and ensures that you get the best possible results from your efforts.

Another reason that experiential and process goals are the most important goals is that, unlike outcome goals, they lie entirely within your control. Therefore, focusing on experiential and process goals allows you to reduce the pressure that you may feel from your outcome goals, thus allowing you to better enjoy your dancing and to perform your best. They also help you build your confidence, because the achievement of these goals depends solely on your own daily commitment and effort.

As you begin to develop a goal-setting program, we suggest that you refer back to the discussion of self-knowledge in chapter 2. You can use the performance profiles that you completed there to help you set your goals, especially your training and lifestyle goals. When you review the strengths and areas for improvement identified in your profiles, you can more precisely set goals that build on your strengths and alleviate any limitations.

Goal-Setting Guidelines

The effectiveness of your goal setting depends on whether you understand what kinds of goal to set and how to use goals to enhance your motivation and direction. Here are seven guidelines for getting the most out of your goal setting.

1. **Make your goals self-determined.** All of your goal-setting efforts will be fruitless if you fail to do one key thing: make your goals your own. In other words, your goals must come from deep inside you. If they do, then you will feel a strong need to fulfill them. One potential challenge lies in the fact that a number of people in your dance life may have their own ideas about what goals you should set. These people may include teachers, choreographers, and parents. If you take your goals from them, you won't own the goals and probably won't feel motivated to pursue them. Of course, you can seek out guidance from others who know your dancing, but ultimately the goals that you set for yourself should be truly yours.

   Here are two key questions to help you set self-determined goals. First, are your goals internally or externally focused? Examples of internally focused goals include enjoying personal fulfillment, experiencing excitement

Setting specific goals helps build strength and improve technique.

and joy, gaining mastery, and overcoming challenges. In contrast, externally focused goals address results such as financial rewards, celebrity, and status. Research has found that people who set externally focused goals experience less success and fewer personal benefits than those who set internally focused goals.

Second, do your goals frame your life as being controlled by yourself or by others? Goals that you control can be based on fun, pleasure, or personal values. On the other hand, goals controlled by others include living up to someone else's expectations and appearing in a good light to others. Research has shown that pursuing goals within your own control leads to more success and happiness.

2. **Set goals that are challenging but realistic and attainable.** Set goals that you can attain—but only with time and effort. If you set goals that are too easy, you'll reach them with little effort, and they'll do little for your motivation, confidence, and progress as a dancer. If you set goals that are too difficult, you won't believe that you can achieve them; worse yet, they may set you up for failure, which discourages your motivation and efforts.

3. **Make your goals specific and concrete.** It's not enough to set a goal such as "improving my adagio this year." Goals should be clearly stated *and measurable*. Here's an example: "I want to improve my strength, flexibility, and stability in order to do better extensions and perform with better control during my adagio. I would like to increase my extension by 3 inches [about 7.5 centimeters] and hold it steady for at least 16 counts. In addition, I need to increase my hip, gluteal, and abdominal strength, as well as the intrinsic muscles of my feet, in order to become more stable. I would like to see this improvement within six months."

This goal identifies the tasks required to achieve the goal, specifies the amount of improvement desired, and indicates the time frame in which to achieve the goal. As you can see, the more specific you make a goal, the more useful it is. You can also break it down even further, into categories, to guide you in what to focus on during class and in your cross-training outside of the studio.

4. **Focus on degree of—rather than absolute—goal attainment.** You won't achieve every goal completely, or exactly when you want to, because it's impossible to judge accurately what is realistic for all goals. However, you will almost always make improvements as you pursue a goal. Therefore, in evaluating your progress, focus not on whether you fully reach a goal (absolute attainment) but on *how much* of the goal you achieve (degree of attainment). With this perspective, if you don't reach a goal but do improve 50 percent over your previous level, you view yourself as succeeding, which in turn motivates you to continue pursuing the goal until you achieve it fully.

5. **Make your goal setting dynamic and fluid.** Goal setting is a process that never ends. When you achieve one goal, set another one that is higher or addresses a different area. In this way, you continually encourage yourself to improve. Review your goals regularly, use them to evaluate your progress, and adjust them as needed. In addition, because you can't set goals with absolute accuracy, be open to making changes when necessary. For example, goals that you reach more easily than expected should be immediately reset to a higher level. On the other hand, if a goal turns out to be simply too difficult to achieve, modify it to a more realistic level. Recognizing goals as dynamic and anticipating adjustments allows you to leave behind the detrimental effects of perfectionism and negative self-talk.

6. **Set process goals that lead to outcome goals.** Your process goals should lead progressively to your outcome goals. For example, your lifestyle goals should help you accomplish your training goals, which should lead to your performance goals, which in turn should enable you to reach your yearly goals, which, finally, should allow you to achieve your long-term goals. Following this progression ensures that your process goals always support and encourage your achievement of your outcome goals.

7. **Put your goals on paper.** There is something very powerful about making your goals tangible. Evidence suggests that the combination of putting your goals on paper and keeping a record of your progress increases your motivation and makes you more likely to achieve your goals. Moreover, research suggests that goal setting is most effective when it's prepared as a written contract—including explicit statements of your goals and how you'll achieve them—and shared with others. This approach clearly identifies your goals and holds you accountable for fulfilling the contract. You can complete a goal-setting contract, sign it, and give copies to your instructor, dance partners, family members, or friends. To ensure that you follow the contract, periodically review it and evaluate whether you're pursuing the goals specified in it.

Key Performance Goals

When we ask dancers about their outcome goals for a particular performance, they usually give general statements, such as "I want to have a great performance" or "I want to dance with artistry and heart." Achieving such performance goals, however, requires setting several smaller performance goals that lead you to the great performance you seek.

- **Performance goal 1.** Your first performance goal is to get through your training program and rehearsals in a healthy state so that you arrive at the performance fit, rested, free of injury and illness, and having enjoyed your preparations. This goal may seem obvious, but we have met many dancers who missed a performance or arrived unprepared because they were overtrained, injured, sick, or so tired from training that they were unable to enjoy their performance.

- **Performance goal 2.** Your next performance goal is to come to the venue ready to perform your best. We have both been fortunate enough to work with a number of dancers as they prepared for a major production. At the start of our work with these dancers, we told them that when they arrived at the theater, they should be able to say to themselves, "I am as prepared as I can be to dance my best." You can't control everything that happens during a performance; for example, the condition of the stage depends on other people. But being as well prepared personally as you can be puts you in a position to dance your best. Making this statement means that you have put the necessary time and effort into your physical, technical, artistic, and mental training to achieve your performance goals.

- **Performance goal 3.** This goal addresses what you do *during* the performance—specifically, it calls on you to maintain consistent focus (on the task at hand, moment to moment) and intensity throughout your performance. At this point, don't change anything in your preparations, in your time offstage, or in your choreography. Whatever you did in rehearsals, do onstage.

- **Performance goal 4.** This goal addresses the end of the performance. Your goal here should be to maintain your energy, artistry, and physicality until the curtain drops. Few things are more inspiring and exciting than to turn, jump, and lift with the same energy at the end of a performance as you did at the beginning.

- **Performance goal 5.** Here is a goal that most dancers don't even think about but that we recommend strongly: Revel in the dance! During your performance, the most important goal that you should strive for is to thoroughly enjoy the experience, feel personally satisfied with your efforts, and to express it so strongly that the audience feels it too.

- **Performance goal 6.** Only after accomplishing your other performance goals should you focus on your outcome goal for the performance. Remember that your result occurs at the end of the performance; therefore, focusing on it during the performance can only distract you from achieving your other goals. When the curtain falls and you have taken a moment to revel in your performance, only then can you look at your performance and see whether you achieved your outcome goal.

Charting Your Progress

One of the most motivating aspects of goal setting is the fact that it enables you to work toward and achieve goals. When your efforts are rewarded with improvement, you experience immense satisfaction and validation. To foster these positive feelings, chart your progress in various parts of your training. For example, if your goal is to improve your turns, track how long you can balance on one leg without wobbling, as well as how many turns you accomplish each day. You can also track the instances when your foot placement was wrong, thus throwing off your turn, and what you need to focus on to move forward. You might identify, for instance, a strength imbalance in your hips or abdominal muscles, then track the exercises and repetitions that you do to strengthen the relevant muscle.

You can also get regular feedback about the pursuit of your goals from a number of sources: teachers, choreographers, artistic directors, video analysis, physical testing, and prime dance profiling (see chapter 2). When this feedback consistently shows improvement in various aspects of your training, that information bolsters your motivation by confirming that you are progressing toward your goals.

Use the prime dance Goal Setting worksheet in the web resource to write down your goals according to the guidelines described in this chapter. If you're uncertain of what your goals should be, ask someone who knows what you're working toward, such as your teacher or choreographer.

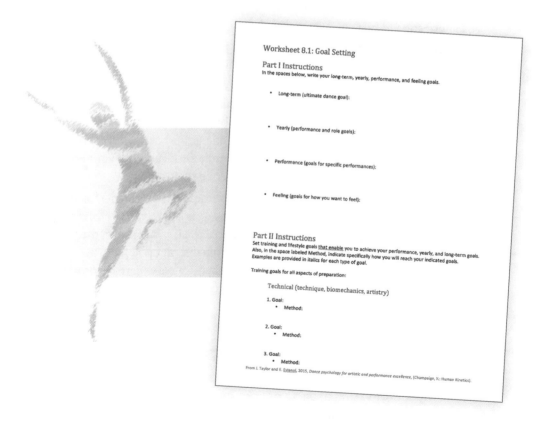

Worksheet 8.1: Goal Setting

Part I Instructions
In the spaces below, write your long-term, yearly, performance, and feeling goals.

- Long-term (ultimate dance goal):

- Yearly (performance and role goals):

- Performance (goals for specific performances):

- Feeling (goals for how you want to feel):

Part II Instructions
Set training and lifestyle goals that enable you to achieve your performance, yearly, and long-term goals. Also, in the space labeled Method, indicate specifically how you will reach your indicated goals. Examples are provided in italics for each type of goal.

Training goals for all aspects of preparation:

Technical (technique, biomechanics, artistry)

1. Goal:
   - Method:

2. Goal:
   - Method:

3. Goal:
   - Method:

From J. Taylor and E. Estanol, 2015, *Dance psychology for artistic and performance excellence*, (Champaign, IL: Human Kinetics).

Center Stage: Ray

Creating a Plan to Achieve Prime Dance

Ray, an 18-year-old contemporary dancer, was doing an apprenticeship in a regional company. Since setting his sights on dance after seeing a local production of *Swan Lake*, he had progressed quickly and enjoyed many opportunities to perform, both in his local dance studio and in competition. Now, his apprenticeship helped him see that he might have a professional dance career, but he also recognized that he would need to become more focused in order to reach his goals. To that end, he read everything he could get his hands on about effective goal setting and arranged to work with Jim.

Ray identified his long-term goal as becoming a leading contemporary dancer in a major company. He knew that in order to realize this dream, he would need to set an intermediate goal of either getting a contract with his current company within the next year or auditioning for other companies. He also knew that he faced strong competition from two other apprentices and that he would have to become more consistent in his performances, more committed in his classwork, and more skilled in his technique and artistry.

With Jim's help, Ray identified his strengths (jumps, overall technique, and handling pressure during performances) and the areas that held him back (poor eating and sleeping habits and limited flexibility and stamina). Based on this information, Ray set performance goals of getting cast in leading roles in two major company productions. He set training goals of increasing his flexibility by 10 percent by the end of the season and his stamina by 30 percent. He also committed to a new eating regimen designed by the company nutritionist and to getting at least eight hours of sleep per night.

Ray wrote down his goals, gave copies to his teacher and parents, and posted them in his bedroom and locker so that he would often be reminded of them. As the performance season unfolded, he tracked his progress and rewarded himself for staying committed to his goals. He continued working hard, and his technique and fitness continued to improve. By the end of the season, he had earned the opportunity to dance two leading roles as an understudy.

ENCORE

- Goal setting is essential for achieving prime dance because motivation without goals is like wanting to get somewhere without knowing where to go.

- Important types of goals to set for your dance include long-term, yearly, performance, training, lifestyle, fulfillment, and feeling.

- Guidelines for goal setting include making your goals self-determined, making your goals challenging but attainable through hard work, making your goals specific and concrete, focusing on degree of (rather than absolute) goal attainment, making your goals dynamic and fluid, setting process goals that lead to outcome goals, and putting your goals on paper so you can chart your progress.

- Your goals for each performance should include arriving healthy and prepared to dance your best; maintaining your ideal focus and intensity throughout the performance; having enough energy to sustain your physicality, technique, and artistry until the curtain falls; and reveling in the performance when you finish.

References

Bandura, A., & Cervone, D. (1983). Self-evaluative and self-efficacy mechanisms governing the motivational effects of goal systems. *Journal of Personality and Social Psychology, 45*, 1017–1028.

Bandura, A., & Simon, K.M. (1977). The role of proximal intentions in self-regulation of refractory behavior. *Cognitive Therapy and Research, 1*, 177–193.

Bennett, J.G., & Pravitz, J.E. (1982). *The miracle of sports psychology*. Englewood Cliffs, NJ: Prentice Hall.

Berardi, G. (2005, February). Better late than never: Six pros on starting later in life. *Dance Magazine*. http://www.dancemagazine.com/issues/February-2005/Better-Late-Than-Never-Six-Pros-On-Starting-Later-In-Life

Carron, A.V. (1984). *Motivation: Implications for coaching and teaching*. London, Ontario:

Sports Dynamics.

Doyle, L., & Landers, D. (1980). *Psychological skills in elite and subelite shooters*. Unpublished manuscript.

Duda, J.L., & Hall, H. (2001). Achievement goal theory in sport: Recent extensions and future directions. In R.N. Singer, H.A. Hausenblas, & C.M. Janelle (Eds.), *Handbook of sport psychology* (pp. 417–443). New York: Wiley.

Erez, M., & Zidon, I. (1984). Effects of goal acceptance on the relationship of goal difficulty to performance. *Journal of Applied Psychology, 69*, 69–78.

Gould, D. (2010). Goal setting for peak performance. In J.M. Williams (Ed.), *Applied sport psychology: Personal growth to peak performance* (pp. 133–148). Palo Alto, CA: Mayfield.

Gould, D., Dieffenbach, K., & Moffet, A. (2002). Psychological characteristics and their development in Olympic champions. *Journal of Applied Sport Psychology, 14*(3), 172-204.

Halliwell, W. (1978). Intrinsic motivation in sport. In W.F. Straub (Ed.), *Sport psychology: An analysis of athlete behavior* (pp 171-192). Ithaca, NY: Mouvement.

Laporte, R.E., & Nath, R. (1976). Role of performance goals in prose learning. *Journal of Educational Psychology, 68*, 260-264.

Latham, G.P., & Baldes, J.J. (1975). The "practical significance" of Locke's theory of goal setting. *Journal of Applied Psychology, 60*, 122-124.

Locke, E.A. (1966). The relationship of intentions to level of performance. *Journal of Applied Psychology, 50*(1), 60-66.

Locke, E.A. (1968). Toward a theory of task motivation and incentives. *Organizational Behavior and Human Performance, 3*, 157-189.

Locke, E.A., & Bryan, J.F. (1969). The directing function of goals in task performance. *Organizational Behavior and Human Performance, 4*, 35-42.

Locke, E.A., Cartledge, N., & Knerr, C.S. (1970). Studies of the relationship between satisfaction, goal setting, and performance. *Organizational Behavior and Human Performance, 5*, 135-158.

Locke, E.A., & Latham, G.P. (1985). The applications of goal setting to sports. *Journal of Sport Psychology, 7*, 205-222.

Locke, E.A., Mento, A.J., & Katcher, B.L. (1978). The interaction of ability and motivation in performance: An exploration of the meaning of moderators. *Personnel Psychology, 31*, 269-280.

Locke, E.A., Shaw, K.N., Saari, L.M., & Latham, G.P. (1981). Goal setting and task performance: 1969-1980. *Psychological Bulletin, 90*, 125-152.

Schunk, B. (1984). Enhancing self-efficacy and achievement through rewards and goals: Motivational and informational effects. *Journal of Educational Research, 78*, 29-34.

Sheldon, K.M., Ryan, R.M., Deci, E.L., & Kasser, T. (2004). The independent effects of goal contents and motives on well-being: It's both what you pursue and why you pursue it. *Personality and Social Psychology Bulletin, 30*(4), 475-486.

Taylor, J., & Schneider, T. (2005). *The triathlete's guide to mental training*. Boulder, CO: Velopress.

Taylor, J., & Taylor, C. (1987, September). Mental attitude: Goal setting. *Dance Teacher Now*, 8-10.

Weinberg, R.S. (1984). Mental preparation strategies. In J.M. Silva III & R.S. Weinberg (Eds.), *Psychological foundations of sport* (pp. 145-156). Champaign, IL: Human Kinetics.

Imagery

"In using imagery, I try to compress the material in such a way that I can get as many levels into one image as can be packed into it. I try to make each image as evocative as I can, on as many levels as possible, so that a person can hook into one level or another, or more than one. It is like a mosaic with bits of information, which can be put together in different ways so that each person comes away with something individually meaningful."

Meredith Monk, choreographer

Mental imagery is a powerful, and often neglected, tool for improving your dance training and performance. It is used by virtually all great dancers in every style of dance, and its value is supported by considerable scientific research. Imagery is beneficial because it influences every contributor to prime dance: It increases motivation by allowing you to see and feel yourself giving your best effort and reaching your goals. It builds confidence by enabling you to imagine yourself dancing with good technique, gracefulness, virtuosity, aplomb, and artistry. It improves intensity by allowing you to see and experience stress and use psych-up or psych-down techniques to control it. It enhances focus by identifying important cues and letting you rehearse prime focus. And it enables you to generate positive emotions in response to seeing and feeling yourself dancing your best.

Imagery also improves your technical, performance, and artistic skills. It ingrains the image and feeling of correct technique and provides imagined repetition of properly executed choreography. Imagery enables you to practice your choreography with the appropriate intensity, artistry, and expressiveness. It also allows you to perform your roles in your mind so that when opening night arrives, you feel as if you have already danced the role many times before. This practice increases your confidence and lowers your performance anxiety.

Many people in the dance world refer to this tool as visualization. In our view, however, this term places too much emphasis on the visual component, whereas the power of mental imagery goes well beyond its visual aspects. The most effective imagery involves feeling the movement from within and experiencing a complete, multisensory reproduction of the performance.

You can use imagery in several settings to help you achieve prime dance. In classes where you focus on improving your technique, you can use imagery to enhance your technical skills and enhance the quality of your training. As part of your rehearsals, you can use it to ingrain the choreography and practice the relevant artistic expression. In addition, you can use mental imagery as part of your pre-performance routine.

Developing Imagery Skills

Using imagery is a skill that, like a dance technique, develops with practice. Few dancers use imagery optimally at first; indeed, it is common to struggle with it initially. This experience may discourage you and lead you to believe that imagery can't be beneficial to you. However, if you're patient and put in the needed time and effort, your imagery will improve and become a valuable tool. For a good analogy, recall the first time you tried to pirouette; at first, it probably didn't work wonderfully, but you continued to practice until it became more like second nature. Imagery works the same way, and commitment and consistent practice allow you to see the benefits of using it in your dancing.

The first step in developing your imagery skills is to assess yourself by using the Imagery Skills Profile worksheet (in the web resource). This profile provides a graphic representation of your imagery strengths and areas to work on. You can use this information to target key areas for improvement through a mental imagery program. To get the most out of your dance imagery, put in the work to fully develop your imagery skills. The quality of your imagery is affected by six major factors: perspective, control, multiple senses, thoughts, emotions, and total imagery.

Dance Imagery Factors

Please rate yourself in each of these categories; the rating scale is defined at the end of each question.

> **Perspective**: Whether imagery "camera" is inside your head looking out through your eyes or outside of you like on video. (1= internal; 5 = both; 10 = external)

> **Vividness (or clarity)**: How clear your visual images are (i.e., blurry or clear). (1 = blurry, unclear 10 = crystal clear)

> **Control**: How well you can control and manipulate your imagery (e.g., see yourself dancing without mistakes). (1 = no control, many mistakes; 10 = total control, flawless dancing)

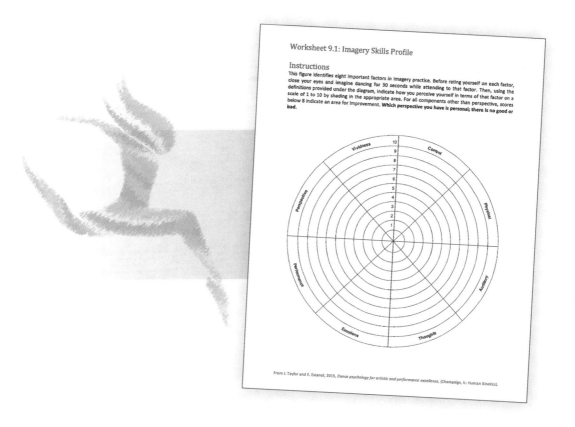

Worksheet 9.1: Imagery Skills Profile

Instructions
This figure identifies eight important factors in imagery practice. Before rating yourself on each factor, close your eyes and imagine dancing for 30 seconds while attending to that factor. Then, using the definitions provided under the diagram, indicate how you perceive yourself in terms of that factor on a scale of 1 to 10 by shading in the appropriate area. For all components other than perspective, scores below 8 indicate an area for improvement. **Which perspective you have is personal; there is no good or bad.**

Physical: How well you can feel the imagined movements in your body. (1 = not at all; 10 = very well)

Auditory: How well you are able to reproduce in your imagery the sounds of an actual performance. (1 = not at all; 10 = very well)

Thoughts: How well you are able to reproduce in your imagery the thoughts you have during an actual performance. (1 = not at all; 10 = very well)

Emotions: How well you are able to reproduce in your imagery the emotions you experience during an actual performance. (1 = not at all; 10 = very well)

Performance: How well you are able to reproduce in your imagery the total experience (e.g., visual, physical, emotional) of an actual dance performance. (1 = not at all; 10 = very well)

You can develop your ability in each of these areas through practice; to help you practice and develop your imagery skills, use the Imagery Exercises worksheet (found in the web resource).

Worksheet 9.2: Imagery Exercises

Exercise 1. Spend 30 seconds imagining yourself dancing—for example, doing a series of turns and jumps or a piece of choreography that you're currently rehearsing. In imagining this scene, use your dominant—that is, either internal or external—perspective. Now imagine the same scene for another 30 seconds but use the other perspective. You may find that only one perspective works for you or that you can use both perspectives equally well. If you do favor one or the other, rely on the perspective that comes most naturally to you.

Exercise 2. Imagine yourself dancing a piece of choreography five times for 30 seconds. In each segment, if you do poorly, rewind and edit your imagery until you get it right. Here's a helpful hint for gaining control over your imagery: We've found that it is difficult for dancers to edit their imagery when they imagine themselves dancing at normal speed—for example, doing a series of arabesque turns during a rehearsal. Therefore, if you have difficulty controlling your imagery, slow it down so that you see and feel yourself dancing in slow motion, even frame by frame. This strategy enables you to exercise greater control over your imagery. As you develop better control in slow motion, progressively increase the speed of your imagery while maintaining good control until you're able to dance without mistakes at your usual speed.

Exercise 3. Watch a recent video of yourself dancing well in a recent class, rehearsal, or performance, then immediately close your eyes and reproduce the video images. As your mental imagery gets clearer, put away the video for a while and repeat the mental images of your performance. If the imagery starts to fade, return to the video until you're able to clearly see yourself dancing on a consistent basis. This exercise helps you ingrain accurate images of how you dance.

Exercise 4. Imagine rehearsing a piece three times for 30 seconds. Each time, focus on a different sound associated with your performance. Once you're able to do so consistently, put all of the sounds together in an integrated imagery sequence.

Exercise 5. Imagine performing a piece of choreography twice for 30 seconds. Each time, focus on feeling your muscles and physical movements. As your dance imagery improves, you may become so immersed in it that your body starts to move without conscious effort.

Exercise 6. Imagine yourself before going on stage to dance an important role in a big production where, in the past, you have used negative self-talk. When you feel the negativity coming on, immediately replace it with positive self-talk, then imagine yourself dancing better with more confidence and virtuosity. Using imagery in this way enables you to benefit from the repetition of positive thinking away from training, thus ingraining new positive thinking skills that you can access when you need them—for example, before a performance about which you have doubts and feel nervous.

Perspective

Imagery perspective refers to the location of your mental camera when you use dance imagery. You can use one of two perspectives. The internal perspective involves seeing yourself from inside your body, looking out as if you were dancing. In this approach, the imagery camera is inside your head looking out through your eyes. In contrast, the external perspective involves seeing yourself from outside your body, as if watching yourself on video. In this case, the imagery camera follows your performance from the outside.

Research indicates that neither perspective is more helpful than the other. Rather, most people tend toward one or the other as a dominant perspective with which they're most comfortable. In addition, some people are equally adept at using both perspectives. Therefore, feel free to use the perspective that's most natural for you and experiment with the other to see if it might help you in different ways.

Control

Once you have a feel for your imagery perspective, you can explore how much control you have over your images. Have you ever done imagery and kept making mistakes, such as falling out of a turn or dropping your partner? Such struggles involve a problem with imagery control—how well you're able to imagine what you want to imagine. Though it's not uncommon for dancers new to imagery to dance poorly in their imagery, this difficulty can be frustrating and puzzling.

Poor imagery control demonstrates the power of the unconscious mind. Imagery is guided by your unconscious beliefs; most directly, it reflects your deepest beliefs about your ability to dance. If you don't have confidence that you can dance well, you won't be able to use imagery to re-create good performances. Therefore, poor imagery control tells you that you need to improve your confidence.

Fortunately, imagery control is a skill that you can develop with practice. If mistakes occur in your imagery, don't just let them go by. If you do, you'll ingrain the negative image and associated feelings, and they will continue to hurt your dancing. Instead, when errors occur in your imagery, immediately rewind the mental video, as it were, and edit it—that is, rerun it until you execute correctly.

Clarity

The clarity of your imagery also influences its value to your dancing. Imagery is most beneficial when it is marked by vivid visual, auditory, and kinesthetic (internal sensation) components. Visual clarity, of course, involves how clearly you see yourself dancing in your imagery. Ideally, your visual images are as clear in your imagery as they are when you're actually performing. Sometimes, however, your visual images may be blurry or you may be unable to see yourself at all in your imagery. In fact, too often, dancers don't even know what they look like while dancing; as a result, they imagine themselves dancing like a training partner or a top dancer they have observed. In either case, the imagery is less helpful than it could be because the dancer is imagining someone else.

One way to develop clear and accurate images of how you dance is to use a video recording. All you need is a few minutes of each piece of choreography to help you ingrain effective imagery. You can also bolster your visual clarity by imagining yourself wearing your usual dance practice clothes or performance costume and locating your imagined self in familiar training or performance settings—for example, the studio where you take classes or the theater where you perform.

Vivid auditory images are also important because sounds play an essential role in dance—for example, the melody, the beat, and an instructor's count or cadence. Yet we believe that the most powerful part of imagery is feeling it in your body. This kinesthetic sense—such as your muscles working, your breathing, your contact with other dancers—deeply ingrains new technical, artistic, and mental skills and habits. One useful way to increase the feeling in your imagery is to combine imagined and real sensations. For example, imagine yourself dancing and, at the same time, move your body with the imagined performance, thus integrating the imagined sensations with physical sensations to give your imagery added power.

Using imagery leads to flawless execution.

Thoughts

What you think during a performance often dictates your motivation, confidence, intensity, focus, and emotions—and, ultimately, how you dance. Imagery gives you the ability to learn new and better ways of thinking during your dance training and performances.

Emotions

As explored in chapter 7, emotions play a vital role in your ability to perform your best. Incorporating them into your imagery helps you strengthen their influence and ensures that you're capable of generating positive emotions when you need them most. In addition, imagining scenarios that have evoked negative emotions in you gives you the opportunity to respond in a more positive way.

Total Imagery

Another key aspect of dance imagery is being able to imagine your total performance. The more completely you re-create your dance training and performance experiences, the more accurate and beneficial the images will be. The most effective imagery reproduces every aspect of your dance performance—the sights, sounds, physical sensations, thoughts, and emotions that you experience during a real performance.

You can incorporate imagery into your dance training in several ways to get the most out of your classes and rehearsals. Just before you begin combinations or a piece of choreography, instead of just thinking about what you want to work on, use imagery to see and feel yourself doing it. Close your eyes and briefly imagine how you want to dance fully and effortlessly. These positive images increase your motivation and confidence, sharpen your focus and block out distractions, and generate positive thoughts and emotions that enhance your efforts.

You can also use imagery when you've finished an exercise or piece of choreography. If your just-completed rehearsal effort was positive, then you want to remember the image and feeling. So when you've finished, close your eyes and use imagery to replay your dancing in order to ingrain the positive image and the associated feelings. If, on the other hand, your effort wasn't of the highest quality, then it is associated with negative feelings and images, and the last thing you want to do is remember it. Nonetheless, those images and feelings are present in your mind and body, and they will be evoked when you begin your next exercise or choreography rehearsal. Thankfully, you can flush them out immediately by editing your imagery so that this time you dance well. This editing process replaces the negatives with positives.

You can also use imagery after your instructor or choreographer gives you feedback. Typically, she or he gives you instruction to improve your technique or artistry, then tells you to think about it before you dance again. But where does thinking occur? In your head, of course. And where does dancing occur? In your body. For this reason, thinking about instruction doesn't always translate effectively into action by the body. Imagery, however, acts as a bridge between the thoughts in your mind and the actions of your body. Therefore, you can use imagery to ingrain instruction into your mind and body. After you receive feedback, close your eyes and imagine yourself making the correction and dancing in the intended way.

Creating an Imagery Program

As with any form of dance training, imagery provides value only if you use it in a manner that is consistent and organized. An imagery program allows you to systematically address key areas that you need to improve in each aspect of your dance. Specifically, you can use imagery to consistently develop the technical, artistic, and mental parts of your dance performance.

Imagery Goals

The first step in developing a dance imagery program is to set goals. They may be technical (e.g., improving your alignment during leg extensions), artistic (e.g., refining your emotional expressiveness), mental (e.g., increasing your confidence), or related to your overall dance performance (e.g., raising the overall quality of a certain role). To identify areas that you would benefit from working on, use the Imagery Goals worksheet in the web resource.

Imagery Ladder

You wouldn't perform in a demanding and pressure-filled situation, such as an audition or show, before first developing yourself as a dancer in simple settings such as classes and rehearsals. This principle of progression also applies to your dance imagery program. Begin by imagining your dance in uncomplicated situations, then progress to increasingly complex settings—

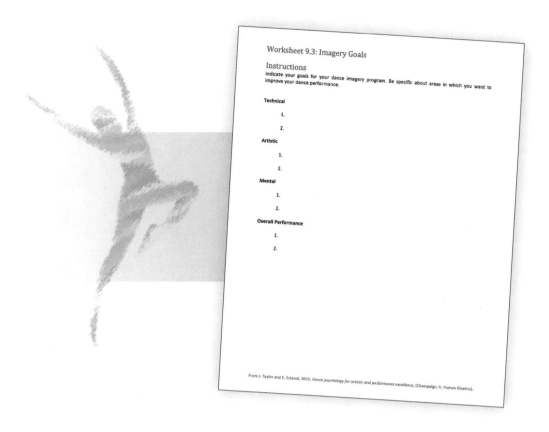

whether in class, rehearsal, or performance—that culminate in imagining yourself dancing in the most important role and performance of your life.

To begin this progression, create a dance imagery performance ladder. Start off doing imagery of your classes where your dance performance is less important. Using the Imagery Ladder worksheet in the web resource, create a ladder of training and performance situations in which you anticipate dancing. Your ladder should begin with the least important training situation—for example, a low-key class—and build up to your most important performance of the season. This ladder enables you to work on areas you've identified in training and performance situations that are increasingly demanding.

Begin your dance imagery program at the lowest rung of the ladder and work your way up until you reach the highest rung. Don't move from one rung to the next until you can dance the way you want to at the current rung. Once you feel solid at a particular rung, stay there for several imagery sessions to reinforce the positive images, thoughts, and emotions and the high-quality dancing.

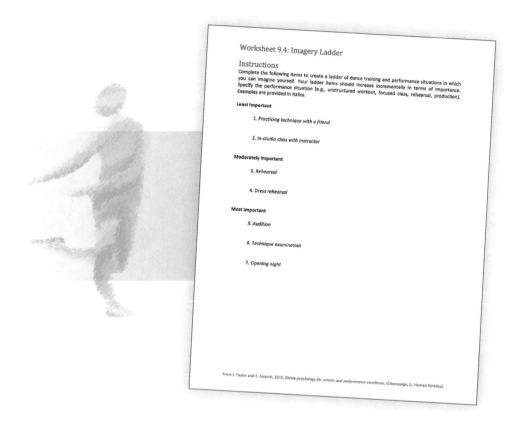

Worksheet 9.4: Imagery Ladder

Instructions

Complete the following items to create a ladder of dance training and performance situations in which you can imagine yourself. Your ladder items should increase incrementally in terms of importance. Specify the performance situation (e.g., unstructured workout, focused class, rehearsal, production). Examples are provided in italics.

Least Important

1. *Practicing technique with a friend*

2. *In-studio class with instructor*

Moderately Important

3. *Rehearsal*

4. *Dress rehearsal*

Most Important

5. *Audition*

6. *Technique examination*

7. *Opening night*

From J. Taylor and E. Estanol, 2015, *Dance psychology for artistic and performance excellence*, (Champaign, IL: Human Kinetics).

Imagery Scenarios

Once you've established your goals and built your dance imagery ladder, you're ready to create training and performance scenarios that you will use in imagery sessions (see the Imagery Scenarios worksheet in the web resource). These scenarios should address real class, rehearsal, and show situations in which you can work on your technical, artistic, mental, and performance goals.

Because dance is an art form that can require hours to complete, it would be unrealistic for you to imagine an entire class or production. Instead, identify seven specific dance situations that you can imagine for a few minutes each. For example, imagine yourself working on your petit allegro or staying positive and motivated during part of a demanding rehearsal. As you move up your dance imagery ladder, imagine using your newly imagined skills in increasingly important dance situations. Eventually, you can imagine your best performance in the most important production of the season.

Your dance imagery scenarios should be training and performance specific. Don't just imagine yourself dancing in a nonspecific location, show, or performance. Rather, imagine scenarios in which you dance at a particular venue (e.g., your usual class studio), in a specific performance (e.g., *The Nutcracker*), and under certain conditions (e.g., during a heat wave). Also, take care to

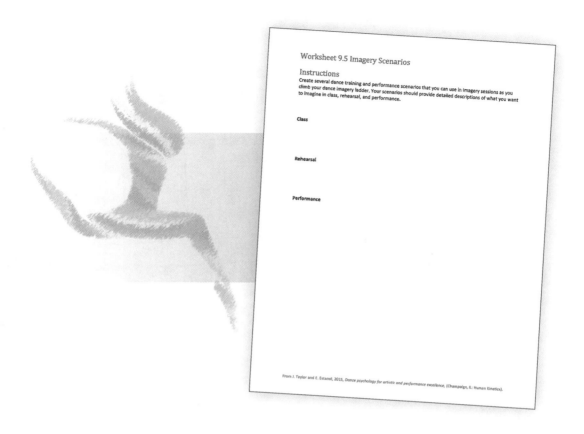

Worksheet 9.5 Imagery Scenarios

Instructions

Create several dance training and performance scenarios that you can use in imagery sessions as you climb your dance imagery ladder. Your scenarios should provide detailed descriptions of what you want to imagine in class, rehearsal, and performance.

Class

Rehearsal

Performance

From J. Taylor and E. Estanol, 2015, *Dance psychology for artistic and performance excellence*, (Champaign, IL: Human Kinetics).

imagine locations, events, and conditions that are appropriate to your level of ability. For example, if you're a dance major in college, don't imagine yourself dancing the lead role in the New York City Ballet production of *Giselle*.

Imagery Log

Because imagery isn't tangible—unlike, for example, weightlifting, in which you can see how much you've lifted—it can be difficult to mark progress in your dance imagery. One way to make it more concrete is to keep a log of your imagery sessions. Doing so allows you to notice improvements as you make your way up your dance imagery ladder. Use the Imagery Log worksheet (found in the web resource) to record relevant aspects of your dance imagery sessions.

The first piece of information to record is which rung of your imagery ladder you are working on. Note a number between 1 and 7 to indicate where you are in your climb up the ladder. Next, rate the quality of the imagery session on a scale of 1 to 10. How clear were the images? How well did you dance? How did you feel about the imagery session?

Now describe your performance—that is, what you worked on and what you imagined during the imagery session. Specify the control you had in the

Worksheet 9.6: Imagery Log

Date	Ladder rung	Quality (on a scale of 1–10)	Performance (what you imagined)	Control (quality of performance)	Senses (visual/auditory/physical) Note: physical refers to what you feel in your body.	Mental (thoughts and emotions)

From J. Taylor and E. Estanol, 2015, *Dance psychology for artistic and performance excellence*, (Champaign, IL: Human Kinetics).

imagery session. Were your imagined performances of high quality, or did you dance poorly?

In addition, rate the quality of your senses in the imagery session. Assign yourself a score of 1 to 10 indicating the clarity of the visual, auditory, and kinesthetic imagery you experienced. Finally, evaluate the mental aspects of your imagery by briefly describing relevant thoughts and emotions that you experienced during your imagery session. Indicate how positive or negative your thoughts and emotions were.

Structure your dance imagery sessions into your regular routine. If you schedule them for a regular time, you're more likely to remember to do them. Find a quiet, comfortable place where you won't be interrupted. Do imagery three or four times a week for no more than 10 minutes per session. Like any form of training, if you do it too much, you'll get tired of it. To augment your session, begin with one of the relaxation procedures described in chapter 5. The resulting deep state of relaxation will help you generate high-quality images and be receptive to the images and feelings you want to ingrain.

Center Stage: Heather

Seeing and Feeling Yourself Experience Prime Dance

Heather considered herself an oddity in the dance world. At age 42, she was much older than the teenagers and twenty-somethings who populate most collegiate ballroom dance programs. But she didn't feel old, and her competitive fires still burned brightly. In fact, she was always looking for ways to get an edge on her competition.

Realizing that her body had its limits, Heather particularly liked to explore how to strengthen her mind. She bought a sport psychology book that included a chapter on mental imagery and, following its suggestions, created an imagery program. The two areas she wanted to work on in her imagery were intensity and pain. Because Heather was very competitive, she sometimes felt overly nervous before a performance. She also knew that if she wanted to push her limits, she would have to learn how to better deal with pain.

Heather scheduled her imagery sessions for Mondays, Wednesdays, and Fridays at 6:15—just before her dinner. In each session, she started with a relaxation procedure described in the book. To reduce her intensity, she imagined herself arriving at the performance venue and going through her pre-performance preparations right up to the start of the performance. She imagined herself feeling confident and using relaxation techniques—such as deep breathing, muscle relaxation, and calming self-talk—to lower her intensity. To better manage her pain, she imagined facing difficult parts of an intense dance routine and using pain-control techniques, such as focusing on positive self-talk, generating positive emotions, and staying relaxed.

Two months later, in her first performance after starting the imagery program, Heather noticed that she automatically used the relaxation strategies she had practiced in her imagery sessions and felt more relaxed before her start. Late in the show, when she was performing her fourth piece of the night, she found herself naturally using the pain-management techniques that she had incorporated into her imagery. As a result, she was better able to tolerate the pain, and she danced with the same intensity as her younger competitors.

ENCORE

- Mental imagery is a powerful tool for improving your dance training and performance.
- Imagery influences dancers psychologically, physically, technically, and artistically.
- Dance imagery is a skill that you can develop through practice.
- Keys factors in maximizing the value of imagery include perspective, clarity, control, thoughts, emotions, and overall reproduction of the dance experience.
- You can maximize the benefits of dance imagery by using it in various ways—away from the studio, in classes and rehearsals, and before and during performances.
- You should develop an organized and comprehensive dance imagery program that includes goals, a ladder of increasingly demanding dance situations, specific dance imagery scenarios, and a log of your dance imagery sessions.

References

Achterberg, J. (1991, May). *Enhancing the immune function through imagery*. Paper presented at the Fourth World Conference on Imagery, Minneapolis.

Bennett, J.G., & Pravitz, J.E. (1982). *The miracle of sports psychology*. Englewood Cliffs, NJ: Prentice Hall.

Bunker, L., & Williams, J.M. (2010). Cognitive techniques for improving performance and building confidence. In J.M. Williams (Ed.) *Applied sport psychology: Personal growth to peak performance* (pp. 235-255). Palo Alto, CA: Mayfield.

Clark, L. (1960). Effect of mental practice on the development of a certain motor skill. *Research Quarterly, 31*, 560-569.

Cohn, P.J., Rotella, R.J., & Lloyd, J.W. (1990). Effects of a cognitive behavioral intervention on the preshot routine and performance in golf. *The Sport Psychologist, 4*, 33-47.

Epstein, M. (1980). The relationship of mental imagery and mental rehearsal on performance of a motor task. *Journal of Sport Psychology, 2*, 211-220.

Estanol, E. (2004). *Effects of a psychological skills training program on self-confidence, anxiety, and performance in university ballet dancers*. Master's thesis, Willard Marriott Library, University of Utah.

Feltz, D.L., & Albrecht, R.R. (1985). The influence of self-efficacy on approach/avoidance of a high-avoidance task. In J.H. Humphrey & L. Vander Velden (Eds.), *Current research in the psychology/sociology of sport* (Vol. 1) (pp. 137-152). Princeton, NJ: Princeton Book.

Feltz, D.L., & Landers, D.M. (1983). The effects of mental practice on motor skill learning and performance: A meta-analysis. *Journal of Sport Psychology, 5*, 25-57.

Feltz, D.L., & Riessinger, C.A. (1990). Effects of in vivo emotive imagery and performance feedback on self-efficacy and muscular endurance. *Journal of Sport and Exercise Psychology, 12,* 132-143.

Franklin, E. (2014). *Dance imagery for technique and performance* (2nd ed.). Champaign, IL: Human Kinetics.

Greenspan, M.J., & Feltz, D.L. (1989). Psychological interventions with athletes in competitive situations: A review. *The Sport Psychologist, 3,* 219-236.

Gregory, W., Cialdini, R., & Carpenter, K. (1982). Self-reliant scenarios as mediators of likelihood estimates and compliance: Does imagining make it so? *Journal of Personality and Social Psychology, 43,* 89-99.

Hall, C.R., Rodgers, W.M., & Barr, K.A. (1990). The use of imagery by athletes in selected sports. *The Sport Psychologist, 4,* 1-10.

Hamilton, S.A., & Fremouw, W.J. (1985). Cognitive-behavioral training for college basketball free-throw performance. *Cognitive Therapy and Research, 9,* 479-483.

Hanrahan, C., & Salmela, J.H. (1990). Dance images: Do they really work or are we just imagining things? *Journal of Physical Education, Recreation, and Dance, 61,* 18-21.

Hanrahan, S.J. (1996). Dancers' perceptions of psychological skills. *Revista de Psicologia del Deporte, 5*(2), 19-27.

Hanrahan, S.J. (2005). On stage: Mental skills training for dancers. In M.B. Andersen (Ed.), *Sport psychology in practice* (pp. 109-127). Champaign, IL: Human Kinetics.

Harris, D.V., & Harris, B.L. (1984). *The athlete's guide to sports psychology: Mental skills for physical people.* New York: Leisure Press.

Klockare, E., Gustafsson, H., & Nordin-Bates, S.M. (2011). An interpretive phenomenological analysis of how professional dance teachers implement psychological skills training in practice. *Research in Dance Education, 12*(30), 277-293.

McKay, D. (1981). The problem of rehearsal of mental practice. *Journal of Motor Behavior, 13,* 274-285.

Nordin, S.M., & Cumming, J. (2005). Professional dancers describe their imagery: Where, when, what, why, and how. *The Sport Psychologist, 19,* 395-416.

Nordin-Bates, S.M., Cumming, J., & Aways, D. (2011). Imagining yourself dancing to perfection? Correlates of perfectionism among ballet and contemporary dancers. *Journal of Clinical Sport Psychology, 5,* 58-76.

Paivio, A. (1985). Cognitive and motivational functions of imagery in human performance. *Canadian Journal of Applied Sport Sciences, 10,* 22-28.

Richardson, A. (1969). *Mental imagery.* New York: Springer.

Rodgers, W., Hall, C., & Buckholz, E. (1991). The effect of an imagery training program on imagery ability, imagery use, and figure skating performance. *Journal of Applied Sport Psychology, 3,* 109-125.

Ryan, E.D., & Simons, J. (1982). Efficacy of mental imagery in enhancing mental rehearsal of motor skills. *Journal of Sport Psychology, 4,* 41-51.

Smith, D. (1987). Conditions that facilitate the development of sport imagery training. *The Sport Psychologist, 1,* 237-247.

Smith, K.L. (1990). Dance and imagery: The link between movement and imagination. *Journal of Physical Education, Recreation, and Dance, 61,* 17.

Suinn, R. (1983). Imagery and sports. In A. Sheikh (Ed.), *Imagery: Current theory, research, and applications* (pp. 503–534). New York: Wiley.

Taylor, J., & Schneider, T. (2005). *The triathlete's guide to mental training*. Boulder, CO: Velopress.

Taylor, J., Horevitz, R., & Balague, G. (1993). The use of hypnosis in applied sport psychology. *The Sport Psychologist, 7*, 58–78.

Weinberg, R.S. (1984). Mental preparation strategies. In J.M. Silva III & R.S. Weinberg (Eds.), *Psychological foundations of sport* (pp. 145–156). Champaign, IL: Human Kinetics.

Woolfolk, R.L., Murphy, S.M., Gottesfeld, D., & Aitken, D. (1985). Effects of mental rehearsal of task motor activity and mental depiction of task outcome on motor skill performance. *Journal of Sport Psychology, 7*, 191–197.

CHAPTER 10

Routines

"Even if I only have 10 minutes, I have to give myself at least 5 minutes of leg elevation. That's my time to focus and think—or even not think at all. It's like the calm before the storm."

Vanessa Zahorian, principal, San Francisco Ballet

R outines are critical tools for improving your dance training and performance. They enable you to be completely prepared—physically, technically, artistically, and mentally—to dance your best. Most dancers use routines before performances to make sure that they're ready to give a great performance. But you can also use routines in other parts of your training,performance, and life to further your dance goals.

You can develop routines through your training to get the most out of your classes. Examples include performing a good warm-up and eating and hydrating properly during long classes in hot, humid studios. Routines can also make your transitions off of the stage smooth, fast, and problem free. In fact, we don't know a single professional dancer in any style of dance who doesn't use routines in some part of his or her training and performance preparation.

Dance involves many factors that you can't control—for example, the theater and the other dancers. But in the areas that you can control, routines help you do so effectively by enabling you to prepare consciously. Areas that you control include your costume and shoes (are they in optimal condition?), your body (are you physically warmed up?), and your mind (are you confident and focused?).

Routines also allow you to make your preparations predictable and know that you're systematically covering every controllable area that influences your performance. For example, you can plan for various eventualities that could arise during a performance. Doing so helps you limit the things that can go wrong and be well prepared when something does; as a result, you can stay focused and relaxed before and during your performances.

All of your preparations involve a consistent narrowing of effort, energy, and focus. Each step closer to your class, rehearsal, audition, or performance leads you to a state of readiness in which you're physically, artistically, and mentally capable of achieving your dance goals.

Routines Versus Rituals

Some folks in the dance world use the term *ritual*, but we prefer *routine* because *ritual* carries connotations that go against what routines are intended to accomplish. Remember, the goal of routines is to totally prepare you for classes, rehearsals, and performances. Everything you do in a routine serves a specific and practical purpose. For example, a routine might include a physical and technical warm-up and a review of choreography, both of which are essential for comprehensive preparation. Routines can also be adjusted as necessary; for instance, if you arrive late to the theater, you can shorten your routine and still get prepared.

In contrast, a ritual is often associated with superstition and includes elements that have no practical effect on performance, such as wearing a lucky hairclip or following a specific route to the theater. The problem with many rituals is that they can be rigid and ceremonial, and a dancer can come to believe that he or she must do the rituals in order to perform well. Then, if something prevents a ritual from being done, the dancer may lose confidence and motivation, which leads to poor dancing. At the same time, rituals do provide some dancers with a sense of familiarity and comfort that may benefit their dancing. Only you can decide whether any rituals you use may serve to help or interfere with your dancing.

Routines offer many benefits for training and performance. First, they help you develop consistency in all areas that affect your dance efforts. Consistency in your preparations leads to consistent thinking, intensity, focus, emotions, and readiness (physical, artistic, and technical). When you use a consistent routine, you are training your mind and body to respond in the same way regardless of the situation—be it a typical class, a rehearsal, or opening night of the biggest role of your life.

Routines are also flexible and can be adjusted to various situations—for example, a delay in the start of a performance. Flexibility in your routine means that you won't be stressed by changes in your preparations and that you're less likely to be affected by performance pressure. Therefore, routines enable you to dance your best in a wide range of situations and conditions.

Routines also provide powerful psychological benefits. They build your confidence by helping you feel more comfortable and in control. Each step of a routine tells you that you're doing what you need to do in order to succeed. In addition, routines help you achieve the ideal intensity that maximizes your dance efforts. By progressing through your routine, you mobilize your body to the level of intensity that enables it to be most effective in a performance. As a result, you feel both relaxed and energized, as well as strong and physically ready to perform. Routines also enable you to avoid distractions and negativity that can hurt your performance; instead, you focus only on factors that help you dance well.

Regardless of whether you're preparing for a first rehearsal at the start of the season or for the most important role of the year, routines signal to you that this is just another performance for which you'll be ready. Ultimately, the goal of routines in training and performance is to ensure that when you start your performance, you're completely prepared—physically, technically, artistically, and mentally—to dance your best.

Training Routines

Though most dancers use some sort of routine before a performance, far fewer use routines to get the most out of their classes and rehearsals. This is a shame, because training routines help you get physically and mentally prepared to benefit as much as possible from these efforts. They also provide you with a good experience in using a routine, so that when you use a routine before a performance you're already comfortable with the process and therefore get the most out of it.

To maximize the quality of your classes and rehearsals, develop both a pre-class routine and a brief training routine. Your preclass routine is important because it sets the tone for your class and ensures that you are prepared for a high-quality effort from the very start. It should include an effective physical and mental warm-up that gets you ready to perform from the first exercise, combination, or piece of choreography.

Your training routine should begin with getting your body ready by warming up, stretching, and checking and adjusting your intensity to ensure that it is primed for a good workout. This part of your routine might include deep breathing to relax yourself for an adagio or lyrical piece or intense breathing and jumping up and down to raise your intensity for a set of turns or jumps.

Common causes of poor training include distractions and lack of focus. Before a class, we often see dancers chatting or looking around rather than focusing on what they need to do in order to get the most out of their efforts. Shortly before you begin a combination or rehearsal piece, stop talking to others and focus on precisely what you want to accomplish in that combination, technique, or segment of your rehearsal—and on what you need to do in order to achieve that goal.

Some dancers use key words to direct their focus to a relevant cue, such as the music or their partner. For example, a dancer might say "up and in" to narrow his or her focus on going straight up and tighten-

Take a moment to focus inward and center yourself before class.

ing the limbs and abdominals while turning. You can help yourself find the needed focus by using the techniques described in chapter 6—for example, controlling your eyes, repeating key words, and maintaining a relaxed body. Elements of your training routine may last only a few seconds, especially focusing routines you use right before performing an exercise. Others can be longer in duration, but it will be time well spent as it will prepare you to get the most out of your training. It will also lay the foundation for pre-performance and transition routines.

Pre-Performance Routines

The next step is to create a pre-performance routine, which is an extended version of your training routine. The overall goal is the same—to be totally prepared to dance your best—but the purpose is different. The specific purpose of the pre-performance routine is to prepare you for a more important, longer, more intense, and more demanding event that can take hours to complete. The routine starts hours before the event, sometimes even the night before, and takes you through the entire event, as well as into the time after. It is weaved through everything else you do, so it doesn't mean you need to add hours to your preparation; it just means you are more intentional and consistent.

All effective routines share some elements, but no certain routine is ideal for all dancers. Rather, you get to decide what to put into your routine and how to structure it, and doing so requires you to consider a variety of practical, physical, and psychological concerns. Developing an effective pre-performance routine is also a progressive process, and it takes time to create one that works for you. The process involves figuring out what you need to do, as well as where, with whom, when, and how you need to do it.

"I have to be onstage warming up 45 minutes before curtain. I do push-ups, crunches, and finishes with balances—passé balances, turned-in, turned-out, arabesque—so I know if I'm on my center. I listen to upbeat, super-cheesy music on my I-pod, and I always have a pre-show cup of coffee, and, last thing, I pop a mint. I don't want to bad-breath my partners!"

Hanna Brictson, River North Dance Chicago

- **What.** Make a list of everything you need to do before a performance in order to be prepared. Common list items include meals, choreography review, physical warm-up, costume check, and mental preparation. Other more personal items might include going to the bathroom, putting on your costume, and doing your hair and makeup. Because dancing is so complex and requires you to prepare for so many elements, you must have a clear and detailed understanding of what you need to do in order to ensure that you don't forget anything. To this end, many dancers with whom we work prepare a list of everything they need to do and what they need to have before a performance, as well as the order in which to do things.

- **Where**. Specify where each step of your routine can best be completed. To identify where you can best accomplish each aspect of your routine, survey the theater prior to opening night. If this is your first time in a production or at a particular theater, don't be shy about asking the artistic director, crew, or veteran dancers to help you get the lay of the land. It is particularly useful to familiarize yourself with the wings and transition areas as you address your focus and intensity needs. For example, if you like to be alone before a performance, is there a quiet place where you can get away from the production activities?

- **Who.** Depending on your focus style (see chapter 6), you may prefer to be either alone or with others before the show. If you prefer being alone, make your style clear to those around you—other dancers, crew members, family members, and friends—so that they give you the solitude to prepare and you can avoid later drama.

  Recognize also that the who component of pre-performance routines begins well before the performance in the form of the people with whom you travel to the venue (whether you come a long or short distance). Decide ahead of time whether you will travel with anyone else—for example, dance partners, family members, or friends—or alone. If you plan to come with others, ask yourself if they're people with whom you feel relaxed and comfortable, who respect your focus and intensity needs, who support and encourage you, who bolster rather than hamper your preparations, and who allow you to adhere to your pre-performance routine.

  Before the trip, communicate your needs (and ask your companions about theirs) so that you can make the best decision for you and avoid any confusion or conflict. Once you're at the venue, nothing is more important to your performance than your preparations. Be particular about who you spend time with and communicate your needs to those around you.

- **When.** Establish a schedule for completing your pre-performance routine. How much time do you need to get totally prepared? Some dancers, usually those who like to perform at low intensity, prefer to arrive at the performance space hours in advance of the opening curtain, thus allowing themselves to take their time and proceed through their routines at a relaxed pace. Others, most often those who perform best at higher intensity, like to arrive closer to performance time and move briskly through their preparations. These decisions are personal; figure out what works best for you. To help you develop your pre-performance routine, use the Personalized Pre-Performance Routine worksheet (found in the web resource).

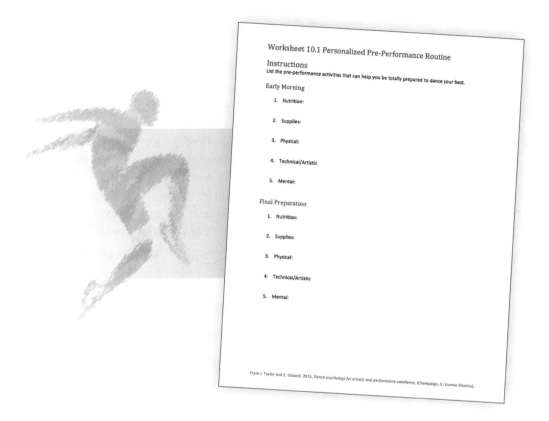

Worksheet 10.1 Personalized Pre-Performance Routine

Instructions

List the pre-performance activities that can help you be totally prepared to dance your best.

Early Morning

1. Nutrition:

2. Supplies:

3. Physical:

4. Technical/Artistic

5. Mental:

Final Preparation

1. Nutrition:

2. Supplies:

3. Physical:

4. Technical/Artistic

5. Mental:

From J. Taylor and E. Estanol, 2015, *Dance psychology for artistic and performance excellence*, (Champaign, IL: Human Kinetics).

- **How.** Try out your pre-performance routine at less important performances (never try a new routine for the first time at your most important performance of the season). Some things may work, and others may not. Over time, you can adjust your routine as you see how your mind and body react and learn what's most comfortable for you and what best prepares you for a performance. For instance, many dancers perspire more when they get nervous or excited. If your body responds in this way, then you may need to apply (or complete) your makeup at the very last moment. Similarly, if you need to use the bathroom several times and are wearing a highly involved costume, you may want to wait as long as possible to put it on in order to avoid asking several people to get you in and out of it before the show even starts.

Finally, remember that pre-performance routines work only if you use them consistently. If you use your routine before every performance, you don't even have to think about doing it. It's simply what you do before a performance, and it ensures that you're totally prepared to dance your best. Once your pre-performance routines are consistent and integrated, they become so ingrained that you may not even need to think much about them; you will just find yourself moving through the steps seamlessly.

Dance Gear Preparation

Dance is a complicated art form that may require considerable gear (costumes, shoes, and makeup, to name a few elements) depending on the dance style and the choreographer's intended look. As a result, forgotten items and gear malfunctions are more the rule than the exception. You can minimize the chance of such problems by actively preparing and organizing your dance gear and the myriad accessories in your pre-performance routine. In developing your routine, know the what, where, and how of making sure that all of your gear is ready. To help you with this task, we provide two lists here: Figure 10.1 lists items that you may need for your performance, and figure 10.2 lists transition-area gear and preparations that you may need to make before and during your performance.

Figure 10.1   Dance Preparation List

Shoes (Depending on Dance Style)

- Slippers
- Pointe shoes (several pairs—some new, some broken in "just right," and some rehearsal or back-up shoes)
- Ribbons sewn
- Dance claws
- Tap shoes
- Jazz shoes
- Dance boots
- Socks
- Warm-up booties

Clothing and Hair

- Several pairs of tights (at least one spare for the relevant dance style)
- Leotards for warm-up and rehearsal
- Nude leotards to wear under costumes
- Nude or other specific underwear
- Specific costume supplements that may not be supplied

- Leg warmers or warm-ups to wear in the theater
- Robe (if desired, to wear while applying makeup or between costume changes)
- Bike shorts (if needed under costume)
- Extra pair (or two) of socks
- Dance belts
- T-shirts
- Dance tights (men)
- Hair gel or spray
- Bobby pins (large and small)
- Hair ties
- Hairnets
- Hair inserts (if needed)
- Hair decorations (if needed, e.g., flowers or feathers)
- Towel(s)
- Any other practice or performance clothing (e.g., knee pads, skirts, shorts, sweatshirts, bodysuits)
- Postperformance clothing, underwear, and shoes
- Sandals (for theater or locker shower)
- Shampoo, conditioner, body lotion.
- Dirty laundry bag (or plastic bag for wet clothes).

Fuel

- Endurance and recovery powder
- Food appropriate for the length of your day and the nature of the rehearsal or performance
- Protein gels or bars, granola bars, dried fruits, and nuts
- Salt or electrolyte tablets
- Water bottle

Makeup Kit

- T-shirt or robe (unless you don't mind spills)
- Hydrating lotion
- Makeup base and concealer (several shades)
- Brown pencils
- Eyeliner, eye-shadow, and mascara
- False eyelashes and glue
- Blush and makeup brushes
- Lip liners and lipsticks

(continued)

Figure 10.1 *(continued)*

- Brown powder for use on eyebrows, filling in hair, or creating contrast in face or body
- Makeup remover fluid and towelettes
- Loose powder

Medical and Supply Kit

- Tape (e.g., for toes, feet)
- Foot protection materials (e.g., toe pads, lamb's wool, plastic, cloth wraps)
- Adhesive bandages
- Athletic tape
- Petroleum jelly
- Baby powder
- Anti-inflammatory medication
- Ice packs or plastic bags for ice
- Taping bandages
- Topical numbing agents (e.g., for lost toenails)
- Shaver
- Sewing kit (including dental floss)
- Extra ribbons and elastics
- Nail clippers
- Nail file
- Clear nail polish (to stop runs in tights or costumes)
- Breath mints or breath strips
- Glue and superglue
- Calamine lotion
- Safety pins (many!)
- Portable music player and noise-canceling headphones

Figure 10.2 Performance Transitions

Transition Supplies

- Costumes
- Towels (small and large)
- Water bottle
- Anti-inflammatory medication
- Adhesive bandages and tape
- Tights

- Undergarments
- Alternate technique shoes
- Snacks

Transition Prep

1. Before the show starts, bring up all the supplies you will need for quick changes and place them where you will need them. Decide which side of the stage will be best (usually where your next entrance is happening), though that decision may be impacted by how crowded that area already is.

2. Lay out your undergarments, tights, costumes, shoes, bobby pins, gels or sprays, and other supplies in the order in which you will use them. Face them the way you will need them in order to avoid putting things on inside-out or backward in the dark.

3. Ask friends or colleagues to help you (if needed) and discuss how they will assist. Involving too many people can complicate things, so be sure that you know ahead of time who will be there to help.

4. Bring a small hand mirror and paper or cloth towels to dry off and check your makeup before you go back onstage.

5. Put on your shoes, and if ribbons need to be tied, secure them so that they don't come undone. You can also use hairspray or rosin to keep them secure.

6. Make sure that your hair and headpieces are fastened securely so that they don't come out of place during turns.

7. Put everything you need on the side of the stage at which you will make your next entrance. If you have several quick changes and enter on opposite sides of the stage, you may need to set up two stations.

8. Practice your routine (during tech or lighting rehearsal) to ensure that you have enough time for all quick changes and, if needed, for going under the stage to the other side.

9. Depending on your time, this may be a moment you use to prepare yourself mentally. You could use deep breathing, imagery, or simply make eye contact with and smile at the dancers opposite you who share the same entrance, letting them know you are ready and synched.

10. Take one or two deep breaths and smile.

Physical Preparation

You can use your pre-performance routine to ensure that you address every component of your physical preparation at the proper time and in the best possible way. Foremost among the physical concerns is your pre-performance nutrition. Eat a nutritious meal of familiar and energy-intensive food two to three hours before your performance. Then perhaps have a snack an hour before the curtain goes up to allow for timely digestion and immediate access to energy. Also, hydrate yourself properly before your performance.

In addition, do a good physical warm-up, which might include a technique class, stretching, and rehearsal of specific parts of the choreography. Identify what will physically prepare you for your performance and determine when and where you will warm up.

Focus

As discussed in chapter 6, you may have either an internal or an external focus style. If you have an internal focus style—meaning that you want to stay totally focused on your preparations—then the goal of your pre-performance routine is to put yourself in a place free of external distractions (whether in the form of people or activities) where you can focus narrowly on getting ready for your performance. For example, you might find a spot backstage, a corner of a dressing room, a nearby studio, or a low-traffic hallway. You may also need to bring noise-canceling headphones, both to block out noise and to let others know to leave you alone as you go through your preparations. We have also known dancers to put a towel over their heads or bring with them a book to let others know that they need to be left alone.

An external focus style, on the other hand, means that you need to keep your focus wide during your preparations in order to keep your mind off of the upcoming performance. If this is your style, then the goal in your pre-performance routine is to put yourself in a place with enough activity that you're unable to focus internally and think too much about the performance. Good possibilities might include the dressing room, the costume shop, or the wings, where you are joined by other dancers, the director, and the production crew. You may also want to identify other dancers with similar needs so that you can cluster together and play games, talk, or listen to music as you get ready. You can have a "mini party" that pumps you up and keeps you out of your head (as long as you are not so loud that you disturb those with an internal focus style).

Intensity

Your pre-performance routine should also be responsive to your intensity needs. This component of your routine includes checking your intensity periodically before the start of the performance and using either psych-up or psych-down techniques (see chapter 5) to adjust it as needed. Set aside time specifically for these strategies in your routine. As you approach the performance, move closer to your prime intensity. The short period just before you go onstage should be devoted to a final check and adjustment of your intensity.

If you perform best at a lower level of intensity, your pre-performance routine should allow you to proceed at an easy pace and include plenty of break opportunities for slowing down and relaxing. Your routine should also put you around other people who are relaxed and low key. If, on the other hand, you perform best at a higher level of intensity, your pre-performance routine can be done at a faster pace and with more energy. Make sure that you're constantly doing something—there should be little time during which you're just standing around and waiting. Put yourself with other people who are energetic and outgoing.

Addressing your intensity needs also involves being aware of how much stress you feel on the morning of a performance. If you tend to get nervous before shows, recognize when the stress becomes a problem, either emotionally or physically, and integrate psych-down strategies (e.g., deep breathing or muscle relaxation) into your pre-performance routine.

> *"Take competing as a big learning experience. You will learn to deal with pressure, which happens all the time in a company when you are asked to fill in for a role last minute. This is a great time to learn to control your emotions and nerves. There's a lot of commotion at competitions, so make sure to take quiet time for yourself, away from the crowd. Listen to your music on an iPod to get ready. Learn from everyone else too: Since you are watching the same variation 30 times, take things you like to benefit your own artistry."*
>
> Jim Nowakowski, demi soloist, Houston Ballet

Transition Routines

Transitions are among the most neglected aspects of dance; they just don't get the attention they deserve. In fact, transitions are sort of the "crazy uncle" of dance. Everyone in the family knows he's there, and they know he can wreck the meal, but the whole family is so busy getting ready and having a good time that he's forgotten until he drops the main dish.

Yet any experienced dancer will tell you that transitions can make or break a performance. They can be brief, smooth, and calming shifts between performances. Or they can be interminable purgatories of stress, distraction, and confusion. Which reality they constitute for you depends on whether you use a transition routine to guide yourself through them. We strongly recommend that you take control of your transitions to ensure that you move to the next phase of your performance as effortlessly as possible.

The first key to a good transition is to set up a well-organized transition area. The transition is a scene of frenetic activity in which gear can be dropped, donned in the wrong order, or just plain forgotten. To prevent chaos in your transitions, know where everything is and in what order you will use each of your dance supplies and costumes without having to think about it. Find a particular spot in the backstage area for your quick transitions and costume changes that you can use for the duration of the show's run. Coordinate with other dancers who have quick changes so that you are not on top of one another, and make arrangements with dancers who are willing to help you. Instruct them specifically ahead of time about what you want them to help you with and what you need to do on your own. Gently turn down offers for extra help at the last minute that might interfere with the routine and flow that you have created.

In addition, practice these transitions as soon as you start rehearsals in the theater as a way of testing how well they will work there. Identify any problems as soon as possible so that you can come up with a workable solution in time to adjust and practice the new routine. At the end of the show, remember to come back and pick up your items, clean the area with due consideration for everyone else, and get organized for the next show.

Consciously refocus and recharge between routines.

Beyond the logistics of your transitions, you must also deal with the psychological and physiological aspects. You can take active steps to ensure that your mind and body are ready to segue from onstage to the wings or the dressing room and back onstage as smoothly as possible. We recommend addressing the four Rs: recover, regroup, refocus, and recharge.

1. **Recover**. As you leave the stage, allow your body to rest, however briefly. In this phase of your transition, take several slow, deep breaths to encourage your heart rate to slow down in anticipation of your return to the stage. If you lower your heart rate by 10 beats per minute during your transition, you enjoy a significant recovery benefit between the parts of your performance. This recovery is especially important after a long or demanding piece that leaves you fatigued and out of breath. If you have enough time, you might also rehydrate or grab a snack. Finally, deep breathing and muscle relaxation can help you focus and better prepare you for the next R.

2. **Regroup**. This phase of your transition routine addresses your emotions. If you're excited and happy about your performance so far, you have a greater chance of performing well in the remainder. If your dancing hasn't gone as well as planned, you may feel any of a variety of negative emotions, such as frustration, anger, or despair. Regrouping allows you to gain awareness of how you feel and how your emotions might affect the rest of your performance. Use the transition as an opportunity to regroup and return to the stage in a better frame of mind. Because emotions exert a powerful influence on your dancing, you can help your performance by using this chance to "get your act together" emotionally while you're off stage.

   The transition also gives you a chance to realize that the way you danced in previous segments of your performance doesn't necessarily relate to how you will dance the rest of the way. For example, doing a poor pas de deux doesn't necessarily mean that you're in for a bad solo at the end of the performance. The one thing that *can* connect different parts of your performance is the emotion that you carry across your transitions. If you're frustrated and angry in the wings, you increase your chances of letting those emotions hurt the rest of your dancing. Angry outbursts also hurt and psych out other dancers. Using your transition to regroup enables you to let go of negative emotions and replace them with positive emotions that help you finish on an upbeat note.

3. **Refocus**. When a performance isn't going well, some dancers have a tendency to focus on how poorly it has gone. If this happens to you, return to a process focus for the next part of your performance. During the refocus phase of your transition routine, start by evaluating the quality of your dancing thus far, then focus on what you need to do so that the rest of your performance goes well. Your focus might be physical (e.g., staying relaxed), technical (e.g., nailing the choreography), or mental (e.g.

remaining positive and motivated). The key is to return to the stage with a clear focus on what you want to do to improve a poor performance—or continue a good one.

4. **Recharge.** Because dance is such a physical art form, your body also needs to be ready to go back onstage. As you wait in the wings before returning to the stage, check your physical intensity to see if it is too high or too low for your best dancing. If it is too high, take deep breaths, relax your muscles, settle your body, and smile before you go onstage. If your intensity is too low, take shorter, more intense breaths and move your body to get your energy up. Either way, the goal of this phase of your transition routine is to ensure that you are physically capable of dancing your best when you return to the stage.

As demonstrated in this chapter, routines offer essential value in ensuring your total preparation for all aspects of your dance experience. However, you can realize the full benefits of routines only if you use them consistently in all areas that affect your dance, including classes, rehearsals, performances, and your life outside of dance. Committing yourself to the use of appropriate routines pays immense dividends in how you dance and how you feel about your dance.

ENCORE

- Routines are critical tools for improving your dance training and performance because they enable you to be completely prepared—physically, technically, artistically, and mentally—to dance your best.

- Rituals can control you, if not mindfully integrated into a flexible routine that you are in full control of.

- Routines are beneficial because they help you develop consistency, can be adjusted to different situations and demands, build confidence and comfort, and get you focused and relaxed.

- Training routines help you get the most out of your classes and rehearsals by ensuring that you are optimally prepared for every exercise, choreography, and run-through.

- Pre-performance routines should include equipment preparation and organization, physical and choreography warm-up, and focusing.

- As you develop your pre-performance routine, attend to the what, who, where, when, and how of it.

- Transition routines that include the four Rs (recover, regroup, refocus, recharge) ensure that your time offstage during a performance is used wisely.

Center Stage: Dahlia

Establishing Routines to Ensure Total Preparation

At age 20, Dahlia relished the complexity of dance. She was first and foremost a hip-hop dancer but enrolled as a modern dance major in order to train in lyrical, jazz, and hip-hop. Her multifaceted talent made her a sought-after dancer for student choreography showcases and ensemble pieces, and she relished these opportunities to learn new choreography.

This diversity, however, often required her to make numerous quick costume changes in a single show. Fortunately, she had her pre-performance routine down to a science. For a typical show, she did a complete inspection of her dance gear two nights before the first spacing rehearsal at the theater: shoes, tights, leotards, T-shirts, socks, and warm-ups. On the night before each performance, she laid out her clothing, prepared her energy drinks and snacks, and packed her dance bag according to a thorough preparation list. She then went to a local restaurant where she and her boyfriend had dinner reservations every night of the production run.

On performance morning, Dahlia arose early for her customary breakfast of half a bagel with peanut butter, a banana, a plain yogurt, and a glass of orange juice. She then did a few calisthenics and stretches before heading to the performance venue, as it was a matinee performance, arriving 90 minutes before the show. She warmed up and checked in with her choreographers and partners for any last-minute run-throughs or practice lifts. She then went to her dressing room, put on her headphones, applied her makeup, and did her hair. Next, she set up a transition area for her three quick changes, laying out her costumes just so. She also had extra tights, bobby pins, and other items—just in case. She then put on her first costume and continued to stretch and keep her body warm. She kept to herself, preferring to stay quiet, calm, and focused.

After dancing well in her first piece, Dahlia ran to her transition area and changed quickly enough to have a bit of extra time. Her partner asked if they could go through a lift, and as they did so his ring caught on her tights and ripped them. He was panicked, but Dahlia simply reminded him to take off all his jewelry, then practiced the lift and quickly changed into her spare tights. The rest of her changes went well, and she was glad that her well-developed routine had kept her calm and on schedule.

References

Bacon, S.J. (1974). Arousal and the range of cue utilization. *Journal of Experimental Psychology, 102*, 81–87.

Bandura, A., & Adams, N.E. (1977). Analysis of self-efficacy theory of behavioral change. *Cognitive Therapy and Research, 1*, 287–308.

Bandura, A., & Cervone, D. (1983). Self-evaluative and self-efficacy mechanisms governing the motivational effects of goal systems. *Journal of Personality and Social Psychology, 45*, 1017–1028.

Bennett, J.G., & Pravitz, J.E. (1987). *Profile of a winner: Advanced mental training for athletes*. Ithaca, NY: Sport Science International.

Brawley, L.R. (1984). Attributions as social cognitions: Contemporary perspectives in sport. In W.F. Straub & J.M. Williams (Eds.), *Cognitive sport psychology* (pp. 212–230). Lansing, NY: Sport Science Associates.

Bunker, L., & Williams, J.M. (2010). Cognitive techniques for improving performance and building confidence. In J.M. Williams (Ed.) *Applied sport psychology: Personal growth to peak performance* (pp. 235–255). Palo Alto, CA: Mayfield.

Burke, S. (2011, January). Teach learn connection: Technique my way—Natalie Desch. *Dance Magazine*. www.dancemagazine.com/issues/January-2011/Teach-Learn-Connection-Technique-My-Way.

Carron, A.V. (1984). *Motivation: Implications for coaching and teaching*. London, Ontario: Sports Dynamics.

Cautela, J.R., & Wisocki, P.A. (1977). Thought-stoppage procedure: Description, application, and learning theory interpretations. *Psychological Record, 27*, 255–264.

Elko, P.K., & Ostrow, A.C. (1991). Effects of a rational-emotive education program on heightened anxiety levels of female collegiate gymnasts. *The Sport Psychologist, 5*, 235–255.

Epstein, M. (1980). The relationship of mental imagery and mental rehearsal on performance of a motor task. *Journal of Sport Psychology, 2*, 211–220.

Gauron, E.F. (1984). *Mental training for peak performance*. Lansing, NY: Sport Science Associates.

Greenspan, M.J., & Feltz, D.L. (1989). Psychological interventions with athletes in competitive situations: A review. *The Sport Psychologist, 3*, 219–236.

Hamilton, S.A., & Fremouw, W.J. (1985). Cognitive-behavioral training for college basketball free-throw performance. *Cognitive Therapy and Research, 9*, 479–483.

Hanrahan, C., & Salmela, J.H. (1990). Dance images: Do they really work or are we just imagining things? *Journal of Physical Education, Recreation, and Dance, 61*, 18–21.

Hanrahan, S.J. (1996). Dancers' perceptions of psychological skills. *Revista de Psicologia del Deporte, 5*(2), 19–27.

Hanrahan, S.J. (2005). On stage: Mental skills training for dancers. In M.B. Andersen (Ed.), *Sport psychology in practice* (109–127). Champaign, IL: Human Kinetics.

Hellstedt, J. (1987). Sport psychology at a ski academy: Teaching mental skills to young athletes. *The Sport Psychologist, 1*, 56–68.

Hunt, M.E. (2011, July). Technique my way: Vanessa Zahorian. *Dance Magazine*. www.dancemagazine.com/issues/July-2011/Technique-My-Way-Vanessa-Zahorian.

Kamata, A., Tenenbaum, G., & Hanin, Y. (2002). Individual zone of optimal functioning (IZOF): A probabilistic conceptualization. *Journal of Sport & Exercise Psychology, 24*, 189–208.

Laporte, R.E., & Nath, R. (1976). Role of performance goals in prose learning. *Journal of Educational Psychology, 68*, 260–264.

Meichenbaum, D. (1975). Toward a cognitive theory of self-control. In G. Schwartz & D. Shapiro (Eds.), *Consciousness and self-regulation: Advances in research* (pp. 223–260). New York: Plenum.

Meichenbaum, D. (1977). *Cognitive behavior modification: An integrative approach*. New York: Plenum.

Molzahan, L. (2012, June). Technique my way: Hanna Brictson—A practical outlook and daily discipline keep this dancer moving. *Dance Magazine*. www.dancemagazine.com/issues/June-2012/Technique-my-way-hanna-brictson.

Richardson, A. (1969). *Mental imagery*. New York: Springer.

Taylor, J., & Schneider, T. (2005). *The triathlete's guide to mental training*. Boulder, CO: Velopress.

Weinberg, R.S. (1984). Mental preparation strategies. In J.M. Silva III & R.S. Weinberg (Eds.), *Psychological foundations of sport* (pp. 145–156). Champaign, IL: Human Kinetics.

Yerkes, R.M., & Dodson, J.D. (1908). The relation of strength of stimulus to rapidity of habit formation. *Journal of Comparative Neurology of Psychology, 18*, 459–482.

Ziegler, S.G. (1987). Effects of stimulus cuing on the acquisition of groundstrokes by beginning tennis players. *Journal of Applied Behavioral Analysis, 20*, 405–411.

CHAPTER 11

Individualized Program

"Then come the lights shining on you from above. You are a performer. You forget all you learned, the process of technique, the fear, the pain; you even forget who you are. You become one with the music, the lights, and indeed one with the dance."

Shirley MacLaine

Would you become a better dancer if you took only class once per month? Would you get stronger if you did Pilates only once every few weeks? Of course not. What enables you to improve technically and physically as a dancer is the fact that you work at it in a consistent and organized way. The same holds true for the mental side of dance. In order to gain its many benefits, you need to develop a mental training program—what we refer to as a prime dance program—that improves your mind much in the same way that dance classes and Pilates improve your technique and fitness.

You know what your goals are and what you need to work on in order to achieve them. The aim of the individualized program is to help you do so in the most efficient and organized way possible. You can develop your own program by taking four steps: design, implementation, maintenance, and evaluation.

Design

The first thing to do in the design phase is to identify your most crucial needs. To identify these areas, use the results from your prime dance profiles (see chapter 2), your instructor's feedback, and your own training and performance experience. Then list your chosen areas on the Areas for Development worksheet (found in the web resource), which serves as a tool to help you focus on key aspects of your dance training and performance.

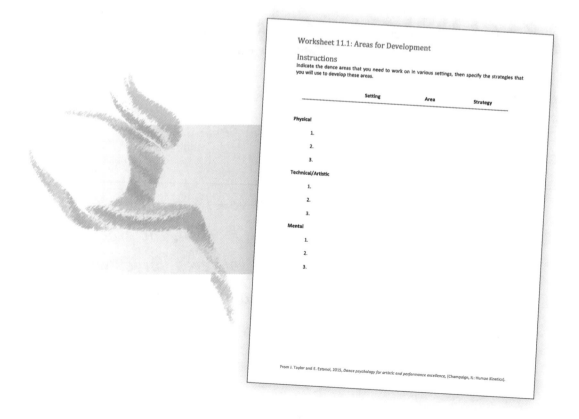

Worksheet 11.1: Areas for Development

Instructions

Indicate the dance areas that you need to work on in various settings, then specify the strategies that you will use to develop these areas.

Setting	Area	Strategy

Physical
1.
2.
3.

Technical/Artistic
1.
2.
3.

Mental
1.
2.
3.

From J. Taylor and E. Estanol, 2015, *Dance psychology for artistic and performance excellence*, (Champaign, IL: Human Kinetics).

Next, specify particular mental training strategies that you can use to develop the areas you've just identified. For example, if you've set goals aimed at improving your confidence, review the confidence-building strategies described in chapter 4. Then narrow those options to two or three techniques that you like the most. You can do so by experimenting with each technique for a few days to see which ones work best for you.

The final part of the design phase involves organizing your prime dance program into a daily and weekly schedule. This step integrates your physical, technical, and mental training into an organized plan; for an example, see table 11.1. To create your individualized plan, use the prime dance Program Planner worksheet (found in the web resource) to address the key aspects of preparation that you've specified in the Areas for Development worksheet.

Implementation

The second phase of the program, implementation, is where you put into action the plan you've just designed. It's best to begin your program as far in advance of your dance season as possible. Starting your program early gives you a chance to develop the most effective program possible and incorporate it fully into your overall dance training program. It also lets you fine-tune the program to best suit your needs. Most important, it gives you sufficient time to fully benefit from the program.

You may feel some concern about the time commitment required for such a program. Even without dance, you probably lead a busy life that includes work or school, as well as family and friends. Adding a comprehensive

TABLE 11.1　**Sample Mental Training Program**

GOAL	STRATEGY	PLACE IN SCHEDULE
Increased motivation	Goal setting	Every Monday
Increased confidence	Positive self-talk	In training and performances
Lower intensity	Deep breathing and muscle relaxation	Before classes, rehearsals, and performances
Increased focus	Key words, imagery	Just before dancing

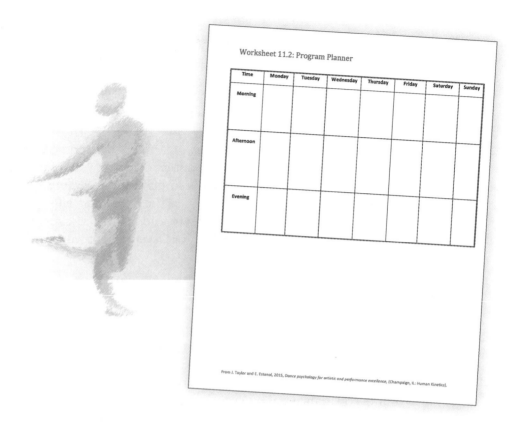

Worksheet 11.2: Program Planner

Time	Monday	Tuesday	Wednesday	Thursday	Friday	Saturday	Sunday
Morning							
Afternoon							
Evening							

From J. Taylor and E. Estanol, 2015, *Dance psychology for artistic and performance excellence*, (Champaign, IL: Human Kinetics).

program to your busy life may seem overwhelming. With all of this in mind, as you establish goals and create your program to meet them, consider what is realistic for the life you lead. No matter how good a program is, it has no value if you don't follow it consistently.

As you settle into your program and integrate it into your overall life, evaluate whether it is manageable. If you find that the program you've created is simply too much, scale it back rather than trying to pull off a time- and energy-consuming feat that you simply can't manage. Reduce your program to the essential elements that allow you to progress in the areas that are most important to you. Over time, the effort and time you put in to developing your program will pay off in increased efficiency and consistency.

Maintenance

The third phase of the program, maintenance, is important because in dance the training never stops. To continue to improve, you must maintain a consistent training program that addresses all aspects of your dance. If you don't maintain your physical conditioning, technique, and artistry through regular use, they will atrophy. The same holds true for mental training. Once you've

Instructors help you learn visually and kinesthetically.

developed a mind-set that allows you to achieve your dance goals for the season, you can adjust your program in order to maintain that high level while also making room for minor improvements.

The quality of your program in the off-season is determined by your commitment to your dancing and your desire to raise your goals at the start of each new season. Some dancers don't do mental training at all during the entire off-season; as a result, they have to work each year to regain their previous season's mind-set. Others maintain a moderate level of mental training that gives them a consistent base to build on when the new season starts. Still others use the off-season to *gain* mental strength and enhance less developed parts of their dancing; to do so, they continue a rigorous program that takes them to a new level of mental fitness for the new dance season.

Evaluation

Finally, to ensure that your program remains fresh and beneficial, we encourage you to continually evaluate it. Self-reflective practice involves looking back at what you have done in order to continue learning and growing. We recommend that you reflect on your program about every six months in order to identify which parts have worked well and which need to be modified or removed. This type of evaluation enables you to regularly make certain that you are getting the most out of your efforts.

Implementing an Organized Mental Training Program

Lucy was a 17-year-old ballet and modern dancer who had been dancing "for the fun of it" for most of her life. She enjoyed performing for an audience and "being transported to another world." As she progressed through her training, teachers and fellow dancers encouraged her to enter competitions. She did so and succeeded both locally and nationally. Her success rested in part on the fact that, though she was focused and worked hard, she never pressured herself but danced simply because she loved performing.

However, as the time approached for Lucy to make decisions about college and apprenticeships, she began to feel anxious when performing. At about the same time, she read about Elena in a dance newsletter and arranged to begin working with her to overcome her nerves. With Elena's help, Lucy set two overall goals: a dance scholarship and an apprenticeship. In her sessions with Elena, Lucy recognized that she needed to make her dancing more consistent while also pushing herself to add an extra turn, especially on pointe. She also wanted to return to dancing with joy and passion and keep her confidence up even when she made mistakes. She recognized that she danced her best when she stayed relaxed with an attitude of fun and excitement.

With Elena's help, Lucy set up a program that incorporated her various goals: technical, physical, artistic, and mental. Her program included the use of imagery, positive self-talk, key words, and a pre-performance routine to help her remain confident and relaxed before performances. She scheduled imagery sessions three times per week that included five minutes of relaxation followed by ten minutes of imagery. She also recorded positive affirmations and feedback from teachers in a notebook. To practice these new mental skills, she auditioned at schools and companies of lesser interest before facing the big auditions that lay ahead.

Lucy's work with Elena paid off with a scholarship at her top choice of school and an apprenticeship with a preferred company. Most important, she was thrilled with her progress as a dancer and the joy that dance brought her.

ENCORE

- Organized and consistent effort enables you to improve your dancing physically, technically, artistically, and mentally.

- In order to maximize the mental side of your dance, you need to develop a consistent and organized mental training program.

- Developing an effective program involves four steps: design, implementation, maintenance, and evaluation.

- The design phase involves identifying your most crucial mental needs from your prime dance profiles (see chapter 2), specifying particular mental training strategies, and organizing them into a structured plan.

- In the implementation phase, you put your program into action by incorporating it into your daily dance training regimen.

- Once your program is integrated in your dance training routine, you enter the maintenance phase, in which you adjust and maintain the program throughout the year.

- In the evaluation phase, it is important to evaluate progress and readjust goals about once every six months.

References

Bacon, S.J. (1974). Arousal and the range of cue utilization. *Journal of Experimental Psychology, 102*, 81–87.

Bandura, A. (1977). Self-efficacy: Toward a unifying theory of behavioral change. *Psychological Review, 84*, 91–215.

Bandura, A. (1986). *Social foundations of thought and action*. Englewood Cliffs, NJ: Prentice Hall.

Bandura, A., & Adams, N.E. (1977). Analysis of self-efficacy theory of behavioral change. *Cognitive Therapy and Research, 1*, 287–308.

Bandura, A., & Cervone, D. (1983). Self-evaluative and self-efficacy mechanisms governing the motivational effects of goal systems. *Journal of Personality and Social Psychology, 45*, 1017–1028.

Bandura, A., & Simon, K.M. (1977). The role of proximal intentions in self-regulation of refractory behavior. *Cognitive Therapy and Research, 1*, 177–193.

Bennett, J.G., & Pravitz, J.E. (1982). *The miracle of sports psychology*. Englewood Cliffs, NJ: Prentice Hall.

Bennett, J.G., & Pravitz, J.E. (1987). *Profile of a winner: Advanced mental training for athletes*. Ithaca, NY: Sport Science International.

Buckroyd, J. (1995). The provision of psychological care for dancers. *Performing Arts Medicine News, 3*, 1.

Buckroyd, J. (2000). *The student dancer: Emotional aspects of the teaching and learning of dance*. London, England: Dance Books.

Carman, J. (2005, September). The silent majority: Surviving and thriving in the corps the ballet. *Dance Magazine*. www.dancemagazine.com/issues/September-2005/The-Silent-Majority-Surviving-and-Thriving-in-the-Corps-de-Ballet.

Caudill, D., Weinberg, R., & Jackson, A. (1983). Psyching-up and track athletes. A preliminary investigation. *Journal of Sport Psychology, 5*, 231–235.

Csikszentmihalyi, M. (1990). *Flow: The psychology of optimal experience*. New York: Harper & Row.

Dowd, I. (1981). *Taking root to fly: Seven articles on functional anatomy*. New York: Author.

Duda, J.L., & Hall, H. (2001). Achievement goal theory in sport: Recent extensions and future directions. In R.N. Singer, H.A. Hausenblas, & C.M. Janelle (Eds.) *Handbook of sport psychology* (pp. 417–443). New York: Wiley.

Epstein, M. (1980). The relationship of mental imagery and mental rehearsal on performance of a motor task. *Journal of Sport Psychology, 2*, 211–220.

Estanol, E. (2004). *Effects of a psychological skills training program on self-confidence, anxiety, and performance in university ballet dancers*. Master's thesis, Willard Marriott Library, University of Utah.

Estanol, E., Shepherd, C., & MacDonald, T. (2013). Mental skills as protective attributes against eating disorder risk in dancers. *Journal of Applied Sport Psychology, 25*(2), 209–222.

Feltz, D.L., & Landers, D.M. (1983). The effects of mental practice on motor skill learning and performance: A meta-analysis. *Journal of Sport Psychology, 5*, 25–57.

Gauron, E.F. (1984). *Mental training for peak performance*. Lansing, NY: Sport Science Associates.

Gould, D., Dieffenbach, K., & Moffet, A. (2002). Psychological characteristics and their development in Olympic champions. *Journal of Applied Sport Psychology, 14*(3), 172–204.

Greenspan, M.J., & Feltz, D.L. (1989). Psychological interventions with athletes in competitive situations: A review. *The Sport Psychologist, 3*, 219–236.

Hamilton, S.A., & Fremouw, W.J. (1985). Cognitive-behavioral training for college basketball free-throw performance. *Cognitive Therapy and Research, 9*, 479–483.

Hanrahan, S.J. (1996). Dancers' perceptions of psychological skills. *Revista de Psicologia del Deporte, 5*(2), 19–27.

Hanrahan, S.J. (2005). On stage: Mental skills training for dancers. In M.B. Andersen (Ed.), *Sport psychology in practice* (109–127). Champaign, IL: Human Kinetics.

Hefferon, K.M., & Ollis, S. (2006). "Just clicks": An interpretive phenomenological analysis of professional dancers' experience of flow. *Research in Dance Education, 7*(2), 141–159.

Hellstedt, J. (1987). Sport psychology at a ski academy: Teaching mental skills to young athletes. *The Sport Psychologist, 1*, 56–68.

Kamata, A., Tenenbaum, G., Hanin, Y. (2002). Individual zone of optimal functioning (IZOF): A probabilistic conceptualization. *Journal of Sport & Exercise Psychology, 24*, 189–208.

Klockare, E., Gustafsson, H., & Nordin-Bates, S.M. (2011). An interpretive phenomenological analysis of how professional dance teachers implement psychological skills training in practice. *Research in Dance Education, 12*(30), 277–293.

Lee, C. (1982). Self-efficacy as a predictor of performance in competitive gymnastics. *Journal of Sport Psychology, 4*, 405–409.

Mahoney, M., & Avener, M. (1977). Psychology of the elite athlete: An explorative study. *Cognitive Therapy and Research, 1,* 135–141.

Martens, R., & Burton, D. (1984). *Psychological skills training.* Unpublished manuscript.

Meyers, A.W., & Schleser, R.A. (1980). A cognitive behavioral intervention for improving basketball performance. *Journal of Sport Psychology, 2,* 69–73.

Miner, J.M., Shelley, G.A., & Henschen, K.P. (1999). *Moving toward your potential: An athlete's guide to peak performance.* Palo Alto: CA; Performance/Personal Solutions.

Orlick, T. (1990). *In pursuit of excellence* (2nd ed.). Champaign, IL: Human Kinetics.

Orlick, T., & Partington, J. (1986). *Psyched.* Ottawa: Coaching Association of Canada.

Rushall, B.S. (1979). *Psyching in sport.* London: Pelham.

Sheets, M. (1966). *The phenomenology of dance.* Madison, WI: University of Wisconsin Press.

Taylor, J., & Schneider, T. (2005). *The triathlete's guide to mental training.* Boulder, CO: Velopress.

Weinberg, R.S. (1984). Mental preparation strategies. In J.M. Silva III & R.S. Weinberg (Eds.), *Psychological foundations of sport* (pp. 145–156). Champaign, IL: Human Kinetics.

Weinberg, R.S. (1988). *The mental advantage: Developing your psychological skills in tennis.* Champaign, IL: Leisure Press.

Williams, J.M. (2010). Integrating and implementing a psychological skills training program. In J.M. Williams (Ed.), *Applied sport psychology: Personal growth to peak performance* (pp. 301–324). Palo Alto, CA: Mayfield.

PART IV

SPECIAL CONCERNS FOR DANCERS

The other parts of this book focus on information and tools that you need in order to dance your best and experience prime dance. This part shifts the focus from dance performance to your *life* as a dancer. Dance can be truly life affirming. At the same time, some aspects of it can be unhealthy, both physically and mentally. You can use the chapters in this part of the book to help ensure that dance plays the healthiest possible role in your life.

Chapter 12 explores the physical and emotional costs of a singular and unremitting commitment to dance. It describes specifically what stress and burnout are and how they develop. It also highlights warning signs—physical, cognitive, emotional, and performance related—so that you can see clearly whether stress and burnout are present in your life. The chapter also discusses their most common causes. It concludes by addressing practical ways for you to prevent and respond to stress and burnout, including physical, mental, and social strategies.

Chapter 13 examines the seemingly ever-present role that pain plays in the life of a dancer. It begins by helping you distinguish between exertion pain and injury pain and offering useful techniques for minimizing your exertion pain. The chapter then shifts to the unsettling effect that injuries can have on dancers, including the emotional toll. Finally, the chapter provides a program to help you stay positive and motivated when recovering from injury, along with a variety of tools that facilitate both the physical and the emotional healing process.

Chapter 14 confronts clearly and empathically one of the most uncomfortable issues that many dancers face: disordered eating. The chapter begins by defining disordered eating and discussing the most common types experienced by dancers. It then describes the risk factors and events that often precipitate the emergence of disordered eating. The chapter also explores the consequences of disordered eating and their effect on physical and mental health. It concludes with a discussion of ways to prevent and treat disordered eating.

Chapter 15 shifts the focus back to the healthiest and most nurturing elements of dance. It begins, however, with a deep consideration of the "dark side" of dance—that is, the unhealthy motivations that can drive dancers, such as self-doubt, anxiety, and fear. It also examines the dark side's physical, emotional, and social dangers, as well as their warning signs. The chapter then takes a happier turn, showing you how to embrace the light side of dance. It describes perspectives and attitudes that can inspire you to enter and live on the light side. Finally, it encourages you to return always to the love and joy you feel in your dancing and to appreciate all of the physical, mental, emotional, and social benefits that dance can give you.

12

Stress and Burnout

"When miseries pile up, I've found that a bit of perspective helps deliver me from the quicksand of discouragement and self-pity. I seek inspiration from those who have shown grace and courage in grave situations—individuals who shatter our ideas about endurance and excellence."

Sascha Radetsky, soloist for American Ballet Theatre,
former principal for Dutch National Ballet

Stress involves a psychological, emotional, or physical reaction to internal or external demands placed on you in dance or another aspect of your life. Despite what many think, stress is an important and highly adaptive (to a point) response to the challenges that you face, both in dance and in life overall. For instance, stress helps you respond physically to the challenges of dance by giving you more energy and stamina when you're confronted with the often-exhausting schedules that dancers must keep. It also sharpens your thinking and focus to help you meet the intellectual demands that dance makes on you.

The difficulties you face in your dance life are usually quite manageable. But when the demands exceed your capabilities and resources, the resulting stress can be debilitating. Take a moment to think of the demands you face in dance. Internal demands can include your perceptions of your ability, your goals and expectations, and your worries and fears. External demands can include pressure to get roles, harsh teachers, conflicts with choreographers and peers, and an unrelenting schedule of classes, rehearsals, and performances.

If the stress you experience is intense and persistent, you may develop burnout as your mind and body become unable to sustain themselves and instead crumple under the weight of demands. Burnout results from breakdown in your ability to cope with constant stress, excessive training loads without appropriate rest periods, or the perception that you're incapable of managing the demands you face. It can last anywhere from a few weeks to a few months. Both stress and burnout are experienced in the following ways:

- You feel psychologically overwhelmed and emotionally vulnerable.
- The quality of your dance declines.
- Your health deteriorates.
- You lose your enjoyment of and motivation for dance.
- Your general quality of life decreases.

Causes of Stress and Burnout

Harmful stress and burnout in dance can result from a wide variety of causes. Still, we have found that some causes are the most common in this art form.

- Psychological causes: low self-esteem, perfectionism, fear of failure, perceived lack of control, poor time management and organizational skills
- Personal causes: poor physical or mental health, financial problems
- Social causes: loneliness; relationship issues such as conflict, breakup, family dysfunction, or overinvolved parents; excessively tough teachers, choreographers, or dance masters or mistresses; unsupportive peers or conflict within a dance school or company

- Environmental causes: demanding classes and rehearsals, long performance seasons, monotonous training routines, overly rigid studio or school rules, perceived training overload, failure to achieve a sought-after goal, academic demands
- Performance causes: role insecurity, technical or artistic deficiencies, difficulty in learning new choreography

This list makes it easy to see why dancers are prime candidates for stress and burnout. In addition, the very characteristics that increase your risk for stress and burnout—for example, being highly motivated, obsessive, a perfectionist, filled with high expectations, prone to extreme self-discipline, and afraid of failure—are often the same as, or similar to, characteristics that are desired and reinforced by the dance world. Therefore, it is crucial that you pay attention to your physical, mental, and emotional well-being in order to dance your best, maintain your health, and ensure your longevity in dance.

Warning Signs

The first step in preventing or minimizing the negative effects of stress and burnout is to become aware of their symptoms. Red flags for stress and burnout fall into four categories (see table 12.1).

Responding to Stress

You can think about stress and burnout much as you would think of the thermometer and thermostat in your home. As discussed in chapter 5, you are well aware of when the temperature in your house is comfortable and when it is too hot, whereupon you adjust the thermostat accordingly. Similarly, you tend to know when your stress is at a comfortable level, and you also need to be able to recognize when it is too high and may lead to burnout. If it gets too high, you can then adjust your stress thermostat—that is, reduce the stress you're experiencing in your dance and in your life as a whole.

Given that stress is a normal part of life as a dancer, you have two options for responding to it. First, you can hope that the stress goes away and doesn't lead to burnout. This attitude, however, can intensify your stress and put you on the road to burnout. Left untreated, stress is more likely to persist than to diminish, and stress that develops into burnout can persist unabated. For this reason, trying to wait it out only prolongs the decline in your dance life; at the same time, it exacerbates your stress and burnout because you feel powerless to counteract your slide. Therefore, though you need not panic when you see warning signs of stress and burnout, you do need to make a dedicated and systematic effort to reverse your downward spiral.

TABLE 12.1 Warning Signs of Stress and Burnout

PHYSICAL	EMOTIONAL	COGNITIVE	PERFORMANCE
• Frequent illness • Frequent injuries • Frequent complaints (e.g., headache, stomachache) • Slow healing of injuries or minor cuts and illness • Decreased appetite (weight loss) • Decreased energy • Sleep disturbance (can't wake or can't sleep) • Frequent or chronic fatigue • Malaise • Gastrointestinal disturbance • Increased susceptibility to asthma and allergies • Changes in heart rate during rest, exercise, and recovery • Increased respiration rate • Changes in blood pressure • Nausea • Increased muscular soreness, pain, or stiffness • Sudden weight changes • Excessive perspiration • Menstrual irregularity • Compromised immune function	• Feelings of depression • General apathy • Decreased motivation • Increased anxiety • Anger • Decreased self-esteem • Emotional instability (moodiness) • Personality changes • Increased irritability • Low tolerance for frustration • Unrealistic expectations • Social isolation or withdrawal • Decreased communication • Increased sensitivity to environmental or emotional stress • Being easily overwhelmed • Fear of competition • Nightmares • More frequent crying • Increased emotional outbursts	• Excessive negativity or self-criticism • Decreased concentration • Frequent mistakes • Failure to remember choreography • Inability to take in large amounts of information • Increased internal or external distractibility • Decreased perseverance • Tendency to give up • Problems with verbal communication • Problems with multitasking • Listless appearance • Lack of engagement • Forgetfulness in daily activities	• Technical problems • Decline in artistry and grace • Decline in quality of dance • Drop in quality of school work

Gaining control of your stress begins with taking the right attitude toward your dance life. This attitude, in turn, starts with love and compassion, which is your first line of defense against debilitating stress. When we talk about love, we mean the love of dance. Let that feeling propel your dance. If you love dance, then you're probably driven by an intrinsic motivation that enables you to experience meaning and fulfillment in your dance. That alone can partially mitigate the stress you experience. This attitude focuses on the process of dance rather than on its outcomes. In other words, you dance, first and foremost, because you enjoy it. The results of your efforts—namely, roles and promotions—are just icing on the cake. Compassion is toward yourself; allowing yourself to practice kindness internally, especially when you feel you are not meeting internal or external expectations. When we feel stress, it is usually a result of our perceived gap between demands placed on us and our capabilities. If the gap is too large, we may begin to doubt our abilities and start focusing instead on our inadequacies, further enhancing the downward spiral. Therefore, practicing self-kindness and compassion, rather than succumbing to criticism and judgment, can be instrumental in decreasing or reversing the downward spiral.

Does this attitude mean that you won't experience stress in your dance? Of course not. But we have found that it does take the edge off of the stress of dance in subtle but substantial ways; moreover, it becomes the foundation for further efforts at mastering your stress.

> *"I put pressure on me. Nobody does it to you but you. I did it because of how I interpreted what was written in the newspaper about me. . . . I was trying to match the image that was written about me. And I got my head way out of proportion instead of just enjoying and loving to dance."*
>
> Judith Jamison, dancer and choreographer

Setting Goals to Reduce Stress and Burnout

Reducing stress and avoiding burnout depend in part on setting realistic goals about how you can respond effectively to these challenges. The first goal you should set is to accept stress as part of the deal in striving for success in dance. Don't try to resist the stress; doing so only makes it worse. If you accept stress as part of your life, it doesn't surprise you when it occurs. In fact, when you assume it's there, you're more able to roll with it rather than trying to push back against it (which is a truly futile effort).

Your second goal is to recognize when stress occurs. Almost without exception, you will find a consistent pattern in the situations, people, and experiences that lead you to experience stress. Just knowing when stress is likely to arise puts you in a better position to respond positively to it. Once you've identified your most common stressors, examine the root causes of the stress—in other words, what sets you off. For example, perhaps you stress out when your teacher criticizes you in class or when you feel overwhelmed by your daily schedule. You can also explore what underlying issues cause your stress, such as perfectionism, self-doubt, and poor time management.

A third goal to aim for is that of committing to looking for solutions rather than wallowing in the problems that cause your stress. When faced with stress, you can make use of several possible solutions. First, you can address the cause of the stress; for example, if you're stressed out about a piece of choreography, you can ask for help from your dance instructor or choreographer.

You can also alter your perception of the stress. Consider two dancers who experience the same stress while learning a demanding role but perceive and react to it in vastly different ways. Dancer A sees the stress as a threat to be avoided and feels overwhelmed and paralyzed by the choreography. In contrast, Dancer B sees the stress as a challenge and feels excited and energized by the difficult steps. Which dancer is going to experience more debilitating stress, and which one is going to rise to the occasion and perform at a high level? Research shows us that the dancers who manage stress best are able to perceive stressful situations not as insurmountable obstacles but as challenges to overcome.

When you are confronted by stress, you can also treat the symptoms. For example, you can use meditation, massage, or exercise to relieve physical manifestations of stress, such as racing heart, shallow breathing, and muscle tension.

Finally, though stress is inevitable in the dance world, the intensity of stress is exacerbated when you feel that you lack the means to respond to it positively—in other words, when you stress out about the stress. Therefore, another way to overcome your stress is to fill a strategic toolbox with stress-relief tools that you can use when you experience stress—for example, calming thoughts, deep breathing, and muscle relaxation. Perhaps you include a particular scent to provide a physical reminder of breath, calming music, and self-affirmations. Physical reminders may help you to remember to employ mental strategies. Having tools that you can use to counteract stress helps you feel more in control and capable of mastering the stress; as a consequence, you also perceive less stress than you otherwise would.

Relieving Stress and Burnout

Because stress and burnout can develop in different ways and their warning signs can vary across individuals, it is essential that you know yourself and listen to your mind, body, and spirit in order to prevent persistent stress from becoming full-blown burnout (use the Dealing With Burnout worksheet in the web resource). Ideally, your school or company is sensitive to the risks of stress and burnout and uses a training and performance schedule that minimizes these risks and allows for rest and recovery when red flags arise. If not, you can still take practical steps to address your concerns. Mastering stress and preventing burnout involve taking control of the stress in your life and proactively doing things that counter their psychological, emotional, and physical causes.

We have created a process that helps you feel empowered to take the necessary steps to alleviate stress and burnout and return to (or even surpass) your previous level of performance. This process can also serve as a way to prevent burnout. Being optimistic about this plan's effect on your recovery is

Worksheet 12.1: Dealing With Burnout

Stress and Burnout Zones

Green zone: You are doing well; you are energetic, resilient, and staying positive when challenges arise.

Yellow zone: Your energy has decreased, you don't enjoy your dancing as much, and you have a hard time staying positive and rebounding from difficulties.

Red zone: You are exhausted, lack energy, and feeling negative.

What is the color of your stress and burnout zone?	
What specific physical, psychological, emotional, or performance signs indicate that you are experiencing unhealthy stress?	
What are the primary stressors you are currently experiencing?	
What underlying issues may be causing your stress?	
In what situations is your stress most likely to occur?	
What changes can you make in your training or rehearsal schedule to reduce your stress?	
What psychological or emotional changes can you make to lessen your stress?	
What sources of social support can you connect with to ease your stress?	

Once you have completed the chart, answer the questions below.

From J. Taylor and E. Estanol, 2015, *Dance psychology for artistic and performance excellence.* (Champaign, IL: Human Kinetics).

helpful to your motivation, adherence, and efforts in overcoming the stress and burnout. This process hinges on providing you with tools to put in your toolbox that you can use to counter the effects of stress and burnout. So even if you are not experiencing burnout at the moment, implementing some of these suggestions may ward off future occurrences.

Maintaining Balance in Your Life

One of the best ways to relieve stress is to engage in activities that provide the exact opposite of what you experience in dance. When dance stress depletes you, find other experiences that produce joy, excitement, meaning, satisfaction, inspiration, and pride in order to refill your tank. Such balance also provides your self-esteem with sources of sustenance other than dance so that, even when your dancing is not going well, you still feel good about yourself in other aspects of your life. Common activities for balance include sports, cultural and spiritual pursuits, cooking, reading, music, travel, movies, crafts, art projects, knitting, and gatherings with family and friends.

Sometimes you just need to relax with a friend to alleviate stress and burnout.

Increasing Your Resources

Stress tends to occur when the demands of a situation exceed your available resources. Therefore, increasing your resources—whether by getting help from others, gaining relevant information and skills, or giving yourself more time—can help you tip the scales back into a healthy balance.

Resting and Recovering

Stress and burnout tear you down and weaken you physically, mentally, and emotionally. In contrast, rest acts to heal your mind, body, and spirit from the damage caused by stress. The type of rest and recovery that you engage in should be determined both by the depth and severity of your stress and burnout and by the ways in which you personally prefer to relieve them. Certain basic measures—getting a good night's sleep, taking naps as needed, eating healthfully, and spending time away from dance—allow your body to rejuvenate itself and be prepared for daily stress.

However, if your stress and burnout are severe and persistent, then you need to take an extended break—away from training and performance and, if possible, in a different environment with different people. This temporary separation from dance can make sense for several reasons. First, one critical component of stress and burnout is the strong negative emotional environment that surrounds you. Emotions such as frustration, sadness, and anger wrap you in an unpleasant cocoon that you cannot escape as long as you remain in the dance environment. Therefore, to alleviate the stress and burnout, you need to put yourself in an environment with a decidedly different emotional tone—one in which you experience joy, excitement, calm, and hope.

Being away from the pressures of the studio gives you an emotional vacation. The change of scenery allows you to gain perspective on your stress and burnout and turn your negative view of your recent dance life into a positive perspective on your future dance life. The break will be most effective if you experience a distinct change of scenery and people. In other words, you should get physical, psychological, and emotional distance from the conditions that caused your stress and burnout.

Stress and burnout are as draining physically as they are emotionally, and the break also enables you to rest, relax, and recharge your batteries. It gives you an opportunity to catch up on your sleep, overcome any lingering illness, and rehabilitate any nagging injuries. Many years ago, Elena took an extended period away from dance to heal injuries plaguing her body. During this time, she picked up her first sport psychology book and became interested in applying sport psychology to dance. Thus, this break not only allowed her body to heal but also enabled her to gain a new perspective on her dance life and provided a new direction for her career and life.

The duration of your time away from dance should be proportional to the seriousness of your stress and burnout. In general, a break of two to five days can be enough to reverse the vicious cycle. If burnout is severe, however, you may need to take a month or two away from your dance in order for the damage to heal.

Eating Well

What you eat and drink provides the energy that fuels your body and helps it resist the debilitating forces of stress. If you put high-quality gas into your car to help it run its best, why not do the same for your body? Unfortunately, the dance lifestyle often allows little time for preparing healthful meals, tempting you instead to eat readily available fast food and rely on caffeine and sugar to keep yourself going. This pattern saps you of energy and makes you more vulnerable to stress. In contrast, eating a healthy and balanced diet every day (with some treats, of course, as a reward for your efforts) bolsters your immune system and gives you the energy to keep on ticking even when your body takes a licking.

Building a Social Support Network

Robust research indicates that social support acts as a buffer against stress. Family, friends, and trusted classmates and colleagues can provide you with emotional support, sympathy, help with problem solving, encouragement, perspective, and distraction from the burdens of stress. Therefore, you should actively build a social support network that you can access when you feel overwhelmed.

Relaxation Techniques

You can also use a variety of practical techniques to help your body and mind counter the stress that they experience. In moments of stress, these strategies reduce the immediate symptoms and help you feel more relaxed and comfortable.

- **Purposeful breathing.** Though simple, the practice of breathing slowly and deeply has a direct effect on a body under stress. Taking additional oxygen into your system slows your heart rate, reduces stress-inducing neurochemicals, eases your pace of movement, relaxes your muscles, and increases your sense of comfort and well-being.
- **Muscle relaxation.** When you perceive a threat to your safety, your muscles tense up to protect your body from damage. Unfortunately, this reaction, which has been hardwired into humans since primitive times, actually has

the opposite effect—that is, it makes us more vulnerable to the stress. You can relieve muscle tension by engaging in relaxation exercises, whether through meditation, yoga, or targeted relaxation practices. As a result, your body is better able to withstand ongoing stress.

- **Music.** Many of us have experienced the profound influence that music can exert on us psychologically, emotionally, and physically. Music can inspire, calm, fire up, and move us. It can transport us from our stressful lives into worlds of tranquility or excitement, either of which, depending on your musical tastes, can take you far away from stress and reinstill in you a sense of ease and comfort.

- **Taking a moment.** In some cases, you don't have time to engage in elaborate relaxation strategies but still need to do *something*. In these situations, it can be enough to just take a brief break. During this respite, you can step back from the stress and take a few deep breaths. You can also look for the source of the stress and find a solution. Afterward, you can return to the formerly stressful situation with a calmer mind, a more relaxed body, and relevant tools that you can use to directly relieve your stress.

Of course, taking these steps toward stress mastery does not eliminate stress from your life. Furthermore, given that you have chosen a stressful profession, we doubt that you want to live a life that is completely free from stress. But that's not what stress mastery is all about; instead, it's about controlling stress so that it doesn't harm your dance or your life. Even more than that, however, you can *harness* stress so that, while others wither under its weight, you stay energized, positive, and focused and keep working hard to move toward your goals.

> *"I'm very excited about dance and love it with a deep passion. I also struggle, tire, and become discouraged. But what has always revived me . . . has been the rebirth of energy each time the creative process is awakened and artistic activity begins to unfold even in some infinitesimal measure."*
>
> Anna Halprin, pioneer in the expressive arts healing movement

Emotional Counseling

As you grapple with the symptoms of stress and burnout, you may feel strong negative emotions that exacerbate those symptoms. To break out of this downward emotional spiral, we recommend that you incorporate both individual and group counseling into your recovery. Individual counseling with a mental health professional who understands dance allows you to express your thoughts and feelings about what you are experiencing to an impartial observer who can offer you perspective and insights for dealing with your stress and burnout. A counselor can also help you develop effective coping skills that you can use to better deal with your symptoms.

Group counseling, on the other hand, allows you to share your experiences of stress and burnout with others who are sympathetic to your plight. These sessions can serve several valuable purposes. First, they can act as a meaningful source of social support during a time when you may feel otherwise unsupported. This support can help mitigate your stress and burnout and address the extreme sense of isolation and loneliness that often accompanies them. It also gives you a strong, centralized source of encouragement and moral and mutual support.

Second, group sessions allow you to share your concerns and realize that your worries and misgivings are natural and expected. Furthermore, these sessions provide a setting in which you can share and compare techniques that you and other dancers have found useful in relieving stress and burnout. Thus, the sessions increase your sense of power and control over your condition.

ENCORE

- Stress involves a psychological, emotional, or physical reaction to internal or external demands placed on you in dance or another aspect of your life.

- Stress occurs when the demands of a situation exceed your capabilities and resources for dealing with them.

- If the stress you experience is intense and persistent, you are likely to develop burnout as your mind and body become unable to sustain themselves under the weight of the demands.

- Stress and burnout can be caused by psychological factors (e.g., low self-esteem, perfectionism), personal factors (e.g., poor health, financial problems), social factors (e.g., overinvolved parents, unsupportive peers), environmental factors (e.g., demanding classes, long performance season), and performance factors (e.g., role insecurity, technical problems).

- Warning signs of stress and burnout can be physical (e.g., fatigue, illness), emotional (e.g., irritability, sensitivity to criticism), cognitive (e.g., low confidence, poor focus), or performance related (e.g., decline in artistry, decline in quality of dance).

- You need to actively counter and gain control of the stress that you experience.

(continued)

Center Stage: Kyle

Finding Joy, Not Stress, in Dance

Kyle, an 18-year-old student on a dance scholarship at a large university, had defied both of his parents by pursuing a life in dance. His parents had assumed that he would follow them in choosing a career in medicine or law. Standing up to them had been hard, and Kyle wanted to show them that he was worthy of their support. In addition, though he was a good student and a committed dancer, he also felt pressure to show the university that he was a good investment, and he spent most of his time in the studio, the classroom, or the library.

Kyle also felt immense pressure to impress a noted Russian choreographer in residence at the university. As the semester wore on, however, Kyle began making mistakes and struggling with the teacher's choreography. Kyle beat himself up emotionally, his confidence shrank as his anxiety grew, and his dancing got even worse. Soon, he was doubting his future as a dancer, and he had little enthusiasm or energy for dance.

Feeling helpless and hopeless, Kyle enlisted the help of a psychologist. Through this work, he recognized the unreasonable pressure that he had put on himself in trying to please his parents and the choreographer. The stress had led him to the edge of burnout. With the psychologist's help, Kyle took several positive steps. First, to get his mind off of dance, he took a week off to visit friends in a nearby city. After a few days of rest and fun, he felt more energetic and optimistic about dance and life in general. He also had a wonderful time at a dance club, where he realized that it had been a long time since he had danced simply for the pleasure of it.

Back on campus, Kyle and his instructor agreed that Kyle would do only two performances for the rest of the semester, take barre only twice a week, and use the remainder of class time to visualize, observe, or do Pilates. Kyle's willingness to seek help and gain control of his stress and burnout made it possible for him not only to recover but also to improve his dance performance. He was thrilled when his parents met him with hugs at the final performance of the season, in which he had a leading role.

Encore *(continued)*

- Overcoming stress and burnout involves accepting them as part of dance, recognizing when you experience them, understanding their causes, committing to finding solutions to those causes, and creating a toolbox for countering stress and burnout.

- Steps for relieving stress and burnout include finding balance in your life, increasing your resources, getting fitter, getting sufficient rest, eating well, and building a social support network.

- Relaxation techniques for treating the physical symptoms of stress and burnout include deep breathing, muscle relaxation, listening to music, and taking a moment away from the stresses of life.

- During times of stress and burnout, consider engaging in individual or group counseling with a trained mental health professional to gain perspective, insights, and support.

References

Beck, A. (1976). *Cognitive therapy and emotional disorders*. New York: International University Press.

Berstein, D., & Borkovec, T. (1973). *Progressive relaxation training: A manual for the helping professions*. Champaign, IL: Research Press.

Brewer, B. (2001). Emotional adjustment to sport injury. In J. Crossman (Ed.), *Coping with sports injuries: Psychological strategies for rehabilitation* (pp. 1–19). New York: Oxford University Press.

Buckroyd, J. (1995). The provision of psychological care for dancers. *Performing Arts Medicine News*, *3*, 1.

Buckroyd, J. (2000). *The student dancer: Emotional aspects of the teaching and learning of dance*. London, England: Dance Books.

Burke, S. (2011, January). Teach learn connection: Technique my way—Natalie Desch. *Dance Magazine*. www.dancemagazine.com/issues/January-2011/Teach-Learn-Connection-Technique-My-Way.

Cresswell, S.L., & Eklund, R.C. (2007). Athlete burnout: A longitudinal qualitative study. *Sport Psychologist*, *21*(1), 1–20.

Feltz, D.L., & Riessinger, C.A. (1990). Effects of in vivo emotive imagery and performance feedback on self-efficacy and muscular endurance. *Journal of Sport and Exercise Psychology*, *12*, 132–143.

Gould, D., Horn, T., & Spreemann, J. (1983). Sources of stress in junior elite wrestlers. *Journal of Sport Psychology*, *5*, 159–171.

Hackney, A.C., Pearman, S.N., III, & Nowacki, J.M. (1990). Physiological profiles of overtrained and stale athletes: A review. *Journal of Applied Sport Psychology*, *2*(1), 21–33.

Hall, C.R., Rodgers, W.M., & Barr, K.A. (1990). The use of imagery by athletes in selected sports. *The Sport Psychologist*, *4*, 1–10.

Hall, K.H., & Hill, A.P. (2012): Perfectionism, dysfunctional achievement striving, and burnout in aspiring athletes: The motivational implications for performing artists. *Theatre, Dance and Performance Training*, *3*(2), 216–228.

Hamilton, L.H. (1998). Advice for dancers: Emotional counsel and practical strategies. San Francisco: Jossey-Bass.

Harris, D.V. (2010). Relaxation and energizing techniques for regulation of arousal. In J.M. Williams (Ed.), *Applied sport psychology: Personal growth to peak performance* (pp. 185–207). Palo Alto, CA: Mayfield.

Hatfield, B.D., & Landers, D.M. (1983). Psychophysiology—A new direction for sport psychology. *Journal of Sport Psychology, 5,* 243–259.

Koutedakis, Y. (2000). Burnout in dance: The physiological viewpoint. *Journal of Dance Medicine & Science, 4*(4), 122–127.

Koutedakis, Y., & Jamurtas, A. (2004). The dancer as a performing athlete: Physiological considerations. *Sports Medicine, 34*(10), 651–661.

Koutedakis, Y., Myszkewycz, D., Soulas, D., Papapostolou, V., & Sullivan I. (1999). The effects of rest and subsequent training on selected parameters in professional female classical dancers. *International Journal of Sports Medicine, 20*(6), 379–383.

Kreider, R.B., Fry, A.C., & O'Toole, M.L. (1998). *Overtraining in sport.* Champaign; IL: Human Kinetics.

Lemyre, P.N., Treasure, D.C., & Roberts, G.C. (2006). Influence of variability in motivation and affect on elite athlete burnout susceptibility. *Journal of Sport & Exercise Psychology, 28*(1), 32–48.

Maslach, C., & Leiter, M.P. (1997). *The truth about burnout.* San Francisco: Jossey-Bass.

Miner, J.M., Shelley, G.A., & Henschen, K.P. (1999). *Moving toward your potential: An athlete's guide to peak performance.* Palo Alto: CA; Performance/Personal Solutions.

Mummery, W.K., Schofield, G., & Perry, C. (2004). Bouncing back: The role of coping style, social support, and self-concept in resilience of sport performance. *Athletic Insight: The Online Journal of Sport Psychology, 6*(3), 1–18.

O'Toole, M.L. (1998). Overreaching and overtraining in endurance athletes. In R.B. Kreider, A.C. Fry, & M.L. O'Toole (Eds.), *Overtraining in sport* (pp. 47–62). Champaign, IL: Human Kinetics.

Poczwardowski, A., & Conroy, D.E. (2002). Coping responses to failure and success among elite athletes and performing artists. *Journal of Applied Sport Psychology, 14*(4), 313–329.

Quested, E., Bosch, J.A., Burns, V.E., Cummings, J., Ntoumanis, N., & Duda, J.L. (2011). Basic psychological need satisfaction, stress-related appraisals, and dancers' cortisol and anxiety responses. *Journal of Sport and Exercise Psychology, 33*, 828–846.

Quested, E., & Duda, J.L. (2010). Exploring the social-environmental determinants of well- and ill-being in dancers: A test of basic needs theory. *Journal of Sport & Exercise Psychology, 32*(1), 39–60.

Quested, E., & Duda, J.L. (2011). Antecedents of burnout among elite dancers: A longitudinal test of basic needs theory. *Psychology of Sport and Exercise, 12*, 159–167.

Radetsky, S. (2012, April). Breaking Free. *Dance Magazine.* www.dancemagazine.com/issues/April-2012/Breaking-Free.

Raedeke, T.D., & Smith, A.L. (2001). Development and preliminary validation of an athlete burnout measure. *Journal of Sport and Exercise Psychology, 23*(4), 281–306.

Rist, R. (2006, March). Dealing with burnout. *Dance Teacher Magazine.* www.dance-teacher.com/2006/03/dealing-with-burnout/.

Schnitt, D. (1990, November/December). Psychological issues in dancers—An overview. *Journal of Physical Education, Recreation, and Dance,* 32-34.

Silva, J.M., III. (1990). An analysis of the training stress syndrome in competitive athletics. *Journal of Applied Sport Psychology,* 2(1), 5-20.

Wehlage, D.F. (1980). Managing the emotional reactions to loss in athletics. *Athletic Training, 15,* 144-146.

Weinberg, R.S., & Ragan, J. (1979). Effects of competition, success/failure, and sex on intrinsic motivation. *Research Quarterly, 50,* 503-510.

13

Pain and Injury

"There are three steps you have to complete to become a professional dancer: learn to dance, learn to perform, and learn how to cope with injuries."

Mikko Nissinen, artistic director, Boston Ballet

As a dancer, you must face the considerable obstacle of pain. In all likelihood, you will experience some degree of pain in every class, rehearsal, and performance—if for no other reason, simply because of the physical demands that dance puts on you. Though pain is unpleasant, it plays an essential and valuable role in your dance training and performance. As you push yourself physically to perform at your highest level, pain gives you valuable information about your dance training efforts and your performance, offering a powerful and persistent physical warning to your body. It's up to you whether you approach pain as an ally that helps you pursue your dance goals or as an enemy that keeps you from realizing your dreams. Your choice depends on your understanding of pain and on whether you gain mastery over pain.

Putting Pain in Perspective

Using pain to your advantage starts with gaining a realistic perspective on it. This process begins with understanding the difference between suffering, injury pain, and exertion pain. Believing that you're suffering in pursuit of artistic expression may inspire you, but the reality is that what you experience isn't suffering. People with cancer suffer, because their pain is severe, long lasting, life threatening, and largely uncontrollable. In contrast, what you normally feel in dance training and performance may not even be pain. Real pain comes from injury. It is similar to suffering and can be severe, but it is not usually life threatening; in addition, it typically doesn't last as long, and it can be controlled much more easily.

What you feel most often in dance, however, is exertion pain or soreness, which is significant physical discomfort caused by efforts in your dance training and performances. It hurts, and it can interfere with your efforts, but it is largely within your control because you can ease the discomfort any time you want to by simply slowing down or stopping. It is always temporary, so even when soreness or exertion pain is extreme, knowing it will pass is also helpful psychologically. For simplicity's sake, though, let's continue to refer to this experience as pain since that term is commonly used for it. But you know now what it really is—mere exertion pain—and that perspective is your first step toward mastering pain.

Distinguishing Injury Pain From Exertion Pain

Due to the rigors of dance training and performance, you will experience some degree of pain on a regular basis during your dance career. Whether a given pain results from injury or exertion, the type of pain you feel determines how it affects you and how you should respond to it. Pain can be either an ally or an enemy depending on the type of pain, how you perceive it, and how you react to it.

Injury Pain

You experience injury pain when you sustain physical damage to a part of your body. Of course, pain that results from injury can have important ramifications for your physical ability to train and perform. It can also hurt you psychologically by reducing motivation and confidence, increasing anxiety, and causing worry and frustration.

Injuries that cause significant pain can be felt in two ways. First, pain due to overuse injuries usually starts with a dull, generalized ache in a certain area of your body. For dancers, common overuse injuries occur in the feet, ankles, lower legs, knees, and hips. Because this pain is usually not acute at first, it is often ignored and may not even be perceived as injury pain. Unlike exertion pain, however, if it is severe enough and is not treated immediately, injury pain becomes more intense, more localized, and more acute. Therefore, if you experience pain that does not abate in a few days, seek medical treatment so that the injury doesn't become a chronic problem that limits your dancing in the long term.

Second, you may experience pain caused by an injury due to an acute incident, such as a fall or twist. This type of injury pain is unmistakable: sudden, intense, and localized. Most dancers recognize when they have "done something," because this type of pain is usually so uncomfortable and intense that it can't be ignored. Indeed, it often prevents them from continuing to dance. Pain resulting from an acute injury usually requires immediate medical attention.

Exertion Pain and Postperformance Pain

Unlike injury pain, most exertion pain is dull and more generalized and doesn't last long after exertion. Therefore, it is produced voluntarily, lies entirely within your control, and can be reduced at will. Another type of exertion pain, referred to as postperformance pain, consists of the soreness and stiffness that you feel after a particularly difficult class or rehearsal in which the exercises or choreography placed unusually strenuous demands on your body.

As compared with injury pain, exertion pain has a decidedly different psychological effect on you. Whereas injury pain seems threatening and can cause considerable distress, exertion pain is often perceived positively as a validation of your effort and even as a source of satisfaction and inspiration. This attitude toward exertion pain breeds increased motivation and confidence, as well as generally positive emotions that can facilitate performance.

Moreover, postperformance pain, though annoying, can also serve as a source of satisfaction and feedback about the intensity of your dance training. That being said, it might be wise to listen to your body and take some conservative action if you are experiencing exertion pain and must return to the studio or the stage the following day. Take time to stretch, use heating pads, and allow yourself to gradually ease into movement.

These simple distinctions between types of pain can help you identify the true nature of the pain you experience in your training and performances. In addition, your understanding of these differences affects how you perceive them (positively or negatively), evaluate them (as benign or harmful), and respond to them (with continued effort, by easing up, or by stopping and seeking medical attention).

Interpreting Pain

The next step in overcoming pain is to understand two facets of it that influence your perception of it: the physical and the psychological. Of course, pain involves a physical experience that you have to tolerate in your training and performances. The pain you feel is real and communicates important messages about your body. But you don't feel pain directly from your body, and this is where the psychological component comes into play. Your mind acts as a filter for the pain. Indeed, the pain you feel is affected by how you interpret it, what you think about it, and what emotions you connect to it. Moreover, the way in which you interpret your pain can either act as an obstacle to achieving your dance goals or propel you to new and higher levels of dance performance.

Ignoring Pain

Many dancers try to ignore pain based on the rationale that if they don't think about their pain, then it won't affect them as much. Instead, these dancers focus on listening to music, talking to classmates or rehearsal partners, or just thinking about other things. This form of distraction can work when pain first appears, especially with exertion pain, which may not be severe and may not have been around for very long. However, ignoring pain as a long-term strategy is both ineffective and harmful. As pain grows and becomes more persistent, it simply can't be ignored. It insinuates itself into your mind and screams to be heard.

In addition, when you ignore pain, you turn away from potentially valuable information about how your body is doing. For example, you may be making a movement that hurts or strains your body, pushing yourself too hard, or risking an injury. Therefore, "spacing out" in dance is never a good option because you must constantly monitor your body and your movements.

Your interpretation of pain is also influenced by other factors that can further complicate your understanding and management of it. For one thing, pain is a subjective experience, and people vary greatly in their tolerance of pain. In addition, pain is affected by a wide variety of physical, psychological, and social influences such as location of pain, intensity, support from others, and how teachers and other dancers talk about pain. Nor can it be directly measured; as a result, it is difficult for others to evaluate the severity of your pain and determine the best way to manage it (pharmacologically or otherwise).

Finally, most highly committed dancers develop a high threshold for pain that can interfere with their ability to recognize when pushing through the pain may be more dangerous than beneficial. Therefore, knowing yourself and tuning in to your body and its signals can make the difference between being held back by pain and dancing your very best.

Pain as Your Enemy

Pain becomes your enemy when you perceive it negatively, as something that threatens you and must be avoided. Negative perceptions of pain often take the form of negative thinking: "Pain is terrible." "Pain means I'm weak." "Pain means I will fail." "This pain means I won't be able to dance." Thinking of pain in this way may cause you to lose confidence and motivation, experience anxiety, and become consumed by the pain—all of which prevents you from dancing your best.

When you're conditioning your body, dancing through all those demanding classes and grueling rehearsals, you may also start to question yourself: "This hurts too much. I hate this. What am I doing here?" As with negative perceptions, research has shown that negative self-talk also increases your pain, reduces your desire to fight through the pain, and limits the benefits that you gain from training.

Similar research has found that pain is also affected by the emotions you connect with it. For example, like all dancers, you've probably felt pain (tiredness or soreness) during a strenuous rehearsal. Perhaps you were frustrated to be hurting and questioned your ability to push through. Perhaps you got angry at yourself for not training harder or not being in "better shape." When you connect such negative emotions with your pain, you feel more pain.

Pain as Your Ally

Making pain your ally is one of the best things that you can do to achieve your dance performance goals. This process starts with recognizing that pain is a normal and necessary part of training and performing. Exertion pain or soreness mean that you're challenging yourself and working hard to move toward your goals.

Pain becomes your ally through experience. If you are new to dance, the increasing pain you feel in your training and performance may alarm you because these uncomfortable sensations are new to you. However, as you gain experience with pain, you become better able to deal with it. You learn how pain affects your body and your mind—what your body feels and how your mind reacts.

One of the most important ways that pain can be your ally is by learning to distinguish injury pain from exertion pain, which allows you to make smarter choices in your dance training. Learn how to manage your pain more effectively—what reduces it and what makes it worse.

Another way to make pain your ally is to use it as information during your classes, rehearsals, and performances. Pain offers you a wealth of valuable information that you can use to get the most out of your dance efforts. It tells you how hard you're working and whether what you're feeling is due to exertion or injury. It also gives you direct information about your pace, technique, body position, posture, nutrition, hydration, and tactics.

Responding constructively to this information can help you in various ways. For example, when you feel faint, you can eat a snack and drink something to nourish and hydrate your body. When you feel the pain of straining too much, you can lower your effort and intensity. And if you experience acute pain, you can inform the choreographer, teacher, or director in order to help him or her understand your alignment and technique or recognize that a movement is dangerous to your body. Thus, using pain as a source of information can help you avoid injury and improve your technique, artistry, and performance.

> *"It's kind of a humbling experience. . . . You remember that you are human and that your body is fragile. I have learned to listen more because I realize now that if I would have listened to my knees and gone to get a second opinion, I could have prevented this moderate-to-severe stage [of degeneration]. I was used to being able to do whatever I wanted. I was used to being able to push my body without a lot of severe consequence. . . . It's something I'm really conscious of now, especially in the way I work."*
>
> Meredith, professional dancer

Mastering Exertion Pain

Exertion pain can hurt your dance both physically and psychologically. Physically, it causes muscle tension, inhibits your movements, interferes with your technique and choreography, and hinders your efforts in classes, rehearsals, and performances. Psychologically, exertion pain can lower your motivation and confidence, alter your intensity, distract you, and produce unhealthy emotions, such as anger and despair. Fortunately, rather than succumbing to exertion pain or soreness, you can employ several strategies to reduce your experience of it, thus enabling you to persist in the face of the discomfort and maintain your highest level of artistry and excellence.

Reframing the Pain

Your instinctive reaction to exertion pain is to see it as a bad thing that must be avoided. In fact, we're hardwired to avoid pain as an indicator of a threat to our survival. As a result, our immediate reaction is to connect pain with negative thoughts (e.g., "this is terrible") and negative emotions (e.g., frustration, fear). Yet, research has found that when we connect pain to negative thoughts and emotions, we feel more pain.

If, on the other hand, we reframe the experience of exertion pain or soreness, we feel less of it. With this fact in mind, instead of seeing pain as an awful thing, you can interpret it positively—for example, as an indication of your great efforts to achieve your goals or as an epic battle to overcome long odds. In turn, these positive thoughts generate positive emotions related to the pain, such as inspiration and pride which, as research has shown, reduce the intensity of pain. Therefore, simply by changing the way you perceive exertion pain, you can make it more manageable.

Breathing Deeply

Perhaps the simplest, most essential, yet most neglected technique for reducing exertion pain is deep breathing. This necessity of life is often overlooked because people do not always understand the relationship between breathing, physiological changes, and the experience of pain.

Deep breathing provides a number of fundamental benefits. Pain inhibits breathing, which lessens blood flow and causes muscle spasms and bracing. Thus the lack of sufficient oxygen in the system leads to more muscle tension and a concomitant increase in pain. Deep breathing, on the other hand, diminishes anxiety and tension by transporting sufficient oxygen throughout the body, relaxes the muscles, and increases generalized parasympathetic nervous system activity. Deep breathing also acts as an internal distraction: If you focus on your breathing, you pay less attention to your pain.

For these reasons, deep breathing can be a valuable addition to various aspects of dance training, including classes and rehearsals. You can incorporate it at the beginning and end of exercises and pieces of choreography in order to slow the arrival of exertion pain and reduce it when it does occur.

Relaxing Your Muscles

Exertion pain produces various forms of muscle tension that restrict blood flow and increase your experience of pain. You can relieve both the tension and the pain by intervening directly through muscle relaxation. Two relaxation techniques—passive relaxation and active (progressive) relaxation—serve as effective tools for reducing muscle tension and increasing an overall sense of physical calm and comfort (see chapter 5).

You can use muscle relaxation in a variety of settings to manage your exertion pain. For example, it is a useful strategy before a class or rehearsal in which exertion pain is likely to occur. Beginning in a more relaxed state slows the rise of exertion pain as your efforts increase. During the session, using muscle relaxation during breaks can help you gain control of exertion pain as soon as it appears, thus enabling you to maintain your efforts through the conclusion of the class or rehearsal.

Muscle relaxation training can also be comforting after a physically demanding class, rehearsal, or performance when exertion pain is high and available resources for managing it are low. Making time to induce relaxation at the end of your dancing provides both physical and psychological benefits. Physically, it decreases exertion pain and helps you return to a general sense of physical comfort and well-being. Psychologically, it diminishes any negative thoughts or emotions associated with your exertion pain, thus helping you view the pain in a positive light that inspires you in your upcoming dance efforts.

Dance-Related Injuries

Given the physical demands of dance, there is little doubt that you will sustain a dance-related injury at some point in your career. Dancers are prone to injury for several reasons. First, dance is often not seasonal; therefore, many dancers rehearse and perform throughout the year. This schedule denies them the opportunity to rest and recover from the stresses of dance. In addition, dance has become so competitive that many dancers feel pressure to dance in spite of an injury rather than take time to rehabilitate and recover. They do so because they fear missing classes and rehearsals and, even worse, losing out on a coveted role or being terminated by a company.

For these reasons, many dancers rationalize the decision to try to dance through their injuries. As a result, they may fall into a routine of dancing while taking painkillers or being taped, massaged, stretched, and sometimes artificially numbed with anesthetic or cortisone shots. However, ignoring pain often allows an injury to worsen and thus proves to be self-defeating; moreover, it can ultimately result in spending more time away from dance and suffering greater setbacks in your dance career.

Fortunately, the medical field has developed surgical and rehabilitative technology to such an extent that full physical recovery can be expected in most cases, even with injuries that would have been career ending just 10 years ago. In reality, however, dancers often do not return to their preinjury level of performance, even when all measurable aspects of the injured area indicate full recovery of stability, strength, and flexibility. This performance deficit may be due to psychological damage related to the injury and a failure to rehabilitate psychological factors that influence performance.

Emotional Reactions to Injury

A severe injury can be devastating because it poses a real threat to your identity as a dancer. If dancing gives you, for example, a great sense of mastery, control, satisfaction, and recognition, then an injury can destabilize your sense of self. The emotions discussed in the following sections are not all experienced by every dancer, nor are they experienced in the same degree by everyone or necessarily in the order in which they are presented here. However, depending on the severity of your injury, you are likely to experience at least some of them to some degree.

Numbness and Denial

At times, the numbness you feel after sustaining an injury can serve as an adaptive emotional response that protects you from immediate shock and turmoil. It allows you to calmly take stock of what has just happened, tune into your body, and make appropriate decisions to respond constructively to the injury. At the same time, this emotional numbness can also enable you to deny the injury, thereby exposing yourself to more damage in the long term. Therefore, it is crucial for you to recognize this numbness as a double-edged sword that is associated with both benefits and risks.

Most studies have found that, in general, dancers are more likely than average to either avoid seeking medical treatment or delay seeking it until their injury progresses to a severe state. Most dancers try to manage the injury themselves, often by dancing through the pain, which ultimately puts them at higher risk for a more severe or even career-ending injury. Therefore, it is best to avoid letting emotional numbness cloud your judgment. Instead, err on the side of caution; doing so can speed up your recovery and your return to dance and thereby reduce the effect of the injury on your dance career.

Fear

As an injury's severity becomes impossible for you to ignore, fear may creep into your psyche. Fear may be the most overwhelming emotion for dancers because it evokes uncertainty and what-if thinking. Fear can also be debilitating because it can paralyze you and prevent you from fully confronting the injury and taking the necessary action to treat it. This fearful state can even escalate to panic if you focus on worst-case scenarios rather than on addressing the injury constructively.

Guilt, Shame, and Jealousy

Though not every dancer experiences guilt, shame, and jealousy, many dancers do struggle with these powerful feelings after an injury. These emotions can arise from your own beliefs and expectations or be triggered by messages received from family members, dance teachers, or peers. Regardless of their source, they can make you feel truly terrible and inhibit your emotional and physical healing.

When an injury results in extended time out of the studio and off of the stage, many dancers blame themselves and feel guilt and shame for being unable to dance. Feelings of guilt might also result from jealousy of other dancers or perception of fault for their own injuries. These emotions can arise from any of several sources. For example, you may worry that the injury will put an end to your dreams in dance. You may fear that you will be seen by your instructor, choreographer, or ballet master or mistress as weak and lacking in commitment and determination. You may also believe that you are letting down your family and friends who have supported you.

Some injured dancers also report feeling jealousy toward peers who are able to continue dancing. Though this reaction is understandable if you are grieving your own body's inability to dance, it indicates an external focus that not only keeps you in an unhealthy emotional state but also prevents you from focusing on what you need to do in order to recover and return to dance as soon as possible. If you experience these feelings, recognize that they are normal parts of the emotional healing process and that you should seek support and professional help so that they don't impede your recovery and return to the stage.

Grief

Injury exacts a powerful emotional toll because it deprives you, at least temporarily, of something that you hold dear. Acknowledge your feelings as a natural part of the injury and rehabilitation process and allow yourself to grieve for your loss. When you deny yourself permission to grieve, you can end up dwelling on the injury, thus failing to put it where it belongs—in the past.

The grieving process is experienced differently and with varying degrees of intensity by different people, but it usually includes feelings of shock, sadness, anger, shame, and guilt. When you allow yourself to go through the journey of grieving, however unpleasant it may be, the process helps you come to terms with your injury and enables you to direct your attention away from the injury and toward your recovery and return to dance.

Psychological Factors in Injury Rehabilitation

In addition to the emotions just described, your mind can also sustain a sort of damage from a physical injury. The areas involved parallel the prime dance pyramid factors addressed throughout this book—the motivation, confidence, intensity, focus, and emotional mastery that are essential to dance performance. Moreover, you can think of injury rehabilitation as a form of performance in itself. With this mind-set, you can apply the same tools that you use to maximize your dance performance in order to maximize your efforts to recover from your injury.

In addition, the prime dance pyramid factors are not distinct entities; rather, they are connected to and influence each other. For example, if you maintain your motivation and confidence during your rehabilitation, you are likely to be less anxious and less prone to negative emotions, such as frustration and despair. In this way, when you improve one psychological area, you may also improve others without direct intervention.

Motivation

Due to the length and intensity of the rehabilitation process, you must establish and maintain a high level of motivation in your recovery efforts. This task is often made difficult by the frustrations associated with injury. In particular, dancers are likely to struggle if they are impatient or have experienced severe disappointment and frustration regarding their progress. Motivation can also be reduced by lack of confidence in the rehabilitation program, anxiety about recovery, and problems with staying focused on progress. In turn, any reduction in motivation interferes with your rehabilitation and delays your full recovery. Lack of motivation can also lead to despair or depression, thus causing you to give up your efforts. For all of these reasons, motivation is the single most important factor in achieving a timely and full recovery.

To develop and maintain your motivation to return to the stage, you can use many of the strategies described in chapter 3, including the three Ds, as well as goal setting, focusing on your long-term goal, establishing a support system, finding a rehab partner, recognizing small victories, and asking yourself daily whether you're doing everything you can to recover fully and return to dance. You may find it particularly helpful to apply the goal-setting process to your rehabilitation. In fact, we encourage you to set goals for

Observing or marking in class while injured can help refine your technique.

every phase and aspect of your recovery in order to maximize your motivation, confidence, and focus as you get healthy and return to dance (this process is discussed in more detail a bit later in the chapter).

Confidence

Confidence is important because it affects all other psychological factors related to injury rehabilitation. Confidence is necessary at two levels of the rehabilitation process. First, when you're injured, you need to have confidence in your ability to adhere to and complete the long and often-painful physical rehabilitation program. A lack of confidence reduces adherence to the program because if you do not believe that you can fully recover, even through an extensive rehabilitation program, it will not seem to be worth the work. Second, you must believe that if you complete the rehabilitation program you will perform again at a high level. Again, if you lack this belief, you will see little reason to work hard in your rehabilitation program.

To rehabilitate the confidence "muscle" that has been damaged by your physical injury, you can use the techniques discussed in chapter 4. These approaches include using positive self-talk and body language, getting support from others, and acknowledging small victories in your recovery efforts (e.g., improving your range of movement or strength).

Anxiety

The experience of suffering a serious injury and going through a lengthy recovery can provoke anxiety in many ways. As a result, your intensity is more often higher rather than lower. The most obvious cause for this anxious intensity is the pain associated with the injury. Inevitably, the rehabilitation program requires you to deal with the pain that results from the injury itself and from the exercises that make up the program. This pain places tremendous stress on your body, which can be very uncomfortable, and it can inhibit the healing process.

Anxiety can also result from doubt and worry about whether you will be able to fully recover from your injury and return to dance. As discussed a bit earlier, the amount of anxiety you experience is affected by your level of confidence in adhering to your rehabilitation program, your level of belief that you can recover fully, and your fears about being unable to return to your preinjury level of dance.

The recovery process also produces anxiety because the injury deprives you of certain aspects of your life that are rewarding and affirming. Now absent from your life are the psychological and emotional rewards of dance; the physical benefits of class, rehearsal, and performance; and the daily camaraderie and friendship with other dancers. Therefore, while you're injured, not only must you endure the difficulties associated with the injury and the recovery themselves, but also you must do so in an environment that is no longer so reinforcing.

As if all of that weren't enough, anxiety does not stop when the rehabilitation program is completed and full recovery seems apparent. To the contrary, it is not uncommon for injured dancers to have new anxiety-provoking worries when they return to the studio and the stage. Foremost among these worries is doubt about their ability to return to preinjury form. Again, this worry relates to confidence, which takes time to rebuild.

You may also fear reinjury during your post-injury training and performance. This worry can hurt your confidence in your ability to dance, inhibit your commitment to complete technique and movement, and distract you from effective performance focus—all of which, ironically, can increase your risk of reinjury. As you can see, then, a vicious cycle of struggles with anxiety, motivation, confidence, and focus can prevent you from reaching and surpassing your preinjury dance form.

The symptoms of anxiety also exert a debilitating effect directly on the body. For example, anxiety produces a restriction of the breathing system, thus impairing the intake of oxygen. Without sufficient oxygen, the body's healing system does not work effectively. Anxiety also causes muscle tension, which increases pain and reduces blood flow to the injured area. Happily, you can actively counter the debilitating physical effects of anxiety by using the methods described in chapter 5, including deep breathing, muscle relaxation, and the use of music, as well as meditation and massage.

Focus

The quality of your rehabilitation is also affected by whether or not you focus effectively. Dancers tend to focus on the negative aspects of an injury rather than on the positive aspects of the recovery. This focus undermines confidence and motivation and results in your giving less than full effort in your program's exercises. A negative focus can also lead to increased worry and anxiety, both of which slow your recovery process.

Focus is also important during postrecovery training and performance. Focusing on the injured area rather than on performance increases the likelihood of reinjury. It also reduces confidence and increases anxiety, which further increases the potential for reinjury. Therefore, in order to maintain your motivation and work effectively during your rehabilitation and postrecovery training, you need to focus on three things: your long-term goals; the particular exercise, technique, or choreography you are engaged in at the moment; and the positive aspects of your recovery and eventual return to dance.

Injury Rehabilitation Strategies

A serious injury produces both physical and psychological damage. Therefore, in order to achieve full recovery, you must implement both a well-organized physical rehabilitation program and a structured psychological rehabilitation program. This psychological program should be similar to the individualized dance program aimed at enhancing your dance performance, and it can follow the same basic procedure (see chapter 11). The psychological component of your rehabilitation program supports your physical efforts to achieve full recovery and heals any psychological damage resulting from the injury (refer to the Pain and Injury Management Strategies worksheet in the web resource).

Your injury rehabilitation program should include five primary strategies for pain and injury management: scheduling, goal setting, relaxation training, dance imagery, and a variety of general prime dance techniques. These approaches enable you to optimize the psychological areas prone to be harmed by an injury, thereby increasing the speed and quality of your recovery process.

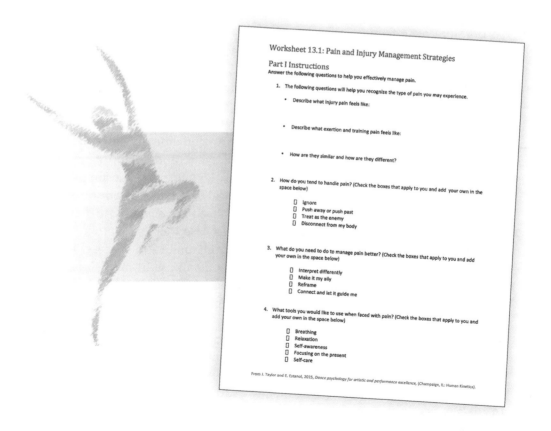

Worksheet 13.1: Pain and Injury Management Strategies

Part I Instructions

Answer the following questions to help you effectively manage pain.

1. The following questions will help you recognize the type of pain you may experience.

   • Describe what injury pain feels like:

   • Describe what exertion and training pain feels like:

   • How are they similar and how are they different?

2. How do you tend to handle pain? (Check the boxes that apply to you and add your own in the space below)

   ☐ Ignore
   ☐ Push away or push past
   ☐ Treat as the enemy
   ☐ Disconnect from my body

3. What do you need to do to manage pain better? (Check the boxes that apply to you and add your own in the space below)

   ☐ Interpret differently
   ☐ Make it my ally
   ☐ Reframe
   ☐ Connect and let it guide me

4. What tools you would like to use when faced with pain? (Check the boxes that apply to you and add your own in the space below)

   ☐ Breathing
   ☐ Relaxation
   ☐ Self-awareness
   ☐ Focusing on the present
   ☐ Self-care

From J. Taylor and E. Estanol, 2015, *Dance psychology for artistic and performance excellence*, (Champaign, IL: Human Kinetics).

Scheduling

Create a schedule that includes all of your appointments with care providers—for example, your physical therapist, doctor, massage therapist, chiropractor, sport psychologist, and nutritionist, as well as any other health care practitioner. This array of appointments can be overwhelming when combined with the other aspects of your life. To ease the pressure, look for compromises, such as doubling up your activities; for example, perhaps you can do some of your mental training during part of a physical therapy or massage session. In addition, make time to eat well and hydrate yourself so that your body can heal properly.

As you manage these various factors, you may need to try several schedules in order to find one that allows you to attend to your body without getting overwhelmed and even more stressed out. To meet this challenge, perhaps another good double-up activity would be to use relaxation and breathing exercises that reduce the stress hormones in your body and thus help it heal.

Goal Setting

To organize an effective prime dance injury rehabilitation program, set a variety of goals that give you direction and focus. As discussed in chapter 8, goal setting provides several benefits, which also apply to recovery from injury. They include increased commitment and motivation, a feeling of increased control over your situation, improved focus on key factors, and a clear path to achieving your goal—in this case, full recovery from your injury.

More specifically, goal setting provides you with deliberate steps in three areas of your rehabilitation: physical, psychological, and performance. Set your physical recovery goals in collaboration with your rehabilitation professional in order to ensure that they are realistic and beneficial to your recovery. Your psychological recovery goals should be based on perceived deficits in your motivation, confidence, anxiety, and focus. Use these goals to address anything in these areas that would inhibit your rehabilitation process. These goals should identify relevant techniques that you can use from this book.

You should also establish performance goals to minimize the deterioration of your current physical, technical, and psychological capabilities. Set goals for your overall physical fitness to help you return to dance in top condition when your recovery from injury is complete. To this end, in addition to your physical therapy, you can engage in a conditioning program. You can also continue to develop yourself as a dancer by working on technique around the injury—for example, working on upper body, arm, and head position while rehabilitating an ankle injury. In setting technical goals, ask your teacher or artistic director what she or he would like to see you improve on. You can address technical skills through dance imagery (see chapter 9), live and video observation of other dancers, and limited practice within the constraints of your recovery.

During your recovery, you can also focus on and improve psychological and emotional areas that affect your performance. Ask your teachers and fellow dancers to help you identify your psychological strengths and areas in which you can improve, and then address them using the many prime dance techniques discussed in this book. You might also seek help from a dance psychologist, who can guide you more completely through your psychological and emotional rehabilitation. The purpose of this approach is to help you be even more psychologically prepared to dance your best when you recover from your injury than you were before it.

Finally, set goals related to your return to the stage. You should not immediately expect to regain your preinjury level or to take on demanding roles. Instead, set a series of performance goals that move you progressively toward your desired level of performance.

Relaxation

Relaxation is an important technique for promoting your healing and return to dance. Research has shown that greater anxiety means slower rehabilitation. As discussed earlier, anxiety can result from a variety of sources related to the difficulty of the rehabilitation process and to concerns about spending time away from the studio and stage. A further difficulty lies in the fact that anxiety may not manifest itself clearly enough for you or others to see it. In fact, you may not feel it distinctly, yet even so it can have a dramatic effect on your rehabilitation process. As a result, it is a good idea to assume that you will experience anxiety and to take proactive steps to address it (see chapter 5 for specific anxiety-relieving techniques).

Healing Imagery

As discussed in chapter 9, mental imagery is a powerful tool for improving the physical, technical, and psychological aspects of your dance. It is also important for your recovery in order to promote healing and regain your preinjury level of performance. There is even some evidence to indicate that imagery may actually assist in the healing process. It has been used to fight cancer and a variety of other illnesses. It has also been shown to alter body temperature and increase blood flow.

To use imagery to enhance your recovery from injury, you need to fully understand the damaged area and how the healing process works. In addition, because imagery is largely visual, you need to have a visual representation of the injured area. Therefore, we encourage you to ask your physician or physical therapist to give you a detailed description of the injury and an illustration of the area, perhaps in the form of X rays or diagrams. With this understanding in mind, you can use the guidance provided in chapter 9 to develop a program of dance imagery for injury, in which you see and feel the injured area healing and becoming whole and strong again.

You can also use imagery to maintain your dance performance even while you're unable to train. This function is valuable because injury not only deprives you of precious training and performance time but also causes you to lose ground that you had gained prior to the injury. You can minimize these losses by implementing a performance-oriented dance imagery program. As discussed in chapter 9, you can use imagery to produce skill and performance improvements without physical practice. Imagery can also help you stay psychologically and emotionally sharp by seeing and feeling yourself continue to perform. Thus, dance imagery allows you to actively continue becoming a better dancer—technically, artistically, and psychologically—during your recovery.

If you're recovering from a serious injury that keeps you away from the studio for an extended period, we suggest that you use healing imagery and performance imagery on alternating days. Most important, your dance imagery should be structured as a regular and necessary part of your rehabilitation program.

Confidence

An injury can take a toll on your confidence. Specifically, doubt, worry, and negativity can conspire to slow your recovery and prevent you from returning to, much less exceeding, your preinjury level of dance. Fortunately, as part of your injury rehabilitation program, you can heal your confidence as you prepare to return to the studio and stage.

Just as negative thoughts can interfere with your recovery, positive thoughts can bolster your rehabilitation efforts. What you say to yourself about your injury and recovery influences you in every psychological area. Positive thoughts help you become more motivated, relaxed, and focused, and they associate positive emotions with what can otherwise be a discouraging experience. Positive self-talk—"I'm getting better every day," "I'm coming back stronger than ever," "I'm working toward my goals"—helps you remain resolute as you continue on the often-bumpy road to recovery.

Associating your rehabilitation with positive emotions is a particularly powerful way to build and maintain your confidence during recovery. It can be difficult to feel good about recovery when you're faced with pain, the absence of something you love, and the resulting isolation. At the same time, your ability to create positive emotions as you heal can benefit you in several ways. If you experience positive emotions, you feel more confident, relaxed, and motivated. As discussed earlier in the chapter, you also feel less pain, because positive emotions release painkilling neurochemicals called endorphins that reduce both the physical reality and the perception of pain. In these ways, positive emotions can make your entire rehabilitation—by definition, an unpleasant experience—a bit more pleasant.

You may wonder, given that you're in pain and not disposed to feel happy, what positive emotions you can realistically generate. We've found two that are most beneficial: inspiration and pride. Inspiration is our favorite positive emotion to experience during recovery from injury. In this framework, you view the pain you feel as part of an epic challenge to overcome your injury and achieve your dance goals. The pain you experience in physical therapy tells you that you're working intensely and progressing toward your dance dreams. The more pain you feel, the more meaning and satisfaction you have after your rehabilitation sessions.

To facilitate this process, we suggest using a two-pronged strategy that combines positive self-talk with positive emotions. When you're in a lot of pain—for example, during a boring and grueling physical therapy session—you can say to yourself, "The more of these boring exercises I do, the sooner I'll be back onstage." Reminding yourself of the reasons for your efforts enables you to feel inspired by the pain.

You can also find inspiration in positive memories, such as challenging classes, mastery of difficult choreography, and outstanding performances you made before your injury. Recalling these exceptional dance experiences—through imagery, photographs, or video—reminds you of your enjoyment of movement, artistry, and music and inspires you to stay committed to your recovery.

Pride is another emotion that you can realistically conjure when you're in pain. Pride is a feeling of satisfaction in your efforts and accomplishments. When you're struggling through a physical therapy session, focus on your ultimate goal. Remember that the effort you're expending and the pain you're experiencing are moving you another step closer to your goal of returning to the stage.

"I was returning to the stage after recovering from a broken foot eight weeks earlier. My body still felt foreign, and I didn't exactly trust it to heed my commands. But as the curtain rose on the stunningly beautiful house with its old-world balconies, there was no turning back. Like Ariadne, the dance's heroine, I had to take those steps into the maze and conquer my own fears—the fear of hurting my body again or that my foot would not respond when I needed it most. As I stood alone onstage, taking that first shift up and down, I felt the audience with me, with Ariadne. They wanted this journey too, for themselves. We all understand the significance of a first step."

Blakeley White-McGuire, Martha Graham Dance Company

Meditation and Mindfulness Practices

We have worked with several dancers who used the strategy of going to a quiet place and engaging in brief meditation when they were really hurting during their rehabilitation. They would close their eyes, take a deep breath, and mentally transport themselves to a place of calm and tranquility. For one dancer, that place was a beach in the warm sun; for another, a mountain meadow; and for a third, her childhood bedroom. In each of these cases, the dancer found a quiet place that gave comfort and eased the pain.

The dancers described these quiet times as being akin to an out-of-body experience in which they became an observer of their pain rather than experiencing it directly. This mental and emotional distancing was most important when they experienced severe pain during a grueling physical therapy session. One moment, their body was in agony and their mind screaming for it to stop. The next moment, in their quiet place, they experienced a shift, in which the pain, though still present, seemed to be at a distance—felt, but only indirectly—and the noise in their mind ceased. This quiet place allowed them to reduce their experience of pain, maintain their effort, and stay committed to their recovery.

Connection and Support

One of the challenges of rehabilitation lies in the fact that it removes a significant part of your social support system. As a result, it can evoke feelings of isolation and loneliness at a time when you most need support. This loss of meaningful contact can hurt your rehabilitation by making you feel more vulnerable. As a result, you are well advised to actively seek out support from various sources, including family members, friends, peers, teachers, and mental health professionals. The people in these groups can provide you with different types of support to bolster your ongoing efforts to recover.

Meaningful Involvement

One of the most debilitating aspects of a serious injury is that it removes you from the environment that fosters your development as a dancer. This disconnection causes you to lose a powerful source not only of support but also of meaning, satisfaction, and joy in your life. It also causes you to stop developing as a dancer. These elements of loss can be harmful physically, psychologically, and emotionally, and we strongly recommend that you find ways, within the confines of your injury, to maintain meaningful involvement in dance.

There are many ways for you to stay connected to your dance life. You can attend classes and work on aspects of your dance that are unaffected by your injury; for example, if you have a knee injury, you can continue to develop your upper-body technique and artistry. You can also focus on your fitness, further developing your strength, stamina, or flexibility in ways that don't interfere with your recovery. When you keep your body moving, whether through dance classes or a conditioning program, you maintain your physicality and your identity as an active person.

Even if you're unable to dance during part of your recovery, you can stay involved by volunteering to assist in classes, rehearsals, and performances. For example, you can help with makeup and costumes during shows. Admittedly, it can be difficult to watch others dance when you cannot, but this participation can also keep you motivated and focused during your recovery and help you stay attuned to dance when you might otherwise lose touch with it. You can also improve your technique and your understanding of all aspects of dance by observing fellow dancers, teachers, and choreographers in classes, rehearsals, and performances. These actions not only encourage a faster recovery and return to dance but can also help you become a better dancer.

Center Stage: Ethan

Working Toward Physical and Mental Recovery

Ethan, a professional jazz dancer, tore the anterior cruciate ligament of his right knee during a rehearsal for a Broadway show. Doubting whether he would ever dance again, he became despondent and pessimistic about his chances for recovery. In addition, because of his lack of confidence in the recovery process, he experienced considerable anxiety, which increased his experience of pain, thus slowing his progress. Ethan also felt isolated and unsupported because the show's director ignored him and he missed his friends from the show.

In Ethan's first few weeks of rehabilitation, these struggles put him well behind schedule, and his prospects for a complete recovery did not look good. At the suggestion of his physical therapist, he agreed to see a sport psychologist who was trained in injury rehabilitation to help him get back on track. The primary objective for the psychologist was to reduce the anxiety that was interfering with Ethan's healing. To that end, he scheduled relaxation training sessions before and after every physical therapy session and gave Ethan a relaxation recording to use every night before going to sleep.

The psychologist also helped Ethan develop a dance imagery program focused on healing and on maintaining his dance skills. In addition, Ethan chose several prime dance techniques to help build his confidence, reduce his anxiety, and maintain his concentration. He also participated in weekly group meetings for recovering athletes and dancers. The support he received at the meetings gave him considerable relief and helped him develop a more positive outlook about his recovery.

Ethan also returned to the studio and participated in class as much as he could with his injury. He found that he was able to work on technical areas, such as upper-body positioning, that he had never had time for before. He also enjoyed being around his friends again. In addition, he spoke to the director of the show and arranged to take on the responsibility of organizing the dancers and preparing them for their cues during rehearsals and performances.

During the remainder of Ethan's recovery process, he maintained a positive attitude and stayed motivated to adhere to his injury rehabilitation program. As a result, he completed his recovery on schedule. Over time, he not only returned to his previous level of performance but also surpassed it and took on new and more demanding roles.

ENCORE

- Virtually all dancers experience an injury at some point in their career that keeps them out of the studio and off of the stage for an extended period of time.

- Even though surgical and rehabilitative techniques are now so advanced that most dancers can expect a full physical recovery, they do not always return to their preinjury level of performance.

- A postinjury performance deficit may be due to psychological damage from the injury and a failure to rehabilitate psychological factors that influence performance.

- A serious injury can evoke a variety of emotions that inhibit recovery, including numbness (which may lead to denial), fear, guilt, shame, and jealousy.

- Four psychological factors that can either facilitate or impede recovery are motivation, confidence, anxiety, and focus.

- A high level of motivation is critical for enduring the length, discomfort, and challenges of the rehabilitation process.

- Anxiety hurts recovery by increasing pain, reducing motivation and confidence, and producing physical symptoms that inhibit healing.

- During post-rehabilitation training and performance, you need effective focus in order to maintain the necessary motivation and intensity to attend to your dance performance rather than to the injured area.

- Prime dance for injury rehabilitation pursues the goal of optimizing these four psychological factors (motivation, confidence, anxiety, and focus) to ensure a timely recovery.

- An effective injury rehabilitation program involves using five primary strategies: goal setting, relaxation training, dance imagery, social support, scheduling, and a variety of general prime dance techniques.

- Goal setting helps injured dancers increase their commitment, gives them a sense of control, and focuses them on their rehabilitation. It includes two phases: psychological recovery and the return to performance.

- Relaxation training is aimed at reducing the anxiety and pain that inhibit the healing process.

- Dance imagery can be used to promote the healing process and minimize deterioration of dance skills and artistry.

- Social support includes three areas that facilitate recovery: support among injured dancers, group discussions with dancers who have recovered from injury, and continued involvement of injured dancers in the life of the studio.

- Developing a schedule of your rehabilitation-related activities that both effectively meets your recovery needs and is also time efficient and not stressful is essential.
- Prime dance training can be used to address your cognitive, emotional, and behavioral responses to your injury.

References

Achterberg, J. (1991, May). *Enhancing the immune function through imagery*. Paper presented at the Fourth World Conference on Imagery, Minneapolis.

Bandura, A., & Cervone, D. (1983). Self-evaluative and self-efficacy mechanisms governing the motivational effects of goal systems. *Journal of Personality and Social Psychology, 45*, 1017–1028.

Banes, S. (1980). *Terpsichore in sneakers: Post-modern dance*. Boston: Houghton Mifflin.

Beck, A. (1976). *Cognitive therapy and emotional disorders*. New York: International University Press.

Berstein, D., & Borkovec, T. (1973). *Progressive relaxation training, a manual for the helping professions*. Champaign, IL: Research Press.

Brawley, L.R. (1984). Attributions as social cognitions: Contemporary perspectives in sport. In W.F. Straub & J.M. Williams (Eds.), *Cognitive sport psychology* (pp. 212–230). Lansing, NY: Sport Science Associates.

Brewer, B. (2001). Emotional adjustment to sport injury. In J. Crossman (Ed.), *Coping with sports injuries: Psychological strategies for rehabilitation* (pp. 1–19). New York: Oxford University Press.

Buckroyd, J. (1995). The provision of psychological care for dancers. *Performing Arts Medicine News, 3*, 1.

Buckroyd, J. (2000). *The student dancer: Emotional aspects of the teaching and learning of dance*. London, England: Dance Books.

Burke, S. (2011, January). Teach learn connection: Technique my way—Natalie Desch. *Dance Magazine*. www.dancemagazine.com/issues/January-2011/Teach-Learn-Connection-Technique-My-Way.

Carman, J. (2005, September). The silent majority: Surviving and thriving in the corps the ballet. *Dance Magazine*. www.dancemagazine.com/issues/September-2005/The-Silent-Majority-Surviving-and-Thriving-in-the-Corps-de-Ballet.

Crossman, J., & Jamieson, J. (1985). Differences in perceptions of seriousness and disrupting effects of athletic injury as viewed by athletes and their trainers. *Perceptual and Motor Skills, 61*, 1131–1134.

Danish, S.J. (1986). Psychological aspects in the care and treatment of athletic injuries. In P.E. Vinger & E.F. Hoerner (Eds.), *Sports injuries: The unthwarted epidemic* (pp. 345–353). Littleton, MA: PSG.

DePalma, M.T., & DePalma, B. (1989). The use of instruction and the behavioral approach to facilitate injury rehabilitation. *Athletic Training, 24*, 217–219.

Dowd, I. (1981). *Taking root to fly: Seven articles on functional anatomy*. New York: Author.

Duda, J.L., Smart, A.E., & Tappe, M.K. (1989). Predictors of adherence in the rehabilitation of physical injuries: An application of personal investment theory. *Journal of Sport and Exercise Psychology, 11*, 367–381.

Edwards, J. (2012, September). Technique my way: Katherine Fisher—Improving stamina in body and mind. *Dance Magazine*. www.dancemagazine.com/issues/September-2012/Technique-My-Way-Katherine-Fisher.

Eldridge, W.D. (1983). The importance of psychotherapy for athletic-related orthopedic injuries among athletes. *International Journal of Sport Psychology*, *14*, 203–211.

Feltz, D.L., & Riessinger, C.A. (1990). Effects of in vivo emotive imagery and performance feedback on self-efficacy and muscular endurance. *Journal of Sport and Exercise Psychology*, *12*, 132–143.

Flatow, S. (1982). Starting over. *Ballet News*, *6*, 16–18, 40.

Hardy, C.J., & Crace, R.K. (1990, May/June). Dealing with injury. *Sport Psychology Training Bulletin*, *1*, 1–8.

Harris, D.V. (2010). Relaxation and energizing techniques for regulation of arousal. In J.M. Williams (Ed.), *Applied sport psychology: Personal growth to peak performance* (pp. 185–207). Palo Alto, CA: Mayfield.

Hatfield, B.D., & Landers, D.M. (1983). Psychophysiology—A new direction for sport psychology. *Journal of Sport Psychology*, *5*, 243–259.

Ievleva, L., & Orlick, T. (1991). Mental links to enhanced healing: An exploratory study. *The Sport Psychologist*, *5*, 25–40.

Kay, L. (2012, January). Technique my way: Katherine Crockett—Respecting her body, devoted to her craft. *Dance Magazine*. www.dancemagazine.com/issues/january-2012/Technique-My-Way-Katherine-Crockett.

Kübler-Ross, E. (2005). *On grief and grieving: Finding the meaning of grief through the five stages of loss*. New York: Simon & Schuster.

Luke, A., & Micheli, L.J. (2000). Management of injuries in the young dancer. *Journal of Dance Medicine and Science*, *4*(1), 6–15.

Lynch, G.P. (1988). Athletic injuries and the practicing sport psychologist: Practical guidelines for assisting athletes. *The Sport Psychologist*, *2*, 161–167.

Mainwaring, L., Kerr, G., & Krasnow, D. (1993). Psychological correlates of dance injuries. *Medical Problems of Performing Artists*, *8*, 3–6.

Mainwaring, L., Krasnow, D., & Young, L. (2003). A teacher's guide to helping young dancers cope with psychological aspects of hip injuries. *Journal of Dance Education*, *3*(2), 57–64.

McDonald, S.A., & Hardy, C.J. (1990). Affective response patterns of the injured athlete: An exploratory analysis. *The Sport Psychologist*, *4*, 261–274.

McEwen, K., & Young, K. (2011). Ballet and pain: Reflections on a risk-dance culture. *Qualitative Research in Sport, Exercise, and Health*, *3*(2), 152–173.

Nagrin, D. (1988). *How to dance forever: Surviving against the odds*. New York: Harper Collins.

Newman, B. (1982). *Striking a balance: Dancers talk about dancing*. Boston: Houghton Mifflin.

Pedersen, P. (1986). The grief response and injury: A special challenge for athletes and athletic trainers. *Athletic Training*, *21*, 312–314.

Radetsky, S. (2012, April). Breaking Free. *Dance Magazine*. www.dancemagazine.com/issues/April-2012/Breaking-Free.

Rotella, R.J., & Heyman, S.R. (2010). Stress, injury, and the psychological rehabilitation of athletes. In J.M. Williams (Ed.), *Applied sport psychology: Personal growth to peak performance* (pp. 338–355). Palo Alto, CA: Mayfield.

Sarno, J. (1984). *Mind over back pain*. New York: Morrow.

Schnitt, D. (1990, November/December). Psychological issues in dancers—An overview. *Journal of Physical Education, Recreation, and Dance*, 32-34.

Selby, C.L., & Reel, J.J. (2011). A coach's guide to identifying and helping athletes with eating disorders. *Journal of Sport Psychology in Action*, 2(2), 100-112.

Simonton, O.C., Matthews-Simonton, S., & Creighton, J.L. (1978). *Getting well again*. New York: Bantam.

Singh, S. (2011). The meaning of pain during the process of embodiment: A case study of trainee modern dancers' experiences of pain. *Sport, Education, and Society*, 16(4), 451-465.

Taylor, J., & Schneider, T. (2005). *The triathlete's guide to mental training*. Boulder, CO: Velopress.

Teitz, C.C. (1984). First aid, immediate care, and the rehabilitation of knee and ankle injuries in dancers and athletes. In C.G. Shell (Ed.), *The dancer as athlete* (pp. 79-81). Champaign, IL: Human Kinetics.

Wasley, D., & Lox, C.L. (1998). Self-esteem and coping responses of athletes with acute versus chronic injuries. *Perceptual and Motor Skills*, 86, 1402.

Wehlage, D.F. (1980). Managing the emotional reactions to loss in athletics. *Athletic Training*, 15, 144-146.

Weiss, M.R., & Troxel, R.K. (1986). Psychology of the injured athlete. *Athletic Training*, 21, 104-109, 154.

Wiese, D.M., & Weiss, M.R. (1987). Psychological rehabilitation and physical injury: Implications for the sports medicine team. *The Sport Psychologist*, 1, 318-330.

Wiese-Bjornstal, D.M., Smith, A.M, Shaffer, S.M., & Morrey, M. (1998). An integrated model of response to sport injury: Psychological and sociological dynamics. *Journal of Applied Sport Psychology*, 10(1), 46-69.

Williams, J.M., & Roepke, N. (1993). Psychology of injury and injury rehabilitation. In R.N. Singer, M. Murphey, & L.K. Tennant (Eds.), *Handbook of research on sport psychology* (pp. 815-839). New York: Macmillan.

Yukelson, D. (1986). Psychology of sport and the injured athlete. In D.B. Bernhart (Ed.), *Clinics in physical therapy* (pp. 175-195). New York: Churchill Livingstone.

Disordered Eating

> *"When I was around 14, I was anorexic, but I had to find a way to deal with it. Now I treat my eating and body the same way: with that respectful attitude of "you get out what you put in." I know I can best help my body speak to my soul by treating it with respect. I want to dance for as long as possible—and look and feel great doing so."*
>
> Katherine Crockett, principal dancer, Martha Graham Dance Company

*D*isordered eating is one of the biggest risks faced by dancers, particularly women. Though few dancers develop a clinically defined eating disorder (ED), many engage in some form of dysfunctional eating due to the physical aesthetic woven into the fabric of much of the dance world, especially in ballet. Quite simply, many choreographers, dance masters and mistresses, and dancers themselves expect dancers to look a certain way.

Although this aesthetic is changing in some parts of the dance world—for example, under the influence of noted choreographer Mark Morris—the perceived need to sculpt a certain type of body drives many dancers to eat in unhealthy ways. For a significant number of those dancers, this change in eating behavior results in clinically diagnosable eating disorders with dangerous implications for their physical, psychological, and emotional health. Moreover, in some cases, this harmful eating causes severe health problems and even death.

Our concern for dancers' health has been heightened by public and private accounts of struggles related to eating disorders. Examples include the highly publicized death of 22-year-old ballerina Heidi Guenther, autobiographical accounts such as that of Gelsey Kirkland, and ongoing anecdotal reports from current dancers. We encourage the dancers with whom we work to become informed about their eating habits and, most important, to make good choices about their diet and health.

This chapter first presents the diagnostic criteria for each eating disorder described in the current (fifth) edition of the *Diagnostic and Statistical Manual of Mental Disorders* (DSM-5), the "bible" of psychological diagnoses, which is published by the American Psychiatric Association. Often, athletes and dancers have a narrow idea of what constitutes an eating disorder; as a result, they may underestimate the severity of disordered eating behaviors in which they commonly engage. Our hope is that you will be able to recognize any disordered behaviors in which you may engage, as well as the associated risks, and then be willing to seek appropriate help.

The second part of the chapter provides a broader understanding of the complexity of eating disorders, describes the risks factors contributing to their development, notes associated features, and makes recommendations for what to do if you suspect that you or a friend may be struggling with an eating disorder. The chapter also teaches you how to recognize unhealthy eating patterns and validates your efforts to fuel yourself properly. Finally, the chapter offers guidance for seeking help to get yourself back on the path to healthy eating.

Common Eating Disorders

Eating disorders are not either-or matters; rather, they lie along a continuum made up of varying degrees of unhealthy behavior related to body weight and appearance (see figure 14.1). The term *disordered eating* is used specifically to

Figure 14.1   Continuum of varying degrees of unhealthy behavior related to disordered eating.

describe unhealthy behaviors along this continuum that can lead to eating disorders per se and threaten your psychological, emotional, and physical health.

Here are some of the unhealthy ways in which dancers may attempt to manipulate their weight: skipping meals; eating "healthy" in a rigid manner; cutting out entire food groups; exercising compulsively; never taking a day off; using diet pills, laxatives, or diuretics; going from extremes of restrictive eating to overeating; bingeing, purging, fasting, or eating erratically; and smoking or chewing gum to avoid meals. These types of disordered eating behavior can lead you down a slippery slope to a harmful eating disorder.

Eating disorders are complex medical and psychiatric illnesses that go beyond body or weight dissatisfaction and lead to destructive patterns of eating behavior. To summarize quickly, these problems are disorders of both too much and not enough. They usually involve a high drive to do too much, a need for order and control, as well as a sensitivity to feeling emotions too strongly, often causing great distress. The behaviors of the eating disorder are attempts to regulate this sensitivity, but, due to the drive that people with eating disorders often have, they take things to an extreme. As a result, guilt and shame keep them in a state of secrecy, often feeling "not good enough."

These disorders are often accompanied by anxiety, depression, obsessive-compulsive thoughts and behavior, an eerie detachment from reality, and, in extreme cases, dissociative disorders. For example, when one young dancer was confronted with the damage that she was doing to her body and the risk of dying from her illness, her response was this: "At least the pallbearers will be able to lift my coffin without hurting themselves."

Indeed, eating disorders constitute one of the leading contributors to mortality among psychiatric disorders, and their prevalence is on the rise, particularly among adolescent and young adult women living in a culture in which thinness is revered. Studies have found that athletes are about 13 percent more likely than members of the general population to develop eating disorders. More specifically, many studies have indicated that dancers are particularly vulnerable, due to the intense pressure they experience regarding their weight and appearance.

In fact, research has shown that dancers (and participants in other aesthetic sports, such as figure skating) are at the highest risk (20 percent) for developing eating disorders. Studies have reported prevalence rates of eating disorders in dancers that range from 7 percent to 45 percent. For example, a study conducted by Elena in 2008, involving more than 200 dancers in professional schools and companies, found that fewer than 10 percent of the dancers admitted to a current or past diagnosis of an eating disorder. However, 55 percent of female dancers and 27 percent of male dancers admitted to being currently dissatisfied with their weight. These findings indicate that many dancers experience pressure to lose weight and conform to a certain physical aesthetic.

Diagnostic Criteria and Descriptions

The DSM-5 defines "feeding and eating disorders" as illnesses "characterized by persistent disturbance of eating or eating-related behavior that results in the altered consumption or absorption of food and that significantly impairs physical health or psychosocial functioning." The manual presents diagnostic criteria for the following disorders in this category: rumination disorder, avoidant/restrictive food intake disorder, anorexia nervosa, bulimia nervosa, and binge eating disorder—all of which are mutually exclusive, meaning that only one of them can be diagnosed at a time. It also includes diagnostic criteria for pica, which can be diagnosed concomitantly with any of the other disorders. Since the DSM-5 was recently released and introduced a new way of diagnosing eating disorders, we provide the diagnostic criteria for each disorder in the sections that follow. However, it is likely that many dancers may not fit some of the categories described.

Rumination Disorder

The essential feature of rumination disorder is the repeated regurgitation of food after feeding or eating over a period of at least one month. Previously swallowed food that may be partially digested is brought up into the mouth without apparent nausea, involuntary retching, or disgust. The food may be rechewed and then ejected from the mouth or reswallowed. For diagnostic purposes, regurgitation should be frequent, occurring at least several times per week (typically daily). The diagnostic criteria include the following:

- Repeated regurgitation of food persists for at least one month. Regurgitated food may be rechewed, reswallowed, or spit out.
- The repeated regurgitation is not attributable to an associated gastrointestinal or other medical condition (e.g., gastroesophageal reflux, pyloric stenosis).

- The eating disturbance does not occur exclusively during the course of anorexia nervosa, bulimia nervosa, binge eating disorder, or avoidant/restrictive food intake disorder.
- If the symptoms occur in the context of another mental disorder (e.g., intellectual disability or another neurodevelopmental disorder), they are sufficiently severe to warrant additional clinical attention.

Avoidant/Restrictive Food Intake Disorder

As the name implies, the main diagnostic feature of avoidant/restrictive food intake disorder (ARFID) is avoidance or restriction of food intake. The diagnostic criteria include the following:

- An eating or feeding disturbance (e.g., apparent lack of interest in eating or food; avoidance based on the sensory characteristics of food; concern about aversive consequences of eating, such as developing a stomach ache) is manifested by persistent failure to meet appropriate nutritional or energy needs associated with one (or more) of the following:
  - Significant weight loss (or faltering growth or failure to achieve expected weight gain in children)
  - Significant nutritional deficiency
  - Dependence on enteral feeding or oral nutritional supplements
  - Marked interference with psychosocial functioning
- The disturbance is not better explained by a lack of available food or by an associated culturally sanctioned practice.
- The eating disturbance does not occur exclusively during the course of anorexia nervosa or bulimia nervosa, and there is no evidence of a disturbance in the way in which the person's body weight or shape is experienced.
- The eating disturbance is not attributable to a concurrent medical condition and not better explained by another mental disorder. When the eating disturbance occurs in the context of another condition or disorder, the severity of the eating disturbance exceeds that routinely associated with the other condition or disorder and warrants additional clinical attention.

This classification is helpful because it is relevant to children, adolescents, and adults. The food avoidance or restriction may be based on sensory characteristics of the food, such as color, smell, texture, temperature, or taste. This behavior has been described as "restrictive eating," "selective eating," "choosy eating," "perseverant eating," "chronic food refusal," and "food neophobia" and may manifest as a refusal to eat particular brands of food.

The classification is beneficial also because, though individuals with ARFID may exhibit behaviors similar to those of individuals with anorexia nervosa, they have neither a distorted nor a negative body image. Their behaviors are merely a reflection of their food sensitivities, though these behaviors may cause equally significant impairment and potential harm to their health and well-being.

Anorexia Nervosa

Although the term *anorexia nervosa* (AN) means "lack of appetite," it is a rather misleading label because individuals with anorexia are generally hungry—literally starving, in fact—yet they deny their hunger. This denial is a key characteristic of the disorder, and it often hinders identification and treatment. Indeed, many individuals struggling with AN resist admitting that they have it, often until it is too late. The diagnostic signs include the following:

- Restriction of energy intake relative to requirements leads to a significantly low body weight in the context of age, sex, developmental trajectory, and physical health. Significantly low weight is defined as a weight that is less than minimally normal or, for children and adolescents, less than that minimally expected.

- The specification of severity is based on body mass index (BMI) for adults and BMI percentile for children and adolescents. The ranges used have been derived from the World Health Organization's categories for thinness. The level of severity may be increased to reflect clinical symptoms, degree of functional disability, and the need for supervision. Here are the ranges for adults:
  - Mild: BMI $\geq$ 17
  - Moderate: BMI = 16 to 16.99
  - Severe: BMI = 15 to 15.99
  - Extreme: < 15

- The person experiences intense fear of gaining weight or becoming fat or engages in persistent behavior that interferes with weight gain, even though he or she is at a significantly low weight.

- The person exhibits disturbance in the way in which her or his body weight or shape is experienced, undue influence of body weight or shape on self-evaluation, or persistent lack of recognition of the seriousness of the current low body weight.

Specifiers include severity level, as well as either restricting subtype or purging subtype. Restricting subtype involves the restriction of intake or use of starvation as the sole means of weight control. Purging subtype consists of compensatory behaviors to control weight, such as vomiting, excessive exercise, and the use of diet pills, laxatives, or diuretics.

Although these are the only diagnostic criteria presented in the DSM-5 for AN, several other psychological features are associated with it. They include the following:

- Extreme desire for control that contributes to a "rule-bound" mentality (i.e., rigid beliefs about weight and food)
- Low self-esteem
- Perfectionism
- High achievement
- Lack of assertiveness
- Extreme thinking
- Strong need for external validation
- Extreme sensitivity to criticism
- Constant internal criticism
- Feelings of guilt, shame, and embarrassment
- Overarching feeling of inadequacy despite significant evidence of competence

Bulimia Nervosa

As described by the DSM-5, the diagnostic criteria for essential features of bulimia nervosa (BN) are as follows:

- Recurrent episodes of binge eating as characterized by both of the following features:
  - Eating, in a discrete period of time (e.g., within any two-hour period), an amount of food that is definitely larger than what most individuals would eat in a similar period of time under similar circumstances
  - A sense of lack of control over eating during the episode (e.g., a feeling that one cannot stop eating or control what or how much one is eating)
- Recurrent inappropriate compensatory behaviors in order to prevent weight gain, such as self-induced vomiting; misuse of laxatives, diuretics, or other medications; fasting; or excessive exercise

- Binge eating and inappropriate compensatory behavior that both occur, on average, at least once a week for three months
- Self-evaluation that is unduly influenced by body shape and weight
- Occurrence not exclusive to episodes of anorexia nervosa

Specifiers of severity include the following (average number of episodes of inappropriate compensatory behavior per week):

Mild: 1 to 3

Moderate: 4 to 7

Severe: 8 to 13

Extreme: 14 or more

Associated features include an obsessive desire for self-control while demonstrating a noticeable lack of control in behavior. The result is erratic eating behavior that oscillates between periods of extreme control and restriction and periods of extreme lack of control and bingeing. Individuals with bulimia also have a compulsive preoccupation with their weight and appearance and spend much of their time thinking about food. They experience intense periods of guilt and shame following binge-and-purge episodes and often isolate themselves as they experience depression and anxiety. Despite an inner world filled with turmoil, people with bulimia tend to be outgoing and social, masking their discontent with an appearance of happiness to conceal their feelings of worthlessness and shame.

Individuals with BN are vulnerable to other addictive behaviors, such as drinking and drug use. Unlike individuals with anorexia, who are consistently very thin, individuals with bulimia often exhibit variability in their physical appearance, ranging from slightly underweight to slightly overweight. For this reason, they are more difficult to identify and diagnose than those with anorexia. Important physical signs of bulimia include bloodshot eyes, knuckle scars, puffy face and cheeks, discolored teeth, water retention and bloating, irritability, moodiness, fast eating, and frequent trips to the bathroom following a meal.

Binge-Eating Disorder

Binge eating disorder (BED) occurs in normal-weight, overweight, and obese individuals. It is more prevalent among individuals seeking weight-loss treatment than in the general population. Unlike individuals experiencing bulimia nervosa, people with BED do not engage in compensatory behavior; therefore, their weight continues to increase, as do the well-documented health concerns associated with obesity. The diagnostic signs of BED include the following:

- Recurrent episodes of binge eating as characterized by both of the following features:
  - Eating, in a discrete period of time (e.g., within any two-hour period), an amount of food that is definitely larger than what most people would eat in a similar period of time under similar circumstances
  - A sense of lack of control over eating during the episode (e.g., feeling that one cannot stop eating or control what or how much one is eating)
- Binge-eating episodes associated with three (or more) of the following:
  - Eating much more rapidly than normal
  - Eating until feeling uncomfortably full
  - Eating large amounts of food when not feeling physically hungry
  - Eating alone because of feeling embarrassed by how much one is eating
  - Feeling disgusted with oneself, depressed, or very guilty afterward
- Marked distress regarding binge eating
- Binge eating that occurs, on average, at least once a week for three months

Binge eating is not associated with recurrent use of inappropriate compensatory behavior as in bulimia nervosa and does not occur exclusively during the course of bulimia nervosa or anorexia nervosa. Specifiers of severity include the following (number of binge episodes per week):

Mild: 1 to 3

Moderate: 4 to 6

Severe: 8 to 13

Extreme: 14 or more

Pica

The essential feature of pica is the eating of one or more nonnutritive, nonfood substances on a persistent basis over a period of at least one month that is severe enough to warrant clinical attention. Typical substances ingested in pica tend to vary with age and availability and include paper, soap, cloth, hair, string, wool, soil, chalk, talcum powder, paint, gum, metal, pebbles, charcoal, ash, clay, starch, and ice. The diagnostic criteria include the following:

- The eating of nonnutritive, nonfood substances persists for at least one month.
- The eating of nonnutritive, nonfood substances is inappropriate to the developmental level of the individual.

- The eating behavior is not part of a culturally supported or socially normative practice.
- If the eating behavior occurs in the context of another mental disorder (e.g., intellectual disability, autism spectrum disorder, schizophrenia, or medical condition [including pregnancy], it is sufficiently severe to warrant additional clinical attention.

Other Specified Feeding or Eating Disorder

The criteria for other specified feeding or eating disorders (OSFED) was developed to encompass individuals who exhibit symptoms of the eating disorders just described but do not fully meet the criteria for diagnosis. This category is used in situations in which the clinician chooses to communicate the specific reason that the presentation does not meet the criteria for any specific feeding and eating disorder. However, the person's behaviors still create distress or put the individual at psychological or medical risk (e.g., all of the criteria except one are met for any of the EDs).

Unspecified Feeding or Eating Disorder

The criteria for unspecified feeding or eating disorder (UFED) are very similar to those for OSFED. The difference is that the UFED diagnosis is used in instances in which the clinician chooses *not* to communicate the specific reason that the presentation does not meet criteria or in which there is not enough time or enough information to do so.

Subclinical Eating Disorders

Another term, *anorexia athletica*, was developed to describe a subset of behaviors that do not meet DSM-5 criteria for an ED diagnosis but are severe enough to put the individual at risk for physical harm. While anorexia athletica is not identified in the DSM-5, the existence of subclinical disorders in general is. Additionally, these disorders still carry the same potential for negative consequences as the fully identified disorders do. The category serves to place individuals who are experiencing negative consequences and are sick, but who may not neatly fit into one of the other categories. The criteria have not been acknowledged in the DSM-5 but are espoused by most clinicians and researchers who work with athletes and dancers. Although many of the criteria resemble those of AN, individuals in this group do not typically display the psychological or emotional disturbances associated with the clinically defined eating disorders. Nonetheless, treatment is warranted if the following symptoms are present.

- Loss of more than 5 percent of expected body weight (or failure to meet expected weight gain for one's height)
- Delayed menarche (i.e., late onset of menstrual function)
- Amenorrhea (menstrual dysfunction)
- Gastrointestinal complaints
- Absence of medical illness or affective disorder to explain weight loss
- Body image distortion
- Excessive fear of weight gain or becoming obese
- Restriction of energy intake
- Use of purging methods
- Binge eating
- Compulsive exercise (often in addition to a grueling training regimen)

Risk Factors for Eating Disorders

As understanding of eating disorders has grown, researchers have come to recognize that multiple factors can contribute to the development of an eating disorder. Therefore, attributing the development of an eating disorder to a single cause, such as dance participation, would be an oversimplification and would interfere with our ability to identify and treat the disorder. It would also do a disservice to the dance community and understate the benefits of dance participation.

Indeed, eating disorders are among the most complex of all psychiatric illnesses because they are often multifaceted and multifactorial. In other words, they affect multiple areas of a person's life (e.g., physical, psychological, and emotional) and usually involve multiple contributing factors. Therefore, participation in dance alone does not contribute to an eating disorder. However, dance participation (especially in a negative environment) in combination with other factors *may* influence the development of an eating disorder.

Understanding the risk factors related to eating disorders is important for several reasons. First, you can recognize that these are serious and complicated illnesses that must be addressed quickly and effectively. Second, you can gain a comprehensive understanding of the factors that may contribute to their development. Third, and most important, if you see risk factors in your own habits or life experience, you can acknowledge them and take active steps to address them in order to maintain your health and continue your dance career as an affirming part of your life. Use the Examine Your Risk Factors worksheet (in the web resource) to help you identify any potential issues or warning signs.

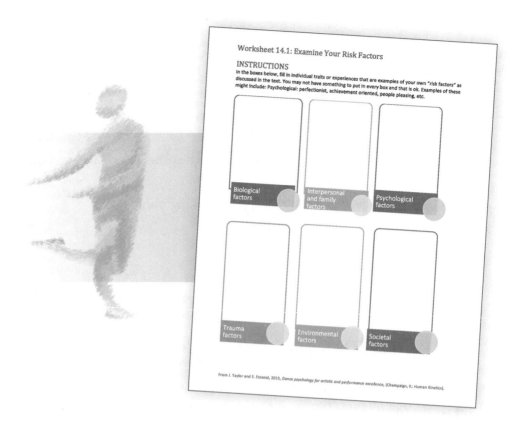

Gender, Age, and Puberty

Research indicates that 10 times more women than men suffer from eating disorders; therefore, gender is considered one of the most important risk factors. At the same time, men are also vulnerable to eating disorders, and unhealthy eating in men should not be ignored. Still, hormonal factors related to being female appear to play a key role in the development of eating disorders, as do cultural pressures related to the physical appearance of women.

Although eating disorders can develop at any time, they are most likely to emerge in adolescence. Females in particular can be made vulnerable to eating disorders by the intense physiological, psychological, and social changes that they experience during adolescence. Another component that may increase susceptibility is the fact that dance places a high value on a particular body type that many women, particularly after puberty, are unable to attain.

Biological Factors

Research has established that having an immediate female relative with an eating disorder increases a person's chances of developing an eating disorder by as much as 10 times. Genes have been estimated to influence the development

Dancers need adequate nourishment for optimal focus and stamina.

of an eating disorder by 46 percent to 78 percent. Other genetic associations include having family members who have struggled with depression, anxiety, obsessive-compulsive disorder, mood disorder, or alcohol or substance abuse. A strong genetic link has been made between alcohol use and eating disorders. We often see, among people with an eating disorder, that a parent or other family member struggles with alcohol or substance disorders.

Researchers are now studying the relationship between eating disorders and certain neurochemicals that regulate mood and appetite (e.g., serotonin, dopamine) as well as hormones (e.g., estrogen, melatonin, thyroid, and growth hormones). Dysfunction in the neurochemical systems regulating mood, satiety, and hunger have been identified as risk factors that also contribute to the emergence of, and difficulty in treating, eating disorders.

Recognizing the contribution of genetic and biological precursors to eating disorders can reduce the self-blame that many sufferers feel. Without this perspective, they may come to believe that the disorder is their fault, and this perception can exacerbate their feelings of inadequacy and shame.

Temperament and Personality

Temperament and personality have been studied extensively as they relate to the development of eating disorders, and a number of factors have been found relevant in dancers. As the study of these factors has deepened, we have moved away from the term *personality* and espoused the term *temperament* as referring to a more enduring collection of traits. It remains unclear whether dancers with these attributes are attracted to the structure and discipline of dance or whether they developed these qualities through the rigorous experience of participation in dance.

Be that as it may, there is no doubt that many dancers are achievement oriented, competitive, driven, hard working, diligent, disciplined, perseverant, people pleasing, sensitive, highly tolerant of pain, detail oriented, perfectionistic, and possessed of a highly active mind. In fact, many of these traits, which have been found to be associated with eating disorders, also allow dancers to thrive in an art form that is intense, competitive, and demanding. The same has been found true of other athletes who participate in aesthetic sports, such as gymnastics, figure skating, and synchronized swimming. These attributes enable people to push themselves to high levels of success. When taken to the extreme, however, they can manifest in harmful forms, such as eating disorders.

Differences have been identified between dancers who remain healthy and those who develop an eating disorder. Specifically, those who develop an ED are more likely to

- be harm avoidant (fearing conflict),
- be perfectionistic,
- have low self-esteem,
- use polarized thinking,
- be self-critical,
- exhibit compulsiveness and rigidity (especially regarding eating and exercising),
- exhibit high need for control,
- be restless,
- exhibit social withdrawal, and
- experience depression, anxiety, or other mood disorders.

These traits lead to increased self-criticism, body dissatisfaction, drive for thinness, distorted body image, need for control, and obsessive-compulsiveness, all of which are common risk factors for eating disorders.

Other common temperamental qualities in people with anorexia include the following:

- High self-control
- High persistence
- Low level of novelty seeking
- Constriction of affect and emotional expressiveness
- Anhedonia (decreased pleasure in things that were previously pleasurable)
- Rigidity of thinking
- Reduced social spontaneity

Traits seen in individuals with bulimia include the following:

- High impulsivity
- Sensation or novelty seeking
- Extremes of intense emotion
- Attention-control deficit
- Difficulty in expressing emotions through language
- Excessive fear of criticism and rejection
- Distrust of others

Be aware that seeing some of these personality or temperamental attributes in yourself does not mean that you are doomed to develop an eating disorder. At the same time, if you find that these traits cause you strong and persistent discomfort in your dancing or your life, you may want to seek help from a parent, dance teacher, or therapist to ensure that your dance remains a positive and healthy part of your life.

Cultural Factors

The role of cultural pressures in the development of eating disorders has been a primary focus among researchers. Although societal pressure alone does not cause eating disorders, it is widely viewed as an important contributor. Eating disorders are most prevalent in Western societies, in which the cultural emphasis on thinness for women is evident in all forms of media, including television, film, and the web, as well as magazines. More specifically, research has shown that articles about diet and weight loss, images of thin women, and the reading of celebrity and women's magazines are the most common predictors of eating-disordered symptoms in young women. These pressures are typically magnified for dancers because, in addition to the cultural forces just described, dancers face additional pressure for unhealthy thinness in dance culture itself.

Social Factors

Families have often been unfairly blamed for the emergence of eating disorders in dancers. The stereotype of "stage parents" who pressure their young daughters to be thin so they can advance their dance careers often exacerbates the cultural pressures that young women already feel. Not every dancer who develops an eating disorder comes from a dysfunctional family. Nonetheless, research has shown that many dancers and individuals who develop eating disorders do have a parent who is overbearing or controlling.

Some of these families also struggle with physical or sexual abuse, alcoholism or substance abuse, mental health issues, divorce, or high levels of conflict in the household. The resulting emotional distress can impair the development of a positive sense of self, autonomy, and healthy coping strategies. The destabilizing effects of this type of family life may lead dancers with personality risk factors to internalize the turmoil. The lack of control that young people may feel in a dysfunctional family may cause them to exert power over their own lives by controlling their weight, appearance, and diet.

Other characteristics that have been correlated with eating disorders include parents who are highly critical of their own bodies or other people's weight and parents who constantly diet and try to lose weight. The literature also commonly mentions mothers who are overprotective and overly involved in their children's lives and fathers who are distant or absent but demanding. Dancers who develop eating disorders also perceive that their parents have high expectations, which may lead an individual to fear making mistakes and disappointing his or her parents. These types of parental behavior do not automatically cause young dancers to develop eating disorders. Instead, individuals are put at risk by the combination of these parental behaviors with inborn and learned characteristics in the individuals themselves. It is important to point out, however, that if an individual develops an eating disorder, it does not mean that his or her parents exhibit these traits and vice versa; the presence of these traits does not necessarily mean a dancer will develop an eating disorder.

Peers can also exert significant influence. Research examining friendship and eating disorders has found that peers can have either a negative or positive effect. On one hand, friends can be another source of expectation, pressure, and unhealthy role modeling. At the same time, they can also exert a protective influence on dancers by offering support, comfort, and unconditional acceptance that counterbalance unhealthy cultural or family pressures.

Precipitating Events

Though no single event can trigger an eating disorder, for those dancers who exhibit some of the risk factors just described, a significant experience can act as the first domino in a sequence that leads to the disorder. Over the years, dancers have told us of many precipitating events that have led to the development of an eating disorder. Of those, the following are related to dance:

- Receiving a critical comment about body weight or appearance from a peer, teacher, choreographer, or parent—perhaps even being told directly to lose weight in order to dance
- An important dance event (e.g., audition, performance, examination)
- Concern about being selected for a particular role
- Being unable to fit into a tight or revealing costume
- Joining a summer program or new company
- Failing to be chosen for a coveted role
- Sustaining a serious injury
- Being dismissed from a dance school or company

Other precipitating events that can trigger eating disorders include traumatic life experiences, such as bullying; loss of a close friend; conflicted or divorcing parents; death of a parent; or emotional, physical, or sexual abuse.

We have yet to meet a dancer who told us that he or she intentionally chose to develop an eating disorder. What we have heard most often is that dancers experienced profound feelings of sadness, anger, anxiety, fear, confusion, despair, and lack of control and that the emergence of an eating disorder was their attempt, however unhealthy, to reestablish control, ameliorate their untenable emotions, and regain some degree of psychological and emotional stability. Our hope in highlighting how these risk factors arise is twofold—first, that you will be able to identify any of these factors that may exist in you (use the Self Check-In worksheet in the web resource as a guide); and second, that, when a stressful or traumatic event occurs, you can recognize the signs of trouble and seek appropriate help in order to respond to the distress in a healthy way.

Consequences of Eating Disorders

When dancers fall victim to a clinically diagnosable eating disorder, they trigger a cascade of threats to their physical, psychological, and emotional integrity. Indeed, an eating disorder affects every level of your dance and personal life.

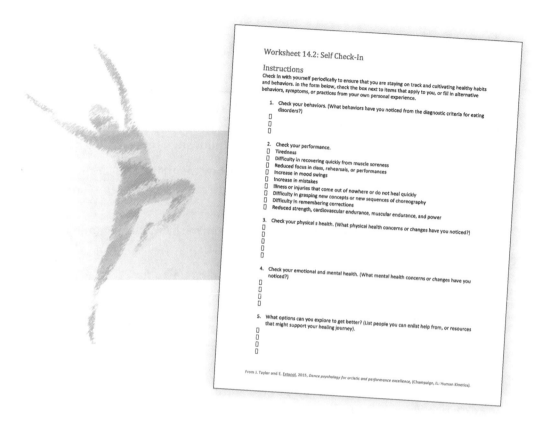

Worksheet 14.2: Self Check-In

Instructions

Check in with yourself periodically to ensure that you are staying on track and cultivating healthy habits and behaviors. In the form below, check the box next to items that apply to you, or fill in alternative behaviors, symptoms, or practices from your own personal experience.

1. Check your behaviors. (What behaviors have you noticed from the diagnostic criteria for eating disorders?)
   ☐
   ☐
   ☐

2. Check your performance.
   ☐ Tiredness
   ☐ Difficulty in recovering quickly from muscle soreness
   ☐ Reduced focus in class, rehearsals, or performances
   ☐ Increase in mood swings
   ☐ Increase in mistakes
   ☐ Illness or injuries that come out of nowhere or do not heal quickly
   ☐ Difficulty in grasping new concepts or new sequences of choreography
   ☐ Difficulty in remembering corrections
   ☐ Reduced strength, cardiovascular endurance, muscular endurance, and power

3. Check your physical s health. (What physical health concerns or changes have you noticed?)
   ☐
   ☐
   ☐
   ☐

4. Check your emotional and mental health. (What mental health concerns or changes have you noticed?)
   ☐
   ☐
   ☐
   ☐

5. What options can you explore to get better? (List people you can enlist help from, or resources that might support your healing journey).
   ☐
   ☐
   ☐
   ☐

From J. Taylor and E. Estanol, 2015, *Dance psychology for artistic and performance excellence*, (Champaign, IL: Human Kinetics).

Crash Dieting

To attain and maintain a healthy physique, you need to commit to a lifestyle change involving your relationships with food and exercise. This commitment means altering various aspects of your life that need to be sustainable over time to promote your overall health and well-being. Yet we rarely hear discussions of lifestyle change as it relates to body weight or appearance. Instead, dancers most often speak, with great trepidation, of the need to "go on a diet," which is usually seen as an intense, temporary regimen of decreased food intake and increased exercise.

However, simply using the word *diet* sets dancers up for failure because, as the research demonstrates, diets rarely work. They don't produce the permanent change in eating and exercise behaviors that are necessary for sustained weight loss and healthy weight maintenance. It is also well documented that periods of extreme dieting lead to a craving for food because the body isn't getting the nutrients that it needs. This deprivation, in turn, often leads to a vicious cycle of denial and gorging.

In addition, because the illness deprives the body of good nutrition, it can affect brain functioning in terms of the ability to hold an accurate perception of self and make good choices. In other words, a person can get into an eating disorder mind-set simply by restricting food intake to the point that the illness takes over. Though this is a rare occurrence, you need to know that the act of "crash dieting," when extreme, can in itself become immediately dangerous.

Impaired Dance Performance

One of the reasons that dieting is reinforcing for many dancers is that, initially, the food restriction enhances one's body image and perceptions of performance. Early on in a diet, most dancers experience a period in which they feel more energetic and are better able to focus on their dance, which increases their feelings of control and confidence and reduces their feelings of worry and anxiety. This psychological and emotional shift causes many dancers to feel "lighter" and gives the impression of improved dancing.

However, this honeymoon phase is short lived. If you continue to restrict your food intake in an unhealthy way, your health and dance performance are almost certain to slowly deteriorate. Sadly, instead of realizing that this course of action isn't working, many dancers recall the initial perceived benefits and double down on their dieting efforts in the belief that they simply haven't reduced their diet or increased their exercise enough. In addition, these dancers' tendency toward perfectionism, high need for control, and fear of failure can make it unthinkable for them to change course lest they feel like a failure.

Dieting also hurts dance performance by causing your body to break down muscle in order to get the nutrients that are not being supplied by the restricted diet. This loss of muscle, of course, entails a loss of strength and stamina, thus resulting in a decline in the quality of your dancing.

Severe dieting impairs dance performance in several additional ways. Due to the low energy that results from inadequate food intake, you feel increased fatigue, both muscular (e.g., being unable to hold your leg up as long) and systemic (e.g., constantly feeling tired). You also find it more difficult to focus in classes, rehearsals, and performances; in fact, you often feel dull and spacey. These symptoms of an unhealthy diet dramatically reduce your ability to dance with technical precision, artistry, and energy. You are more prone to mistakes, and your ability to connect with your audience diminishes. These breakdowns also make you more vulnerable to illness and injury, which of course can prevent you from dancing at all, thus potentially jeopardizing your role in a particular production or even your spot in a company.

Decreased Physical Health

The profound changes in your body caused by eating disorders trigger many physical problems that, if untreated, can become severe and permanent.

Illness

You are now beginning to understand how a simple thought like "I'm going on a diet" can drastically affect your performance and health. If unhealthy dieting persists, as is the case with an eating disorder, then the immune system can also become compromised. In this case, your body's natural ability to fight illness is reduced because it simply lacks the resources to address any physical demands beyond basic functioning. You may find that you catch colds or other bugs more frequently and that they last longer and take a bigger toll on your body. Other long-term consequences can include gastrointestinal problems, menstrual dysfunction leading to infertility, low bone density, long-term trouble with gums and teeth, osteoporosis, hormonal imbalances, kidney damage, and, in the long run, immune function that is permanently compromised (in the form of auto-immune disorders).

Injury

Injuries are also common among dancers who adhere to a highly restrictive diet or suffer from an eating disorder. The susceptibility to injury often results from what experts have referred to as the female athlete triad (which also applies to dancers): restrictive eating, menstrual dysfunction (amenorrhea), and decreased bone density. The combination of these factors can lead to stress fractures and broken bones, as well as sprains, muscle strains, and torn ligaments and tendons. In addition, when injury occurs, the insufficient nutrition also slows down the healing and rehabilitation process.

Death

Chronic eating disorders can place tremendous stress on the body's many systems. In rare cases, this strain can cause systems to shut down and, without proper treatment, can lead to death.

Mental Health

The psychological effect of eating disorders can also be substantial, though it is often more difficult to identify than the physical effect because psychological and emotional symptoms are less apparent and may appear more gradually. Performance-related psychological problems associated with eating disorders can include a loss of motivation and confidence, an increase in performance anxiety, difficulty in concentrating, and extreme emotional sensitivity.

More important, eating disorders take a significant toll on dancers' mental health. Specifically, considerable research demonstrates a strong relationship between eating disorders and higher incidences of sleeping problems, anxiety, depression, mood disorders, and, in extreme cases, psychosis. The bottom line is that decreased or improper nutrition (or other compensatory behaviors) can take a grave toll on a dancer's body and mind.

Healthy dancers make stellar performers.

Prevention of Eating Disorders

The best way to deal with eating disorders is to prevent them from occurring in the first place. Fortunately, you can take a number of physical and mental steps to reduce your chance of developing an eating disorder. The first step is to gain awareness and understanding of what eating disorders are, how they develop, and how they can affect your dance and your life. In addition to taking in the information provided in this chapter, we encourage you to learn more about eating disorders through other readings and discussions with fellow dancers and dance professionals.

Physical Prevention Methods

Learn as much as possible about how nutrition and exercise affect your health and your dance. In addition, consider meeting with a nutritionist and a personal trainer for help in developing eating and fitness plans that benefit your health and dance training. To get started, review the following basic guidelines that we have learned through years of collaboration with a number of nutritionists and personal trainers.

- Always begin your day with a healthful breakfast that includes protein, grains, and fruit.
- Eat at least three meals a day.
- Never skip a meal.
- Between meals, eat snacks that include fruit, nuts, or cheese. (In general if you eat every three or four hours and include some protein, you will keep your metabolism up and avoid blood sugar crashes.)
- Stay hydrated, particularly during long dance sessions, summer months, and sessions in a hot studio. Avoid caffeine (e.g., in coffee, cola, energy drinks), which acts as a diuretic.
- Add resistance training to your fitness regime to increase your metabolism and burning of fat.
- Pay attention to your hunger and fullness signals and respond to them appropriately.
- Recognize your body's other signals that it needs fuel—for example, fatigue, sleepiness, crankiness, headache, stomachache, decreased concentration, and spaciness.
- Cut or moderate your intake of caffeine and other stimulants.
- Learn how painful emotions and negative thoughts affect your hunger signals.
- Practice grounding techniques to stay connected to your body so that you can recognize its signals and respond appropriately.

Psychological Prevention Methods

Learn about any family history of eating disorders, alcohol or substance abuse, anxiety, mood disorder, depression, or any other psychiatric illness. In addition, be aware of any signs of these conditions in yourself. Get to know yourself and see if you possess any of the temperamental risk factors described earlier in this chapter (e.g., perfectionism, fear of failure, low self-esteem). Notice messages that you receive about body weight or appearance (e.g., "You don't quite have the body type for this role") from parents, dance teachers, or choreographers—and how you react to them. These measures—early awareness, identification, and treatment—can prevent such issues from developing into problems that harm your health and your dance.

In 2009, Elena conducted research exploring whether certain mental skills can be used to decrease the risk of eating disorders—and increase resilience—

among dancers. In the study, the strongest factors protecting against eating disorders were identified as "coping with adversity," "freedom from worry," and "self-confidence." The results demonstrated that using the mental skills discussed throughout this book—for example, relaxation techniques, positive self-talk, mental imagery, and developing a balanced and realistic perspective on your dance life—reduce your chance of developing an eating disorder, depression, or anxiety. These strategies are most beneficial if you incorporate them into your life so that they not only help you improve your performance but also provide a protective effect against the development of eating disorders (use the Prevention and Recovery worksheet in the web resource as a guide).

Other studies have suggested additional factors that can protect you from developing an eating disorder: sense of humor, strong spirituality, optimism, good self-esteem, and good supportive relationships. You can also benefit from recognizing—and accepting—the limits of your genetically endowed body type. No matter what you do, you simply cannot sculpt your body into a form that it was not meant to take. If your body type doesn't fit the physical expectations of a particular dance style, school, or company, don't try to force yourself into that mold through disordered eating. Instead, switch to a dance style, school, or company that respects, embraces, and celebrates the type of body you have. Doing so benefits both your health and your dance!

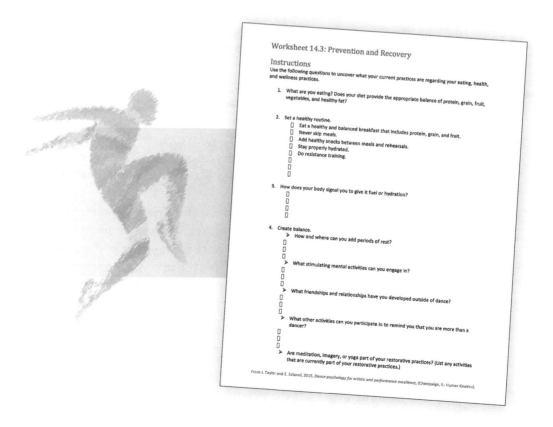

Worksheet 14.3: Prevention and Recovery

Instructions

Use the following questions to uncover what your current practices are regarding your eating, health, and wellness practices.

1. What are you eating? Does your diet provide the appropriate balance of protein, grain, fruit, vegetables, and healthy fat?

2. Set a healthy routine.
   - ☐ Eat a healthy and balanced breakfast that includes protein, grain, and fruit.
   - ☐ Never skip meals.
   - ☐ Add healthy snacks between meals and rehearsals.
   - ☐ Stay properly hydrated.
   - ☐ Do resistance training.
   - ☐
   - ☐
   - ☐

3. How does your body signal you to give it fuel or hydration?
   - ☐
   - ☐
   - ☐
   - ☐

4. Create balance.
   - ➤ How and where can you add periods of rest?
   - ☐
   - ☐
   - ☐
   - ➤ What stimulating mental activities can you engage in?
   - ☐
   - ☐
   - ☐
   - ➤ What friendships and relationships have you developed outside of dance?
   - ☐
   - ☐
   - ☐
   - ➤ What other activities can you participate in to remind you that you are more than a dancer?
   - ☐
   - ☐
   - ☐
   - ➤ Are meditation, imagery, or yoga part of your restorative practices? (List any activities that are currently part of your restorative practices.)

From J. Taylor and E. Estanol, 2015, *Dance psychology for artistic and performance excellence*, (Champaign, IL: Human Kinetics).

"You're dealing with young people who are putting themselves on the line for their art form, and you want to be as supportive as possible. The approach is about making them understand that there are requirements for this career. They don't need to be drastic: They're about health, vitality, energy, and mental alertness. You don't want a starved body or one that has more weight than it can fully articulate."

Cherylyn Lavagnino, Co-Chair, Department of Dance,
NYU's Tisch School of the Arts

Helping Someone With an Eating Disorder

After taking in all of this information, some readers may have thoughts along the following lines: "I'm doing well. I eat healthily and feel good about my body. I don't have these risk factors. However, my friend [roommate, sister, colleague] may have an eating disorder. What should I do?"

It's understandable if you feel concerned about confronting a friend for fear that you'll say the wrong thing or that he or she will get upset at you. Recognize, however, that taking the time and making the effort to talk to this person could save her or his life. Without treatment, eating disorders seldom improve, and they often get worse. In addition, many people who struggle with an eating disorder are too afraid or too embarrassed to ask for help. Some even think that they don't deserve help. In reality, of course, all people deserve the help they need in order to have a healthy life and a healthy relationship with food and their body.

The following guidelines, in the form of do's and don'ts, can help you prepare to confront a friend or loved one about her or his behaviors. First, here are some things to do: Find a quiet and private place where you won't be interrupted. Focus on your feelings and the importance of your relationship with the person (e.g., "I really care about you, and your friendship is very important to me"). Tell the person that you're concerned about her or his health. Mention behaviors that you have noticed and how they may affect the person's health or performance.

Now, here are some things *not* to do: Do not mention appearance or weight; doing so only reinforces ED thoughts and behaviors. Similarly, do not convey any prejudice regarding fatness. If the person mentions feeling fat, help her or him explore fears about being fat and emphasize that self-worth does not depend on appearance. Nor should you assign any blame, shame, or guilt; the person is probably already experiencing these feelings. Also avoid simplistic statements, such as "you just need to eat." Instead, use "I" statements that reinforce your concern (e.g., "I'm worried about you because you're dancing a lot and I haven't seen you eat lunch in a week").

In addition, do not get into power struggles about food or eating. The person may well deny what is happening or tell you that everything is okay. Do not demand that the person change or try to force her or him to do so. Do, however, make clear that the person doesn't need to justify things to you, that you care, and that you want her or him to be healthy and happy. State that you are happy to go with the person for support if she or he wants to talk to a teacher, nurse, or counselor.

After this conversation, if you notice that nothing changes, you may need to express your concerns to someone who holds some authority; for example, an instructor or company director. If your friend gets angry at you for doing so, remember that simply keeping the secret won't keep her or him alive.

Treatment of Eating Disorders

We have included a lot information in this chapter in order to help you recognize any instances in which your eating behavior may constitute a problem. Early recognition enables you to get the help you need, prevent disordered eating from becoming a chronic and debilitating condition, and return to full health more quickly. Bottom line: The earlier you recognize a problem and seek treatment, the better your odds are for a full recovery.

If you have come to the realization that your eating habits are unhealthy and potentially harmful to your physical or mental health, you may be reluctant to reach out to a teacher, choreographer, or director for help. Seeking treatment for an eating disorder can seem threatening to your identity as a dancer and to your goals for a career in dance. You may worry that you will lose out on roles or even be dropped from your dance program. You may also fear that others will judge you harshly, seeing you as weak and incompetent. As a result, you may be tempted keep your realization to yourself.

However, if your disordered eating has a significant effect on your dance or your health, it is imperative that you reach out to people in your life for guidance and support. Most important, key people in your personal and dance lives can assist you in finding the help you need. It is likely that you are not the first dancer in your program or company to suffer from disordered eating. As a result, the chances are good that the dance professionals you work with have experience with eating disorders and therefore can be empathetic to your problems and give you good advice about where to find help.

Ultimately, the decision to tell someone that you may have an eating disorder comes down to trust. You know the relationship you have with your teacher, choreographer, director, parents, and friends. And only you can judge whether these individuals can be relied on to act in your best interest. If you don't feel comfortable talking to anyone in your dance school or company, then seek help from another source—but seek help! Doing so could make the difference in continuing your dance career.

Assembling a Treatment Team

Most dancers we've known find it hard to admit that they suffer from some degree of disordered eating and to seek appropriate help to address the problem. In fact, due to a variety of factors—including the dance culture of "no pain, no gain" and fears of a career setback—dancers are known for denying or hiding eating-related problems. We mention this reality to let you know that we understand that seeking help takes tremendous courage. At the same time, we cannot emphasize enough how important it is that you take this difficult step. Swallow your pride, let go of your fears, and talk to a parent, teacher, friend, or health professional for referrals to people who can help you.

If you suspect you have an eating disorder, we recommend that you work with a team of qualified professionals in three areas: physical health, mental health, and nutrition. Taking a comprehensive approach to eating disorders ensures that you address all of the relevant areas to enable your return to health as safely and as fast as possible.

Physical Health

When you acknowledge that you may have an eating problem, the foremost concern is the potential physical harm. As a result, your first task is to identify a physician who can specifically diagnose the symptoms that you present and recommend a course of treatment that minimizes the potential damage and helps you return to optimal health. It is essential to select a physician with expertise in eating disorders because of the unique symptoms, complications, and consequences that they can cause. Without specialized training and experience, a physician may miss important signs that can compromise your diagnosis and treatment.

Mental Health

Another important part of your treatment team is the mental health professional (MHP), who can identify and treat psychological, emotional, and behavioral causes and consequences. Eating problems begin with thoughts and emotions that drive the individual to an unhealthy shift in eating habits. As discussed earlier in this chapter, disordered eating can be spurred by a range of psychoemotional issues—for example, perfectionism, lack of assertiveness, fear of failure, anxiety, and low self-esteem. An MHP can provide psychotherapy that explores and relieves the thoughts, emotions, and behaviors behind the eating disorder and offer coping strategies for the situations in dance and life that led to it.

In selecting an MHP, the first priority is to find one who has specialized training and experience with eating disorders. A well-qualified professional has the expertise to best identify and address the complexities presented by eating disorders. In addition, an MHP with knowledge and experience of working with dancers possesses a deep understanding of how dance culture can contribute to an eating disorder and therefore is able to offer relevant insights and tools to help you return to full health and continue pursuing your dance goals. If you cannot find an MHP with all of these credentials, seek a sport psychologist with a specialty in eating disorders; she or he will be able to learn about dance culture and guide you appropriately.

Nutrition

Because an eating disorder is, fundamentally, about your relationship with food and eating, another essential member of the treatment team is the nutritionist. This person may also be the most threatening member of your team because she or he will challenge you to change the relationship with food that has become physically and psychologically harmful to both your dance and your life. The main goals of a nutritionist are to help you understand the unhealthy role that food and eating play in your dance and your life and to help you alter your eating habits in a way that is healthful and allows you to continue to work toward your dance goals.

The nutritionist will help you figure out the best combination of foods for healing any damage caused by your disordered eating and returning you to complete physical health. In addition—and for a committed dancer, only slightly less important—the nutritionist can help you develop a plan that provides you with the appropriate balance of nutrients for your body to train and perform at its best. As with both the physician and the mental health professional, a nutritionist with training and expertise in eating disorders is best qualified to address their complicated nature. One who is also experienced with dancers can also provide understanding of the unique physical and nutritional demands of dance.

Types of Treatment

The type of treatment you receive depends on how severe and chronic your symptoms are and on the evident physical or psychological harm. We have found that the mere mention of "treatment" can provoke fear and reluctance in dancers, and it may be helpful to remember that the goal is to return you to full physical and psychological health so that you can continue to pursue your life in dance.

Outpatient Treatment

The three-pronged team of physician, mental health professional, and nutritionist is most common in outpatient treatment. In this approach, you might meet with your nutritionist once a week for ongoing treatment, with your MHP anywhere from one to three times a week, and with your physician every other week or once a month for examination and assessment of progress. The three professionals maintain a collaborative relationship in which they share relevant information and administer an integrated treatment plan. The exact frequency of appointments is determined by the severity of the problem and your motivation level, and it slowly decreases as you move through your recovery.

Intensive Outpatient Treatment

If you are diagnosed with an eating disorder that is health threatening, your treatment team may recommend an intensive outpatient program (IOP). This more urgent course of action is usually taken in response to a recognition that your condition is immediately threatening to your physical or mental health. It usually involves more frequent contact with your treatment team—for example, seeing your MHP several times per week and your physician weekly. This type of program may also involve spending several hours each day in a variety of modalities, including physical examination and testing, nutritional counseling, and individual and group therapy.

Intensive outpatient treatment may require you to take time off from your dance in order to focus on your immediate health concerns. In general, IOPs involve 9 to 20 hours of treatment per week, depending on the severity of the condition and on the individual program. A few programs allow you to continue engagement in school or dance but still require you to spend several hours a day in the program. Though committing to an IOP is certainly a difficult decision, keep in mind the fact that your general health and well-being should be your first priority.

Inpatient Treatment

If your eating disorder is severe enough to threaten your life, your treatment team may advise you to seek inpatient treatment. This recommendation, however scary it may be, must not be ignored. Though it is difficult to accept, you need to recognize that this urgent form of treatment may be your best chance to regain your health and continue to pursue your dance goals. In fact, ignoring this recommendation could cost you your dance career or your life. Some inpatient treatment programs for eating disorders now cater to the unique needs of dancers.

Center Stage: Kara

Taking Behavior to Extremes

Kara was an 18-year old ballet dancer in her first year of college. She had been looking forward to starting college and pursuing her lifelong dream of becoming a professional dancer. She was also glad to be leaving home because her family life was full of conflict.

Though Kara was under the weight limit for partnering classes in her school's dance program, she worried that she would get too heavy after hearing about the "freshman fifteen" that so many of her female classmates were concerned about. Over time, she began to obsess about her weight. She decided to do whatever her classmates were doing—and more.

She started waking up early to take a yoga class before her dance classes. At the end of the school day, she lifted weights or did Pilates. She cut out all junk food and then—shunning knowledgeable sources of good information and favoring peer influence—decided to eat less of everything. She began to lose weight, and her peers and teachers complimented her improved muscle tone and strength.

As the months went by, however, Kara's weight loss continued, and her classmates and teachers began to express concern. Soon, she found herself lacking energy and feeling listless. She began to withdraw from her friends, and her studies suffered. She started getting sick more frequently and sustained a series of minor but persistent injuries so painful that doing jumps brought her to tears.

Finally, the teacher with whom Kara was closest called her into the office and, in a caring yet firm way, confronted her with what she had noticed about her behavior and physical changes. The teacher referred Kara to a mental health professional at the school's health center who specialized in eating disorders. Kara was diagnosed with anorexia nervosa, and the university gave her a leave of absence to address her health problems.

In consultation with her treatment team, and her very concerned parents, Kara entered an inpatient treatment center to accelerate her recovery so that she could be ready to rejoin the program in the following fall term. The experience, though painful, was also life affirming as Kara gained a new perspective on her dance and its role in her life. With dedicated effort, she returned to a healthy weight, regained her dance fitness, and was cast in a lead role in the spring production during her sophomore year.

Options for Finding Help

If you are in need of treatment for disordered eating, here are a few options for finding help:

- Ask your regular primary care physician for a referral to an eating disorders specialist.
- Check with local hospitals or medical centers for referrals or immediate treatment.
- Ask your school counselor or nurse for a referral.
- Call the hotline of the National Eating Disorders Association: 1-800-931-2237.
- Search www.psychologytoday.com for mental health professionals and review the information carefully so that you can select a provider or facility that specializes in eating disorders. You can also call and ask them about their experience with dancers.

We have also included a document with several resources for eating disorder treatment in the web resource.

ENCORE

- Disordered eating can involve skipping meals; engaging in extreme clean eating; cutting out entire food groups; exercising compulsively; using diet pills, laxatives, or diuretics; bingeing and purging; starving yourself for days; smoking or chewing gum to avoid eating meals; and eating erratically.
- Eating disorders recognized in the DSM-5 include avoidant/restrictive food intake disorder, anorexia nervosa, bulimia nervosa, binge eating disorder, rumination disorder, pica, other specified feeding or eating disorder (OSFED), and unspecified feeding or eating disorder (UFED). In addition, anorexia athletica, though not included in the DSM-5, is considered a subclinical presentation of anorexia nervosa in athletes.
- Eating disorders are complex medical and psychiatric illnesses that go beyond body or weight dissatisfaction or erratic eating and can be associated with anxiety, depression, and obsessive-compulsive behavior.
- In avoidant/restrictive food intake disorder, the individual avoids or restricts food intake to an extent that fails to meet requirements for nutrition or energy. The individual does not have a distortion of body image or fear of gaining weight. Restriction is usually associated with sensitivity to texture, taste, smell, temperature, and other food qualities.

- Anorexia nervosa is characterized by a significant loss of body weight or maintenance of body weight at least 15 percent below the ideal level, as well as intense fear of gaining weight, distorted body image and size, menstrual dysfunction, and extremely low caloric intake.

- Bulimia nervosa is characterized by episodes of binge eating followed by purging behaviors that occur at least twice per week for three months, as well as a sense of lacking control during episodes and severe dissatisfaction with one's body image.

- Binge eating disorder has many of the same criteria as bulimia nervosa with the exception that the individual does not engage in compensatory behaviors (e.g., exercise) to lose weight.

- Two other diagnoses—other specified feeding or eating disorder and unspecified feeding or eating disorder—are used when many but not all of the criteria are met for any of the other disorders and the consequences are severe enough to impair health and functioning. The main difference between these two diagnoses lies in whether or not the clinician specifies what type of eating disorder may be involved.

- Anorexia athletica is similar to anorexia nervosa but lacks the associated psychiatric problems related to anxiety and mood.

- Biological risk factors for disordered eating include family history of depression, anxiety, mood disorder, alcoholism, or drug abuse.

- Personality and temperamental traits that predispose dancers to eating disorders include low self-esteem, high achievement orientation, high pain tolerance, perfectionism, lack of assertiveness, a need to please, a tendency toward harm avoidance, lack of emotional expression, polarized thinking, negative emotions, impulsivity, high need for control, novelty seeking, fear of criticism and rejection, and obsessive-compulsive tendencies.

- Sociocultural contributors can include a dance culture that emphasizes thinness and values a certain physical aesthetic.

- Family contributors can include a conflict-ridden home life, an overinvolved mother, a father who is absent or distant yet demanding, dysfunctional communication, parents who diet or are critical of themselves or others who are overweight, and high expectations for achievement.

- Precipitating events can include criticism from a teacher, parent, or peer; failure in an audition or performance; loss of a friend; divorcing parents; and injury.

- Eating disorders harm your relationship with food, your dance performance, and your physical and mental health.

- Physical preventive steps include eating three meals per day (and not skipping meals), snacking between meals, hydrating consistently, and engaging in a resistance training program.

- Psychological preventive steps include learning about your family's history of mental illness, knowing yourself, gaining awareness of the unhealthy messages you may be getting about your dance, using mental skills, developing supportive relationships, and accepting your body type.

- The first step toward achieving health is recognition of the problem.

- A treatment team typically includes a physician, a mental health professional, and a nutritionist. Ideally, each member has specialized training in working with eating disorders and dancers.

- Treatment options include outpatient, intensive outpatient, and inpatient programs that address the wide range of causes of eating disorders and provide many tools for dealing with them.

References

American Psychiatric Association. (2013). *Diagnostic and Statistical Manual of Mental Disorders* (5th ed.). Washington, DC: American Psychiatric.

Beals, K. (2004). *Disordered eating among athletes: A comprehensive guide for health professionals*. Champaign, IL: Human Kinetics.

Beck, A. (1976). *Cognitive therapy and emotional disorders*. New York: International University Press.

Bonci, C.M., Bonci, L.J., Granger, L.R., Johnson, C., Malina, R.M., Milne, L.W., et al. (2008). National Athletic Trainers' Association position statement: Preventing, detecting, and managing disordered eating in athletes. *Journal of Athletic Training, 43*(1), 80–108.

Buckroyd, J. (1995). The provision of psychological care for dancers. *Performing Arts Medicine News, 3*, 1.

Buckroyd, J. (2000). *The student dancer: Emotional aspects of the teaching and learning of dance*. London, England: Dance Books.

Crow, S.J., Peterson, C.B., Swanson, S.A., Raymond, N.C., Specker, S., Eckert, E.D., et al. (2009). Increased mortality in bulimia nervosa and other eating disorders. *American Journal of Psychiatry, 166*, 1342–1346.

Dravenstott, K. (2012, November). Running on empty. *Dance Teacher Magazine.* www.dance-teacher.com/2012/11/running-on-empty/.

Estanol, E. (2009). *Exploring the relationship between risk and resilience factors for eating disorders in ballet dancers*. Doctoral dissertation, University of Utah, Salt Lake City.

Estanol, E., Shepherd, C., & MacDonald, T. (2013). Mental skills as protective attributes against eating disorder risk in dancers. *Journal of Applied Sport Psychology, 25*(2), 209–222.

Garner, D.M., & Garfinkel, P.E. (Eds.). (1997). *Handbook of treatment for eating disorders*. New York: Guilford Press.

Hall, K.H., & Hill, A.P. (2012). Perfectionism, dysfunctional achievement striving, and burnout in aspiring athletes: The motivational implications for performing artists. *Theatre, Dance, and Performance Training, 3*(2), 216–228.

Hamilton, L.H. (1998). *Advice for dancers: Emotional counsel and practical strategies*. San Francisco: Jossey-Bass.

Herbrich, L., Pfeiffer, E., Lehmkuhl, U., & Schneider, N. (2011). Anorexia athletica in pre-professional ballet dancers. *Journal of Sports Sciences, 29*(11), 1115–1123.

Kay, L. (2012, January). Technique my way: Katherine Crockett—Respecting her body, devoted to her craft. *Dance Magazine*. www.dancemagazine.com/issues/january-2012/Technique-My-Way-Katherine-Crockett.

Luthar, S.S. (1991). Vulnerability and resilience: A study of high-risk adolescents. *Child Development, 62*, 600–616.

Luthar, S.S., & Cicchetti, D. (2000). The construct of resilience: Implications for interventions and social policies. *Development & Psychopathology, 12*, 857–885.

McEwen, K., & Young, K. (2011). Ballet and pain: Reflections on a risk-dance culture. *Qualitative Research in Sport, Exercise, and Health, 3*(2), 152–173.

McGuire, K. (2011, July). When words hurt: Dancers discuss how they feel when others criticize their bodies. *Dance Magazine*. www.dancemagazine.com/issues/July-2011/When-Words-Hurt.

McVey, L.G., Pepler, D., Davis, R., Flett, L.G., & Abdolell, M. (2002). Risk and protective factors associated with disordered eating during early adolescence. *Journal of Early Adolescence, 22*(1), 75–95.

Mehler, P.S., & Andersen, A.E. (2010). *Eating disorders: A guide to medical care and complications*. Baltimore: Johns Hopkins University Press.

National Association of Anorexia Nervosa and Associated Disorders. (2014). Eating disorder statistics. www.anad.org/get-information/about-eating-disorders/eating-disorders-statistics/.

Reel, J.J., Jamieson, K.M., Soohoo, S., & Gill, D.L. (2005). Femininity to the extreme: Body image concerns among college female dancers. *Women in Sport and Physical Activity Journal, 14*(1), 39–51.

Rolnick, K. (2011, July). Centerwork: A careful approach—The right way to talk to students about eating disorders. *Dance Magazine*. www.dancemagazine.com/issues/July-2011/Centerwork-A-Careful-Approach.

Schnitt, D. (1990, November/December). Psychological issues in dancers—An overview. *Journal of Physical Education, Recreation, and Dance*, 32–34.

Steck, L.E., Abrahams, M.L., & Phelps, L. (2004). Positive psychology in the prevention of eating disorders. *Psychology in the Schools, 41*(1), 111–117.

Striegel-Moore, R.H., & Bulik, C.M. (2007). Risk factors for eating disorders. *American Psychologist, 62*(3), 181–198.

Striegel-Moore, R.H., & Cachelin, F.F. (2001). Etiology of eating disorders in women. *The Counseling Psychologist, 29*, 635–661.

Sundgot-Borgen, J. (1993). Prevalence of eating disorders in elite female athletes. *International Journal of Sport Nutrition, 3,* 29–40.

Sundgot-Borgen, J., & Torstveit, M.K. (2004). Prevalence of eating disorders in elite athletes is higher than in the general population. *Clinical Journal of Sport Medicine, 14,* 25–32.

Tchanturia, K., Anderluh, M.B., Morris, R.G., Rabe-Hesketh, S., Collier, D.A., Sanchez, P., et al. (2004). Cognitive flexibility in anorexia and bulimia nervosa. *Journal of the International Neuropsychological Society, 10*(4), 513–520.

Tompson, R.A., & Sherman, R.T. (1993). *Helping athletes with eating disorders.* Champaign, IL: Human Kinetics.

15

Dance for Your Life

"*Dancing for me is harder than it used to be, but the rewards are so much richer. . . . I treasure the bond that links all dancers with the unspoken understanding that comes from going through tough challenges individually, yet in the company of others. I am humbled and proud to take my place in the line of those who have gone before me, passing those beautiful pieces of art from dancer to dancer.*"

Gavin Larsen, Oregon Ballet Theatre

*D*ance can be a wonderful, life-enriching experience that provides you with meaning, satisfaction, and joy in an art form that promotes health, cultivates relationships, and extends your physical, psychological, and emotional horizons. It can fuel passion, bolster confidence, engender positive emotions, and encourage a life full of engagement, drive, and focus.

Yet for some, dance becomes a harmful experience that is physically debilitating, emotionally crippling, and socially damaging. Because of the extreme nature of dance—in terms of the commitment needed, the time and energy required, and the physical demands involved—it can be a breeding ground and an outlet for unhealthy aspects of personality that hurt self-esteem, promote obsessiveness, alienate family and friends, and lead to a life of anxiety, frustration, and unhappiness.

Dance attracts some of the healthiest people in the world—people who value movement, artistry, and fitness. It also draws people who are not so psychologically healthy and who want dance to fill a void in their lives. These individuals, rather than immersing themselves in dance, use it as an escape from their problems and demons.

Which group you fall into depends on why you're involved in dance, what you get out of your participation, and how it affects your life as a whole. One simple litmus test for determining whether you've gone to the "dark side" of dance is to answer the following questions: Does your dance hurt your physical health, your relationships, or your emotional well-being? Are you usually tired, sick, or injured? Have your familial, friendship, romantic, and work relationships suffered? Are you angst ridden, irritable, or unhappy more often than not?

Whatever your answers may be, this chapter is devoted to educating you about the dark side of dance in order to help you enjoy the healthy side of this magnificent art form.

Entering the Dark Side of Dance

People who enter the dark side of dance are driven by a variety of unhealthy motivations, including self-doubt, insecurity, and fear. At the center of these motivations is the need to feel better about themselves, safe, and free from anxiety. These individuals believe that by achieving dance success, they'll receive the respect and admiration they want from others, the love and value they crave from themselves, and, ultimately, inner peace. Unfortunately, their involvement in dance can exacerbate these needs rather than relieve them.

Three concerns lie at the heart of the turn to the dark side of dance. Foremost is low self-esteem, in which people view themselves as unworthy of love and respect and lacking in competence. They get involved in dance in an attempt to show how capable they are and how deserving they are of love and respect.

Dance provides them with a modicum of security in an otherwise threatening world. These individuals approach dance from a position of weakness in which they need to be successful in order to feel good about themselves. Unfortunately, because their needs are so great and their expectations so extreme, their participation in dance rarely satisfies them.

People can also be drawn to the dark side by getting overly invested in dance. A person's self-identity can become excessively connected to his or her dance efforts. Ideally, dance should be part of your life, not life itself—just one slice of the pie that is your self-identity, which should also include school or work, family, friends, and other interests and activities. But dance can become the dominant slice of the pie, in which case you may draw most of your beliefs and feelings about yourself from your dance pursuits. The danger of this over-identification arises when things aren't going well in dance—whether due to overtraining, poor performance, failure to get coveted roles, or injury—and you feel bad about yourself, even as if a part of yourself has been removed.

Another group of people who are drawn to dance are perfectionists. Indeed, dance is the ideal art form for perfectionists. Because of its complexity, intensity, rigor, minute details, precise organization, and highly competitive environment, dance satisfies the punctilious needs of individuals whose standards are higher than high. Perfectionists are drawn to dance because it allows them to focus on the smallest details, gives them the sense of control that they crave, and enables them to create an artificial world characterized by the precise structure with which they feel most comfortable.

At the same time, however, dance can be a chamber of horrors for perfectionists. It may appear at first to be a perfect world made up of regimented training, precise movement, immaculately prepared costumes, clearly defined hierarchies, and no room for flaws or missteps. But the real world of dance is much messier. In reality, dance is filled with frustration, pain, mistakes, and failure—the very antithesis of the perfect art form. An opening night that is superbly planned, highly organized, and well structured can quickly devolve into a chaotic experience due to unforeseen events, unanticipated problems, and a constantly changing environment. Therefore, what starts as a dream day for perfectionists can turn into a nightmare of frustration, lost control, and inflexibility.

Perfectionists attach their self-esteem to their achievements, which, no matter how lofty, are never enough to meet the unrealistic standards these individuals set for themselves. Perfectionists aim their often misdirected efforts at achieving the impossible goal of perfection in pursuit of feelings of competence and a happiness and contentment that they so desperately crave.

Dancers who have gone to the dark side persist in their efforts despite their failure to find what they want. Often, these dancers tend to believe that they simply haven't done enough to achieve their goals rather than recognizing that their goals are misplaced. They are also loath to admit defeat in pursuit of their goals because such an admission would only confirm that they are a failure unworthy of love and respect.

Their intense and continuing efforts in dance act as an anesthetic against the painful sense of inadequacy they feel in their lives. When they're training hard and feeling physical pain, they're distracted from their emotional pain. In addition, when they achieve small successes in training and performance, they experience highs that, however brief, offer them a respite from their angst. The poignant truth, of course, is that they—and you, and all of us—are worthy of love, respect, and acceptance regardless of dance achievements.

The most unfortunate reality of the dark side of dance is that all of the efforts that perfection-driven dancers put into their art are ultimately self-defeating. They put so much time and energy into their dance in the belief that they will find what they seek, and they don't realize that they're looking for the wrong things in the wrong places. Not only do they not find what they want, but also they are kept from charting a new course that could lead them to what they're searching for. Furthermore, as they spend more and more time in their dance pursuits, their lives become increasingly unbalanced. They may flounder in school, lose valuable friendships, and have trouble with their families. When all of life becomes dance and it's no longer fun, you have gone too far.

Dangers of the Dark Side

Living on the dark side of dance isn't just a frustrating experience in which you never seem to find what you seek. The dark side also presents a number of very real dangers, the most common of which is overtraining. Because dancers are driven to train and perform, they tend to believe in the "more is better" approach to dance training, which makes them vulnerable to overtraining and to the burnout, illness, and injury that often accompany it.

Another part of the dark side is the association of thinness with increased performance. Dancers view their body as their instrument for art and, as a result, can become obsessive not only about training and technique but also about altering their body to attain that elusive perfect line. For example, as discussed in chapter 14, many dancers fall prey to the life-threatening dangers of disordered eating. Their desire to sculpt their body can also contribute to a host of other dangerous behaviors, such as the use of diet pills, laxatives, cigarettes, and energy drinks.

The desire and pressure to dance at the highest level can also lead dancers to abuse both over-the-counter and prescription drugs (e.g., using beta-blockers to reduce performance anxiety) and even to turn to illegal substances to improve their performance. The use of illegal substances can be especially tempting as dancers pursue top prizes (e.g., at the USA International Dance Competition or the Prix de Lausanne) and, for professionals, coveted roles and financial rewards.

Nor are the dangers of the dark side only physical. Dancers who live on the dark side elevate dance as their highest priority. As a result, they may cause their relationships with family members and friends to suffer from neglect. The desperate commitment made by dancers on the dark side can also cause them to reduce their commitment to school, even to the point of dropping out in order to pursue their dance dreams.

Ultimately, the greatest danger is the price that they pay in unhappiness. Their efforts to find peace and contentment are usually counterproductive. Unless they explore the issues that lead them to the dark side, such as perfectionism and low self-esteem, happiness remains a largely unattainable goal.

Warning Signs of Being on the Dark Side

You may now be asking yourself which side of dance you're on. Few dancers would readily admit that they don't dance for the best of reasons. Even fewer might be aware that they are already on the dark side. We offer a number of warning signs that you can look for in yourself in order to evaluate your relationship with dance.

The strongest indication of being on the dark side is a profound *need* to train that is expressed as a compulsion to work out with excessive frequency, intensity, and volume. If you're on the dark side, you take too many classes and push yourself past exhaustion and pain. One example was seen in a young dancer who, in her attempt to increase her competitiveness at auditions, began taking extra classes, in addition to exercising several times a day and seven days a week. As you might imagine, she quickly became overtrained, burned out, ill, and injured.

If you're on the dark side, you may also resist taking rest days after demanding classes and rehearsals. You may show up to class and rehearsals sick or injured. And you may not eat enough to fuel all of your work in classes and rehearsals in a given day. This need to train also manifests itself in the choices you make about how dance fits into your overall life. Because not training isn't an option, you may devote an inordinate amount of time to dance at the expense of other parts of your life.

To evaluate whether you're on the dark side, you can look for several psychological warning signs. Pre-performance nerves are normal, but if you experience sizable performance anxiety in the days leading up to an audition or show, the dark side may be dictating your reactions. Your anxiety may be a response to a perceived threat in which the way you dance affects how you feel about yourself as a person. In this manner, the dark side transforms every situation in which you can compare yourself to others, whether in training or performance, into a potential threat to your self-esteem.

Another warning sign is excessive self-criticism. When you dance poorly or struggle in part of your dance life, you may punish yourself beyond what is reasonable. You may dwell on it for days and have trouble letting go of your self-criticism. Even if others see your efforts as perfectly adequate, you hold yourself to an unfairly high standard; nothing is ever good enough. Yet when you have a good class or dance well in a performance, you don't balance your criticism of your perceived failures with appropriate praise for your successes; instead, you find minute details to criticize.

Indeed, dancers who have gone to the dark side often get in their own way. They engage in self-defeating behavior, in which they do things that seem to validate them as committed and hard working but that in reality keep them from achieving their goals. For example, they may train so hard that they become sick or injured, which keeps them from having to go to an audition or take on a new role. Their peers would express admiration at these efforts, thereby providing affirmation in the face of failure. Yet their self-sabotage protects their self-esteem by giving them an excuse for their misfortunes while enabling them to avoid the possibility of real failure.

Certain emotions can also serve as warning signs. If you feel anxious, frustrated, depressed, or angry on a regular basis related to your dance, you may be living on the dark side. If the preponderance of your emotions related to dance are negative, that's a red flag that warrants a careful look.

Embrace the light side of dance! Remember why you started dancing in the first place.

Keys to the Light Side of Dance

To ensure that you don't enter the dark side of dance—or that you get out of it as soon as possible—take a healthy perspective on the role that dance plays in your life and maintain a healthy balance between your involvement in dance and the rest of your life. Dance should add to rather than detract from your life as a whole. It should also foster qualities and experiences that enhance other parts of your life, including relationships, school, work, and other activities. Dance should contribute to your growth as a person by helping you develop admirable qualities, such as confidence, passion, and perseverance. It should also discourage less desirable attributes, such as selfishness, perfectionism, and self-doubt. In short, dance should make you a better person.

Being a Human Being, Not a Human Doing

In our achievement-focused and results-oriented culture, many dancers base how they feel about themselves on what they accomplish rather than on who they are. Granted, this conception of a person as a "human doing" may encourage people to work hard and achieve great success, but they rarely find much joy in these accomplishments. Most of human doings' efforts are directed toward accomplishing goals and succeeding as a way to validate their self-esteem and find a respite from the specter of failure from which they are constantly running. But that relief is temporary because they're dependent on their next achievement in order to continue feeling good about themselves. Even though failure is a normal and inevitable part of life, human doings perceive it as an attack on their self-esteem.

Human beings, in contrast, base their feelings about themselves on who they are as a person—the values they hold, the way in which they treat others, the responsible way in which they behave, and the efforts they put in, regardless of the results. Do you work hard, exercise patience, and persist in the face of adversity? Are you kind, thoughtful, and compassionate?

Being a human being rather than a human doing doesn't mean that you lose interest in achieving and being successful. To the contrary, it liberates you from the fear of failure because success and failure are no longer so centrally connected to your self-esteem. The removal of this threat to your self-esteem allows you to pursue success from a position of strength, in which you seek out challenges with gusto, take risks, and fully realize your ability. When you are a human *being*, no pressure—from you or others—interferes with becoming successful. Human beings connect their passions and commitment to their efforts, which results both in success and in tremendous satisfaction and joy in those efforts.

Redefining Success and Failure

The culture of the dance world has defined success and failure in ways that are narrow and limiting and that ultimately interfere with efforts to achieve success and avoid failure. Success has been defined strictly and simplistically in terms of results—for example, winning a coveted role or earning a contract with a professional company. The message is that you must succeed on the culture's terms in order to be valued. If you don't, then your dancing is an insignificant failure. Buying into this definition of your dance participation makes success largely unattainable. At the same time, however, the dance culture has made failing even more intolerable.

When you blindly accept society's narrow definitions of success and failure, you give away your own power to define these aspects of life. Buying into limiting definitions of success and failure rather than choosing definitions based on your own values forces you to go down a path that, for most people, is impossible to navigate—and was never truly yours anyway. This path may also lead you to the dark side of dance.

In order to make dance a truly meaningful and rewarding experience, choose to create your own interpretations of success and failure. Broaden your definition of success to include expending great effort in pursuit of your dance goals; gaining satisfaction and joy in your training; having fun in classes, rehearsals, auditions, and productions no matter how you dance; staying focused on the process of each performance; and achieving personal bests in your dance.

As you broaden your definition of success, narrow your definition of failure. Instead of an unhealthy definition based on criteria such as failing to earn a desired role, disappointing others, being imperfect, feeling incompetent, and feeling unworthy of love and respect, define failure to mean simply not giving your best effort and not enjoying your dance experience. This definition of failure falls entirely within your control, and it doesn't carry the baggage of the more commonly accepted definitions.

In this narrower context, your reaction to dancing poorly certainly still involves feeling disappointment yet also enjoying the experience, letting it go, and using the lessons learned from failure to become more successful in the future. Aim for excellence—not perfection—and recognize that each experience presents you with an opportunity to learn and grow as a dancer and as a person.

Keeping Dance in Perspective

Dance can be an all-encompassing art form. You can become so involved in its many facets (e.g., fitness, technique, artistry, health, training, nutrition, costumes, auditions, performances) that, without realizing it, you can let it take over your life. If dance gains dominance over you—and you begin to set all of your priorities and make all of your decisions based on dance—then your overall life suffers. Beyond the sheer time commitment and practical aspects, the real danger is that you may become overly connected to dance and, as we have discussed, invest too much of your self-esteem in your dance participation. If this happens, you lose perspective on the role that dance plays in your life, and you can be drawn to the dark side.

Keeping dance in healthy perspective benefits not only your training and performance efforts but also various essential aspects of your overall life, including school, work, relationships, and other valued activities. It is critical for you to realize, and accept, the fact that dance can be an important part of your life but is not life itself. With this view, your dancing can still play a central role in your life and be a wonderful source of satisfaction and enjoyment, but it doesn't burden you.

Maintaining Balance

Dance is an art form that can breed imbalance due to its complexity and the demands that is puts on your time and energy. Committing fully to dance while maintaining a healthy life balance constitutes a considerable challenge. Yet that balance is essential to leading a deep, fulfilling, and happy life. Balance involves giving dance a prominent place in your life while also maintaining respect for and engagement in other parts of your life. When your life is well balanced, you devote sufficient time to achieve your dance goals. You also have time to share with family and friends, and you remain fully committed to your school or professional life.

When your life is in balance, you can also spend time enjoying other activities that you value. Moreover, this balance doesn't apply only to a particular day, week, or month. You can also think of it in terms of longer periods of time. For example, over the course of a year, you might tip the scale toward dance for six months, then tip it back to other parts of your life for the remainder of the year.

Maintaining balance is particularly difficult when you're committed to a career in dance. The inordinate amount of time and energy that's necessary to prepare for a life of dance can preclude having true balance. But maintaining some semblance of balance—what we call "balance within the imbalance"—is still a worthy goal. This approach involves finding small opportunities to infuse balance into your otherwise lopsided life.

For example, you might commit one full afternoon on weekends after dance class to spending with your family. Or you might spend one evening a week doing extra schoolwork that you might otherwise neglect due to your long hours in the studio. Or perhaps you catch an early dinner and a movie with friends on Friday night and still go to bed early enough to get a good night's sleep in preparation for a long Saturday of rehearsal.

You might also tip the scale in certain ways during a performance week by sneaking a nap in the middle of the day so that you have the energy to perform that night. Or you might designate some days for rest as you near the end of a grueling performance season. Whatever the particulars, there needs to be a yin and yang—in other words, a doing side (e.g., pursuing, working, achieving) and a nurturing side (e.g., resting, eating, reflecting, being). When one side is neglected, you stagnate; but when you attend to both sides, you flourish.

> *"The dance is over, the applause subsided, but the joy and feeling will stay with you forever."*
>
> W.M. Tory

Developing Healthy Expectations

Living in the results-oriented culture of dance, we tend to create expectations for ourselves based on our results. However, as you may have learned from your experience in dance, you can't always control the fruits of your dance efforts. Even if you give a great effort at an audition, factors beyond your control—for example, the style of dance, the artistic director, the other dancers— may deprive you of the role that you had hoped for. If you believe what this culture says, then you will have to judge yourself as having failed. If, however, you set healthy expectations, you can walk away with your head held high, knowing that you gave your best effort and danced as well as you could and that the role or the company simply was not a good fit.

Developing healthy expectations means setting goals that you have control over and can achieve if you give your best effort. Healthy expectations might focus, for example, on being completely prepared for a performance or enjoying your performance experience. Or they might involve responding well to adversity or persisting when you're really tired. The key is to establish expectations that you can control and that encourage success, excellence, and satisfaction in your pursuit of them.

Striving for Excellence, Not Perfection

We've already emphasized how unhealthy the pursuit of perfection in dance can be and how it ultimately leads neither to real success nor to happiness. Because of the unpredictable nature of dance, perfection is both unattainable and undesirable. As an antidote to perfection, we propose excellence, which we define as doing your best most of time while accepting that things sometimes go wrong and using your mistakes as learning experiences. Excellence embraces the positive qualities of perfectionism—for example, setting high standards and working hard to achieve goals—and rejects its unhealthy aspects, such as viewing failure as unacceptable and criticizing yourself for not living up to impossibly high standards.

Excellence means giving your best effort on any given day, accepting that problems may arise, and adapting to changing situations in a positive way. Thus it relieves you of the burden of trying to make everything perfect, encourages you to pursue your goals as challenges rather than threats, and enables you to remain positive and calm as you constructively deal with the unexpected tests that dance throws at you. Striving for excellence allows you to become flexible, adaptable, and resilient in the face of disappointment, which helps you become mentally tougher and contributes to your long-term growth as a dancer.

Feeling the Love and Joy

Dance should be about love—love of yourself, love of others, love of music, love of movement, love of dance, and love of life. Yet because dance is a competitive art form, it can sometimes turn into a love of results, of a position in a company, of leading roles, and of rave reviews. If you fall in love with these results, you may lose your true love of dance. Without that passion for all things dance, your interest and motivation to train and perform may wane. But if you love the process of dance, the physicality, the artistry, the music, the emotional expressiveness, the exhilaration of performing on a stage in front of an audience, then dance will bring you both love and joy.

We have found that, more often than not, if you love the experience, you'll also get the results you want, even though you aren't focusing on them. If you love training, you put in the time and effort necessary to gain the benefits you need in order to achieve your goals. Because you're not overly invested in your results, you're more confident, relaxed, and focused; less anxious about how you'll dance; and better able to perform up to your ability in auditions, productions, and competitions. The end result is that you have a wonderful dance experience while often getting the results you want.

Joy can be found in the dance experience itself. Enjoy giving your best effort, improving your dance, reveling in the intensity of an audition, and getting to know like-minded people. Dance remains a joy when it serves as an antidote for stress and a healthy escape from the demands of your life. It continues to be joyful when you maintain a positive balance between physical exertion and rest and when your commitment of time to dance doesn't cause you to sacrifice other parts of your life.

Dance is a joy when you feel excited about and look forward to classes, rehearsals, and productions. Find joy by surrounding yourself with other dancers who also get joy from dance. Find joy in the changes you see in your body and mind and the quality of your dancing. Staying continually connected with those feelings is the surest way to gain the maximum joy out of dance.

Appreciating the Benefits

Dance offers you physical, mental, emotional, social, and spiritual benefits. It encourages a healthy and vigorous lifestyle. It allows you to connect with your body, music, and other dancers. It gives you opportunities to demonstrate your motivation, confidence, and focus. You can use it to relieve stress; learn about your emotions; and develop discipline, patience, persistence, and perseverance. Dance also introduces you to passionate, interesting, artistic, and committed people with positive attitudes who share common interests and goals and live in a spirited and energetic way.

In addition, dance has a strong spiritual component that challenges you to push your limits and expand your horizons. It presents you with opportunities to learn essential life lessons that help you grow as a person. Your dance can be a source of profound meaning, satisfaction, and enjoyment. Whoever or whatever you worship, these benefits of dance enable you to get closer to your faith and manifest it more fully in your life. Ultimately, dance offers you many diverse experiences through which you can enhance the quality of your life.

Embracing Prime Dance for Life

To be motivated, confident, relaxed, and focused. To respond positively to stress, frustration, and fear. To overcome the physical challenges of dance. To be your own best ally in classes, rehearsals, and performances. To consistently dance your best under the most demanding conditions. These are the skills that prime dance can help you develop.

Why is prime dance so important to you that you would read this book and put such time and effort into dance? Your answer is a personal one. You may want to have more fun when you dance. Or maybe you want to become the best dancer you can possibly be. Or perhaps you aspire to greatness in dance.

We would like to believe, however, that the most compelling reason you want to achieve prime dance is to master the mental performance described in chapter 1. If you can succeed at the mental performance and remove all of the obstacles that keep you from dancing your best, then so much more is possible.

When you free yourself to dance with grace, spirit, love, and joy, you clear the path to the greatest possible fulfillment, success, and happiness in dance.

It has often been said that dance is, at its core, simply a metaphor for life. If so, in experiencing dance at its purest and deepest, you show yourself how to experience life in the same way. Dance, like life, is filled with challenges, struggles, excitement, failures, disappointments, and, we hope, achievement of your dreams. So, to triumph in dance is also to seize victory in life itself.

Center Stage: Tom

Finding the Light Side of Dance

Tom grew up in a family where both parents were perfectionists who pushed him and his siblings to excel in every aspect of their lives. These high expectations drove Tom to succeed in his educational and dance life, but he paid a price for his achievements. Despite his efforts at perfection and, by most people's standards, his great successes academically and as a dancer, he never felt that he was good enough. In fact, he was terrified of failure and drove himself relentlessly to keep from failing.

By age 21, Tom developed a series of overuse injuries but kept trying to train through them. Eventually, however, these injuries forced him to stop dancing and performing altogether for some time. The resulting void in Tom's life left him feeling frustrated, angry, and depressed. At the urging of his girlfriend, he decided to see a dance psychologist, Dr. E., who worked at his college's counseling center, for help in figuring out what was happening with him.

It quickly became clear to Dr. E. that Tom's unforgiving personality hurt not only his dance efforts but also his overall happiness and well-being. He began to explore with Tom his perfectionism and how it affected his life. For the first time, Tom started to see why he was so perfectionistic and how it interfered with his dance pursuits and caused his general unhappiness. With these realizations in mind, he committed to making some changes.

Over time, Tom's perspectives on dance—and life—were transformed. With Dr. E.'s help, Tom learned that he didn't have to be perfect in order to be loved and respected. Dr. E. helped Tom focus on the wonderful benefits of dance and how dance enhanced his life. Most important, Tom connected more deeply with his love for dance and the joy it brought him—not the extreme effort or the results. For the first time in his life, Tom felt a weight lifted off his shoulders, and he came to believe that he could not only freely pursue healthy goals in dance but also find happiness in life.

ENCORE

- Dance can be a wonderful, life-enriching experience that provides you with meaning, satisfaction, and joy in an art form that promotes health, cultivates relationships, and extends your physical, psychological, and emotional horizons.

- Dance can also be a harmful experience that is physically debilitating, emotionally crippling, and socially damaging.

- Three concerns lie at the heart of the turn to the "dark side" of dance: low self-esteem, overinvestment in dance, and perfectionism.

- The dangers of being on the dark side of dance include overtraining, disordered eating, unhealthy or neglected relationships, and unhappiness.

- Watch for warning signs of being on the dark side of dance: an obsessive need to train; life imbalance; performance anxiety; excessive self-criticism; self-sabotage; and persistent negative emotions, such as fear, frustration, sadness, and anger.

- Here are eight keys to the light side of dance: avoiding the pitfall of basing your self-worth on dance; defining success and failure in healthy ways; maintaining a healthy perspective toward dance; maintaining balance in your life; establishing healthy expectations; striving for excellence rather than perfection; feeling love and joy in your dance; and appreciating the many benefits that you can gain from dance.

References

Achterberg, J. (1991, May). *Enhancing the immune function through imagery*. Paper presented at the Fourth World Conference on Imagery, Minneapolis.

Beals, K. (2004). *Disordered eating among athletes: A comprehensive guide for health professionals*. Champaign, IL: Human Kinetics.

Beck, A. (1976). *Cognitive therapy and emotional disorders*. New York: International University Press.

Bennett, J.G., & Pravitz, J.E. (1982). *The miracle of sports psychology*. Englewood Cliffs, NJ: Prentice Hall.

Buckroyd, J. (1995). The provision of psychological care for dancers. *Performing Arts Medicine News*, *3*, 1.

Buckroyd, J. (2000). *The student dancer: Emotional aspects of the teaching and learning of dance*. London, England: Dance Books.

Estanol, E. (2004). *Effects of a psychological skills training program on self-confidence, anxiety, and performance in university ballet dancers*. Master's thesis, Willard Marriott Library, University of Utah.

Estanol, E. (2009). *Exploring the relationship between risk and resilience factors for eating disorders in ballet dancers*. Doctoral dissertation, University of Utah, Salt Lake City.

Estanol, E., Shepherd, C., & MacDonald, T. (2013). Mental skills as protective attributes against eating disorder risk in dancers. *Journal of Applied Sport Psychology, 25*(2), 209–222.

Gould, D., Dieffenbach, K., & Moffet, A. (2002). Psychological characteristics and their development in Olympic champions. *Journal of Applied Sport Psychology, 14*(3), 172–204.

Graham, M. (1974). A modern dancer's primer for action. In S.J. Cohen (Ed.), *Dance as a theatre art: Source readings in dance history from 1581 to the present* (pp. 135–142). New York: Dodd, Mead.

Hall, K.H., & Hill, A.P. (2012). Perfectionism, dysfunctional achievement striving, and burnout in aspiring athletes: The motivational implications for performing artists. *Theatre, Dance, and Performance Training, 3*(2), 216–228.

Hays, K. (2002).The enhancement of performance excellence among performing artists. *Journal of Applied Sport Psychology, 14,* 299–312.

Hefferon, K.M., & Ollis, S. (2006). "Just clicks": An interpretive phenomenological analysis of professional dancers' experience of flow. *Research in Dance Education, 7*(2), 141–159.

Holm, H. (1979). Hanya speaks. In J.M. Brown (Ed.), *The vision of modern dance* (pp. 71–82). Princeton, NJ: Princeton Book.

Hunt, M. (1992, April). Return of the prodigal mentor: Benjamin Harkarvy. *Dance, 4,* 52–56.

Kay, L. (2012, January). Technique my way: Katherine Crockett—Respecting her body, devoted to her craft. *Dance Magazine.* www.dancemagazine.com/issues/january-2012/Technique-My-Way-Katherine-Crockett.

Koutedakis, Y. (2000). Burnout in dance: The physiological viewpoint. *Journal of Dance Medicine & Science, 4*(4), 122–127.

Koutedakis, Y., & Jamurtas, A. (2004). The dancer as a performing athlete: Physiological considerations. *Sports Medicine, 34*(10), 651–661.

Kreider, R.B., Fry, A.C., & O'Toole, M.L. (1998). *Overtraining in sport.* Champaign, IL: Human Kinetics.

Kroll, W. (1979). The stress of high-performance athletes. In P. Klavora & J.V. Daniel (Eds.), *Coach, athlete, and the sport psychologist* (pp. 211–219). Toronto: University of Toronto.

Larsen, G. (2009, September). Why I Dance. *Dance Magazine.* www.dancemagazine.com/issues/september-2009/Why-I-Dance.

Loren, T. (1978). *The dancer's companion: The indispensable guide to getting the most out of dance classes.* New York: Dial Press.

Luthar, S.S. (1991). Vulnerability and resilience: A study of high-risk adolescents. *Child Development, 62,* 600–616.

Luthar, S.S., & Cicchetti, D. (2000). The construct of resilience: Implications for interventions and social policies. *Development & Psychopathology, 12,* 857–885.

Lyle, C. (1977). *Dancers on dancing.* New York: Drake.

Mahoney, M., & Avener, M. (1977). Psychology of the elite athlete: An explorative study. *Cognitive Therapy and Research, 1,* 135–141.

Mummery, W.K., Schofield, G., & Perry, C. (2004). Bouncing back: The role of coping style, social support, and self-concept in resilience of sport performance. *Athletic Insight: The Online Journal of Sport Psychology, 6*(3), 1–18.

Newman, B. (1982). *Striking a balance: Dancers talk about dancing.* Boston: Houghton Mifflin.

Orlick, T. (1990). *In pursuit of excellence* (2nd ed.). Champaign, IL: Human Kinetics.

Orlick, T., & Partington, J. (1986). *Psyched.* Ottawa: Coaching Association of Canada.

Poczwardowski, A., & Conroy, D.E. (2002). Coping responses to failure and success among elite athletes and performing artists. *Journal of Applied Sport Psychology, 14*(4), 313–329.

Pulinkala, I. (2011). Integration of a professional dancer into college. *Research in Dance Education, 12*(3), 259–275.

Reivick, K., & Shatte, A. (2002). *The resilience factor: 7 essential skills for overcoming life's inevitable obstacles.* New York: Broadway Books.

Scanlan, T.K., Stein, G.L., & Ravizza, K. (1989). An in-depth study of former elite figure skaters: Sources of enjoyment. *Journal of Sport and Exercise Psychology, 11*, 65–83.

Seligman, M.E.P. (1990). *Learned optimism: How to change your mind and your life.* New York: Pocket Books.

Seligman, M.E.P. (2002). *Authentic happiness: Using the new positive psychology to realize your potential for lasting fulfillment.* New York: Free Press.

Steck, L.E., Abrahams, M.L., & Phelps, L. (2004). Positive psychology in the prevention of eating disorders. *Psychology in the Schools, 41*(1), 111–117.

INDEX

Note: The italicized *f* and *t* following page numbers refer to figures and tables, respectively.

ABOUT THE AUTHORS

Jim Taylor, PhD, is a long-time sport psychologist and a consultant, speaker, and author who has worked with dancers for three decades. He is also a coauthor of *Psychology of Dance*, a predecessor of this book, and has consulted with Miami City Ballet. He is a member of the American Psychological Association and the Association for Applied Sport Psychology. Taylor received a PhD in psychology from the University of Colorado at Boulder. He enjoys skiing, running, and cycling.

Elena Estanol, PhD, MFA, is a counseling sport psychologist, speaker, peak performance, wellness, and ADHD coach and executive director of Synapse Counseling, LLC, a wellness center that provides cutting-edge sport psychology services, eating disorder and ADHD treatment to dancers, athletes, and performing artists in Fort Collins, CO. She has spent most of her life dancing, teaching, and choreographing dance. She is a frequent consultant to dance schools, companies, and teams. Estanol is a member of the American Psychological Association, the Association for Applied Sport Psychology, and the International Association for Dance Medicine and Science. She received her PhD in counseling psychology, MS in sport psychology, and MFA in kinesiology, choreography, and pedagogy from the University of Utah. In her leisure time, she enjoys hiking, yoga, dancing, writing, and aerial silks (aerial dance).